GOD, GUNS GUITARS & WHISKEY

An Illustrated Guide To Historic Nashville, Tennessee

2nd Edition

Mark Zimmerman
Author of Guide to Civil War Nashville

God, Guns, Guitars & Whiskey: An Illustrated Guide to Historic Nashville, Tennessee – 2nd Edition
ZIMCO Publications LLC

Copyright © 2019, 2012 by Mark Zimmerman

All rights reserved.
All Text, Photographs, and Maps by the Author Unless Otherwise Noted.

No part of this book may be reproduced or transmitted in any form or by any means — electronic or manual, including photocopy, scanner, email, CD or other information storage and retrieval system — without written permission from the author, except for personal use or as provided to the news media and book sellers. Visitor attractions may reprint the feature specific to them, giving credit to *God, Guns, Guitars & Whiskey: An Illustrated Guide to Historic Nashville, Tennessee.* For other permissions, contact ZIMCO Publications LLC.

Printed in the United States of America.
First Printing 2019.

ISBN: 978-0-9858692-3-6

The text in this book, which is published to inform and entertain, should be used for general information and not as the ultimate source of educational or travel information. Most of the attractions listed in this book can be found on the Internet with the latest relevant travel information. Every effort has been made to ensure the accuracy and relevance of information in this book but the author and publisher do not assume responsibility for any errors, inaccuracies, omissions or inconsistencies within. Any slights of people, places, or organizations are strictly unintentional.

The names of organizations and destinations mentioned in this book may be trade names or trademarks of their owners. The author and publisher disclaims any connection with, sponsorship by, or endorsement of such owners.

Other books by Mark Zimmerman:
Guide to Civil War Nashville, 2nd Edition
Gone Under: Historic Cemeteries of Nashville, Tennessee, 2nd Edition

ZIMCO Publications LLC
Nashville TN 37214
Email: info@zimcopubs.com
Website: zimcopubs.com

INTRODUCTION

Tour of Historic Downtown Nashville .... Page 4
Historic Sites of West, North, South, East Nashville 71
Historical Markers of Davidson County 136

In using this book you will soon discover that Nashville, the capital of Tennessee, offers a treasure trove of fascinating historic sites to explore. In the process you will learn the stories of our ancestors, the journeys they undertook, and the trials and tribulations they encountered. Along the way you will explore museums of all types, historic buildings and significant architecture, antebellum mansions, monuments and memorials, sculptures and public art, battlefields, artifacts, and markers.

This guide begins with a walking tour of historic downtown Nashville that spotlights more than 70 sites. The tour will take you from the historic riverfront to the centers of municipal and state government, along Church Street with its eclectic architecture, down the Victorian-era warehouse row, and then up Broadway, home to many of Nashville's music venues—from symphony halls to honky tonks. The full tour will take several hours; you may wish to pick and choose your destinations to create a shorter route. This section also includes feature articles on the Tennessee State Capitol and Ryman Auditorium and a listing of Native-American historic sites.

The next section covers nearly 100 historic sites of Nashville-Davidson County outside the downtown area and includes a feature article on the Tennessee Centennial Exposition and a listing of African-American historic sites. A table of contents and 14 maps can be found beginning on page 71. Descriptions and articles include Centennial Park, Music Row, Vanderbilt University and other West End attractions; the North Nashville and Germantown historic districts; the College Hill and South Nashville districts; several Civil War sites; and historic Edgefield and East Nashville.

Several historic sites are marked as Five-Star Attractions—these are landmarks of distinction and most are full-featured tourist sites which cater to visitors. Some historic sites are privately owned and not open to tourists; visitors should respect private property rights and owners' privacy.

The final section contains the text and locations of 240 historical markers in Nashville-Davidson County.

More information on most historic sites can be obtained by searching the appropriate name or topic on the Internet. Call beforehand to make sure all information is up-to-date. Also, maps and routes can change; for the best experience purchase a recent road or street map or use the latest GPS device. Always be careful when driving and always be aware of your surroundings for safety's sake.

4 God, Guns, Guitars & Whiskey: *An Illustrated Guide to Historic Nashville, Tennessee — 2nd Edition*

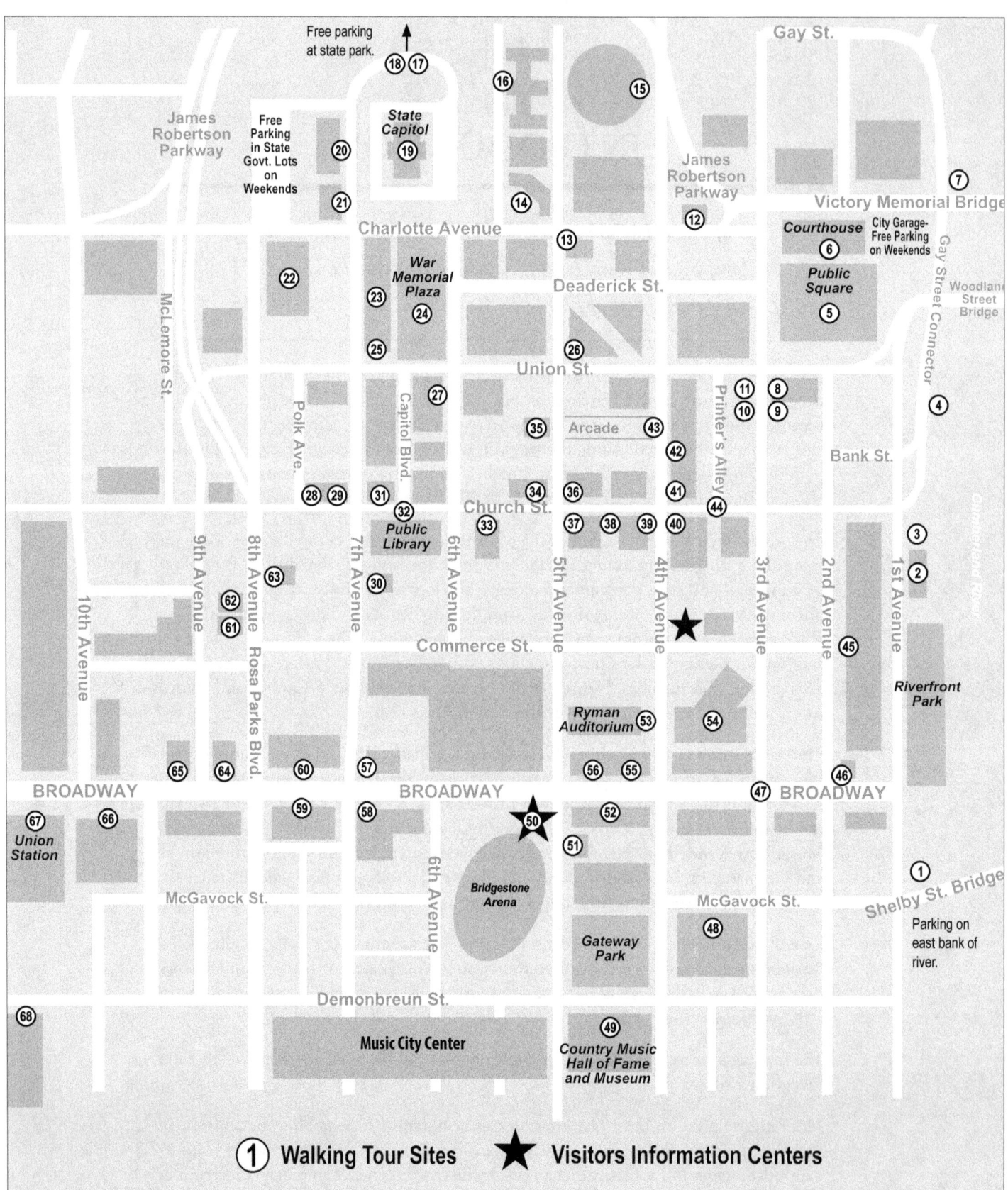

For Contemporary Tourism Sites, See visitmusiccity.com

Tour of Historic Downtown Nashville

① Riverfront and Shelby Street Bridge......Page 6-7
② Fort Nashborough 8
③ Founders Statue 9
④ Timothy Demonbreun Statue 9
⑤ Nashville Public Square 10
⑥ Davidson County Courthouse 10
⑦ Victory Memorial Bridge / Railroad Bridge 12
Native-American Historic Sites 13
⑧ Stahlman Building 14
⑨ Federal Reserve Building 14
⑩ Nashville Trust Building 14
⑪ American Trust Building 14
⑫ Morris Memorial Building 16
⑬ St. Mary's Church 16
⑭ John Sevier State Office Building 17
⑮ Musicians Hall of Fame and Museum 17
⑯ People of Tennessee Sculptures 18
⑰ Bicentennial Capitol Mall State Park 19
⑱ Tennessee State Museum 24
⑲ Tennessee State Capitol and Grounds 27
⑳ State Library and Archives 35
㉑ State Supreme Court Building 35
㉒ Tennessee Tower 35
㉓ War Memorial Building 36
㉔ War Memorial Plaza 37
㉕ State Museum-Military Branch 39
㉖ Chet Atkins Statue 40
㉗ Hermitage Hotel 40
㉘ Doctors Building 41
㉙ Bennie-Dillon Building 41
㉚ James Robertson Hotel 41
㉛ Castner-Knott Building 42
㉜ Nashville Public Library 42
㉝ McKendree Methodist Church 43
㉞ Saint Cloud Corner 43
㉟ Kress Building .... Page 44
㊱ Fifth Third Bank Building 44
㊲ Downtown Presbyterian Church 45
㊳ Cohen Building 46
㊴ L&C Tower 46
㊵ Old First National Bank Building 47
㊶ Noel Hotel Building 47
㊷ The Men's Quarter 48
㊸ The Arcade 49
㊹ Printers Alley 49
㊺ Market Street Historic District 51
㊻ Silver Dollar Saloon 51
㊼ Broadway Historic District 52
㊽ Schermerhorn Symphony Center 53
㊾ Country Music Hall of Fame and Museum 54
㊿ Visitors Center (Bridgestone Arena) 55
(51) Underground Railroad House 56
(52) Ernest Tubb Record Shop 56
(53) Ryman Auditorium 57
(54) AT&T Building 61
(55) Gruhn Guitar 61
(56) Tootsie's Orchid Lounge 62
(57) Masonic Grand Lodge 62
(58) First Baptist Church 62
(59) U.S. Customs House 63
(60) Hume-Fogg High School 64
(61) Frost Building 65
(62) The Standard at Smith House 65
(63) Berger Building 66
(64) Old Methodist Publishing House 66
(65) Christ Church Cathedral 67
(66) Frist Center for the Visual Arts 67
(67) Union Station 68
(68) Cummins Station 69

Note: Most sites and buildings reflect the historic names associated with them.

① Cumberland Riverfront

The *General Jackson* paddlewheeler showboat churns upriver to its home at Gaylord's Opryland Hotel in this view looking southward (upstream) from the Shelby Street Pedestrian Bridge. The graceful arched bridge is the Korean War Veterans Memorial Bridge. Behind the arched bridge are the last remaining structures of the old General Hospital, being redeveloped on Rolling Mill Hill. At lower left is an abandoned derrick once used by the Nashville Bridge Co.

Ghost Ballet for the East Bank Machineworks is the title of this provocative abstract sculpture on the east bank of the Cumberland River next to LP Field and directly across the river from Lower Broadway. The 100-foot-tall metal sculpture uses an old barge-launching gantry crane as its foundation. The design by renown New York City sculptor Alice Aycock resembles a bright-red roller coaster to some observers, but the sculptor likens it to two colliding spiral galaxies representing the sense of a vortex of energy, within historical context. The public-art sculpture cost $330,000 and was funded by the "Percent for the Arts" program. It was dedicated in July 2007.

The Cumberland River, named by explorer Dr. Thomas Walker for William Augustus, Duke of Cumberland, runs 700 miles from Lechter County, Ky. to its confluence with the Ohio River at Smithland, Ky., draining a watershed of 18,000 square miles. Old Hickory Dam is located on the Cumberland about 25 miles upstream from downtown.

The Nashville Bridge Company was created in 1902 by Arthur J. Dyer, a Vanderbilt University engineering graduate. The riverfront company fabricated steel for several Nashville landmarks in the early 1900s, including the Arcade, Nashville Trust Building, and the Hermitage Hotel. Over the World War Two years their 700 workers built nearly 100 ships, including 14 submarine chasers, two minesweepers, and 67 specialty barges. The ships were launched by sliding them sideways down metal rails and into the river with a tremendous splash. The ships then traveled downriver to New Orleans, where they were outfitted for seagoing duty. In the late 1940s the company met the demand for bridge construction, and later barges, towboats, bridge overpasses, and fabricated steel for the NASA service tower of the Saturn missiles. LP Field occupies the former site of Nashville Bridge, which now operates as Trinity Marine downstream in Ashland City.

1 Shelby Street Bridge

The Shelby Street Bridge was dedicated on July 5, 1909 and was originally known as the Sparkman Street Bridge. It was designed by Howard M. Jones, the Chief Engineer of the Nashville, Chattanooga, and St. Louis Railway. The bridge is 3,150 feet long and was the first bridge in North America to use concrete arched trusses (on the approaches). Closed to vehicular traffic in 1998, it reopened as a pedestrian bridge in 2003 at a cost of $15 million. It is reportedly the longest pedestrian bridge in the world. The bridge is wheel-chair accessible, and features benchs and four observation platforms. At night the bridge is spectacularly lit from underneath. The bridge has been used as a backdrop for several music videos.

The graceful, arched Gateway Bridge opened downtown in 2004 and was renamed the Korean War Veterans Memorial Bridge. It handles the vehicular traffic that formerly used the Shelby Street Bridge.

The Jefferson Street Bridge downriver was an exact copy of the Sparkman Street Bridge and opened in 1910. It was demolished in 1990 and replaced with a modern structure now known as the Kelly Miller Smith Bridge, named in honor of the famous local civil-rights leader.

The first bridge across the Cumberland was completed in 1823 and used until 1851. This was the bridge used by the Cherokee Indians forced to march on the Trail of Tears to the Oklahoma Territory. The wooden covered bridge extended from the northeast corner of the Public Square to Main Street across the river. Reportedly, a flock of sheep was lost in crossing when the lead sheep jumped out a bridge window and all the others followed. The site is now occupied by the Victory Memorial Bridge, which was built in 1955 at a cost of $4 million and dedicated to the 752 Nashvillians killed in World War Two (memorials to those killed in the Korean and Vietnam wars were later added).

The 700-foot-long Suspension Bridge that connected Nashville and the City of Edgefield (now East Nashville) was built in 1853. An argument over the proposed location led to a pistol duel between local newspaper editors. Architect Adolphus Heiman designed it but resigned after changes were made. Part of it collapsed in 1855, killing a boy and seven horses. The bridge was destroyed during the Civil War. After the war, the Suspension Bridge was restored and used until 1886, when it was replaced by the Woodland Street Bridge. This bridge was rebuilt in 1965, although the original abutments were retained.

The Railroad Bridge opened in 1859, built for the joint use of the Louisville and Nashville Railroad and the Edgefield and Kentucky Railroad. The bridge was partially burned in 1862 by retreating Confederates but rebuilt and fortified within months by the U.S. Army Corps of Engineers. Later rebuilt with steel trusses, the railroad bridge remains in use today, still incorporating its unique swing-span center section.

Upstream are the Silliman-Evans interstate highway bridge, the railroad bridge at Shelby Park, the Briley Parkway Bridge (1965) at Pennington Bend, and the Old Hickory Boulevard Bridge (1929). The newest is the pedestrian suspension bridge linking Shelby Bottoms Park in East Nashville with the Two Rivers greenway in Donelson.

Downstream are the Interstate 65 bridge, the Ashland City Highway bridge, the railroad bridge, and the Briley Parkway bridge at Cockrill Bend.

Before bridges, there were ferries; six were licensed as early as the 1780s to operate in Nashville. The last ferry service ceased operations in 1990.

② Fort Nashborough

A replica of Fort Nashborough is located on the riverfront at 170 First Avenue North. Owned by the Metro Nashville Board of Parks, the fort is open daily for self-guided tours at no charge. The replica, built in 1930, is one-fourth the size of the original two-acre fort and located slightly closer to the river.

Hundreds of Indian warriors led by Dragging Canoe assaulted Fort Nashborough on the morning of April 2, 1781. Dragging Canoe was the son of Cherokee chieftain Attakullakulla and the fiery leader of renegades who chose not abide by the Sycamore Shoals Treaty of 1775. Dragging Canoe's followers were known as the Chickamaugans.

Dragging Canoe's plan was to wipe out the settlers at Nashborough and then attack the remaining Cumberland settlements. A small band of Indians drew James Robertson and 20 men out of the fort and then ambushed them. The settlers dismounted to fight, and their horses galloped back towards the fort. The horses divided another band of Indians who had positioned themselves between the settlers and the fort. The horses were coveted by the Indians, and many began chasing them.

Watching from the fort, Charlotte Robertson, James' wife, set loose fifty hounds kept in the fort. The dogs attacked the Indians, and the settlers were able to retreat to the safety of the fort. Five whites were killed and three wounded, including one of Robertson's sons, who was scalped but survived. At 10 a.m., the Indians retreated out of rifle range. That evening, after being fired upon by the fort's lone swivel-gun, the Indians left. Thus, the quick thinking of Charlotte Robertson saved the day for the settlers at what has come to be known as the Battle of the Bluffs.

Fort Nashborough was named for Brigadier General Francis Nash of North Carolina, who fought alongside James Robertson at the Battle of Alamance in 1771. Nash had also previously served as a clerk in the North Carolina Court presided over by Judge Richard Henderson. Nash was mortally wounded at the Battle of Germantown, near Philadelphia, in October 1777.

In July 1784 the Davidson County Court shortened Nashborough to Nashville, reflecting a preference for the French ville over the British borough. The town was incorporated in 1806.

Davidson County (1783) was named for Brigadier General William Lee Davidson of North Carolina, a distinguished officer of the Revolutionary War. He served at Valley Forge and was killed in action at Cowan's Ford, N.C., in 1781.

③ Founders Statue

On Monday, April 24, 1780, the two founders of Nashborough, James Robertson (1742-1814) and John Donelson (1718-1785), shook hands on the bluff overlooking the Cumberland River. Robertson and his men arrived via an overland route from what is now East Tennessee on Christmas Day, 1779 and walked across the frozen river. Donelson led an expedition of flatboats along a perilous river route, enduring many hardships, and arrived in April 1780. One of his daughters, Rachel, who survived the trip, later married a young lawyer named Andrew Jackson.

On May 1, 250 of the settlers signed the Cumberland Compact, which established a simple representative form of wilderness government. The fortified settlements, or stations, of Middle Tennessee were ruled by a 12-man Tribunal of Notables.

> "The Fertility of the Soil, and Goodness of the Range, almost surpass Belief; and it is at present well stored with Buffalo, Elk, Deer, Bear, Beaver &c, and the Rivers abound with Fish of various Kinds. Vast Crowds of people are daily flocking to it."
> Richard Henderson, writing about the Cumberland territory

The settlements had been planned by land speculator Richard Henderson, aka Carolina Dick, who had purchased much of what is now Middle Tennessee from the Indians in 1775. The Cumberland settlements were attacked by hostile Indians until 1795. During the four years following the Cumberland Compact, one third of the signers were killed in battles with Indians.

The statue by Puryear Mims stands north of Fort Nashborough. Robertson is on the left; Donelson on the right. The statue's base lists the signers of the Cumberland Compact.

④ Timothy Demonbreun Statue

Timothy Demonbreun (1747-1826) was a French-Canadian fur trader and explorer who first came to the French Lick (Nashville) in 1769. To escape the hostile Indians he often resided in a cave on the bluffs overlooking the Cumberland River (the entrance to the cave can still be seen today from the river).

As lieutenant commandant of the Illinois Territory he lived in Kaskaskia on the Mississippi River with his wife and five children. He also resided in Nashville, beginning permanently in 1790, with his common-law Indian wife and their three children. They resided at what is now Third and Broadway, marked today by a historical marker. Nashville's "first citizen" operated a prosperous mercantile business on the public square. His burial site is unrecorded.

The statue of Jacques Timothe Boucher de Montbrun by sculptor Alan LeQuire was dedicated in 1996 and is located just north of the city's Bicentennial Park along the Gay Street Connector.

The first Europeans in the Middle Tennessee area were French fur traders and English or German long hunters, so named because they spent long periods of time on their hunts. The fur trappers established a trading post at the French Lick (the area immediately north of what is now downtown) in 1714. The post was operated by Charles Charleville, who knew the Cumberland River as the Chauvenon.

Nashville Public Square

A new park was dedicated at Nashville's Public Square in 2006, on the city's 200th anniversary. The level-lawn park replaced a surface parking lot that stood in front of the courthouse for 30 years. The park includes a Founders' Pavilion between the Public Square and the Cumberland River. The pavilion is connected to the park and the underground parking garage by a pair of towers representing Nashville's historic founders James Robertson and John Donelson. Atop the pavilion are panels along the overlook that review and highlight the history of the city. Informative historical markers line the south edge of the park.

Davidson County Courthouse

The Davidson County Courthouse is the fourth such structure on the Public Square site, built in the Art Deco style and dedicated on Dec. 8, 1937 as a Depression-era Public Works Administration project.

In 2007 the courthouse was re-dedicated after extensive remodeling and the creation of the Public Square Park with oval lawn and historical interpretive signage throughout. Surface parking was replaced by an underground garage. Garage parking is free to the public on weekends.

The first courthouse was a log cabin dating back to 1783, before Tennessee was a state (Davidson was a county of North Carolina). In the mid-1800s, William Strickland Jr., the son of the famed architect, designed a courthouse that looked much like the State Capitol, minus the tower.

Today's courthouse abounds with symbolism. Cornice figures of a lioness, a snake, and a bison represent Protection, Wisdom, and Strength, respectively. Six figures on the bronze doors by sculptor Rene Chambellan allude to the American qualities of Courage, Loyalty, Law, Justice, Security, and Wisdom. The three etched glass panels above the doors represent the three great law-givers: King John of England, Moses, and Justinian. Colorful murals in the lobby by artist Dean Cornwell represent industry, agriculture, statesmanship, and commerce.

In 1963, the Nashville city and Davidson County governments merged to form a consolidated government. Thus, City Hall is also located in the courthouse.

Courthouse Monuments and Artwork

FOUR LARGE MURALS of red, yellow, and gold adorn the County Courthouse lobby, featuring heroic male and female figures representing Agriculture, Commerce, Industry, and Statesmanship imposed on maps of Nashville. The Art Deco murals were created in 1937 by illustrator Dean Cornwell (1892-1960), whose commissions include the Los Angeles Public Library, the Eastern Airlines Building in Rockefeller Center, and the U.S. Post Office in Raleigh, N.C. Cornwell also produced in 1941 the murals depicting the Discovery of Tennessee and the Development of Tennessee at the John Sevier State Office Building.

"To the Heroes of 1776 Not dead, but living in deeds such lives inspire."

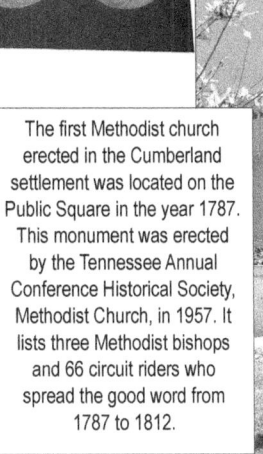

The first Methodist church erected in the Cumberland settlement was located on the Public Square in the year 1787. This monument was erected by the Tennessee Annual Conference Historical Society, Methodist Church, in 1957. It lists three Methodist bishops and 66 circuit riders who spread the good word from 1787 to 1812.

Entrance Doors in Art Deco Style.

⑦ Victory Memorial Bridge / Railroad Bridge

The Victory Memorial Bridge (right) opened in January 1956 to serve as a memorial to Tennesseans who lost their lives in World War Two. A monument and plaque attest to that fact at the west end of the 1,900-foot-long bridge near the courthouse. A dedication ceremony in honor of the war dead was held May 30, 1964, presided over by Mayor Beverly Briley. Bronze plaques list the 752 Davidson Countians who fought and died in World War Two. Later, plaques listing the 71 soldiers killed in the Korean War and the 107 killed during the Vietnam War were added. The bridge connects Main Street in East Nashville with James Robertson Parkway downtown. During construction, a bridge painter, formerly employed as a sponge diver in Greece, claimed to have fallen 100 feet from the bridge into the river and survived, twice.

Visible to the north, downstream from the Victory Memorial Bridge, is the Railroad Bridge (below), originally built in 1859 of stone piers and wooden superstructure, with its revolving center span which allowed tall vessels to pass. The bridge was burned by retreating Confederates in 1862, but quickly rebuilt by occupying Union forces, who reinforced it with palisades and gun turrets. Later the bridge was rebuilt with a steel superstructure, but retaining the historic stone piers. Visible downstream from the railroad bridge is the Kelly Miller Smith Bridge at Jefferson Street.

Native-American Historic Sites

Clee's Ferry Site *(Cleeces Ferry Road off Annex Avenue in Charlotte Park, West Nashville).* This site is on the banks of the Cumberland River, particularly the north bank. The white sand-like material is actually river mussel shells piled on the bank for thousands of years by Indians who lived there. The Clee's Ferry shell mound stretches for about 100 yards along the river, and extends from 100 to 200 yards away from the river bank. The Cumberland was once much narrower than it is today. All four prehistoric periods are represented at the Clee's Ferry site. Paleo-Indians hunted mastodon here during the last Ice Age. Archaic, Woodland, and Mississippian Period villages and towns were located here. The site was occupied more or less continuously for the past 9,000 years.

Ganier Site *(located to the southeast of the Clee's Ferry parking lot).* During the 1960s, excavations were made here to collect information about the site before it was destroyed by residential construction. This work revealed that Native Americans lived here during the Archaic, Woodland, and Mississippian Periods. During the Archaic and Woodland Periods, Indians had small campsites here that were probably occupied seasonally. They made temporary camps at good hunting or fishing places, and to gather certain plants at different times of the year. The Ganier site was occupied from around 1200 A.D. to 1450 A.D.

Noel Cemetery *(area of Granny White Pike and Clifton Lane)* was a large Mississippian-era burial ground that contained 3,000 graves. This was just one of several other cemeteries of comparable size in the Nashville area. Mississippian Indians usually lined their burials with large limestone slabs. This type of burial is called a stone-box grave.

By the early 1900s the burial ground had been completely destroyed by looters. Even the remains of the people buried here were taken away. A large number of artifacts from the Noel Cemetery can be seen at the Tennessee State Museum.

Today, residential neighborhoods cover the area once known as the Noel Cemetery, and I-440 cuts through the otherwise quiet neighborhood. The Battle of Nashville Monument was recently moved here from its former location.

Nashville Mound *(area of Bicentennial Capitol Mall State Park)* was a Mississippian Period platform mound that was about 10 feet high and 30 feet across at the base. Early accounts say stone-box graves surrounded the pyramid-shaped mound. This burial ground stretched all the way to the river, about six blocks away. Around 1710 a French trader built a trading post on the Nashville Mound to trade with the Shawnee who lived in the area at that time. A historical marker near the intersection of Jefferson Street and 5th Avenue commemorates the trading post.

Shawnee Settlements *(Fifth and Jefferson at north end of Bicentennial Mall Park)* The Great French Lick historical marker fails to mention that the French trading post built near the intersection of Jefferson Street and 5th Avenue was built to trade with the Shawnee who lived in the area in the early 1700s.

Fort Nashborough *(foot of Broadway at the Cumberland River)* is a replica of the white settlers' first fort. See full article on page 8.

Buchanan's Station *(historical marker at Elm Hill Pike and Massman Drive)* was built near Mill Creek soon after Fort Nashborough was constructed. The Chickamaugan Indian towns formally declared war on the United States in September of 1792. On Sept. 30, 1792 at midnight, a force of 280 Chickamaugans led by John Watts attacked the fort at Buchanan's Station, about four miles east of Fort Nashborough. The sharpshooters in the fort, numbering about 20 men, were able to kill or wound many of the Indian leaders, including Watts and his brother Unacata; Little Owl, brother of Dragging Canoe; Shawnee Warrior, who had led 30 Shawnees; Tallotiskie, leader of 83 Creek warriors; and Chiachattalla, who had unsuccessfully tried to set the roof of the station on fire with a torch. The Indians retreated when settlers at Fort Nashborough fired their cannon, signaling that help was on the way.

The Chickasaw Treaty *(historical marker at Morrow Road and Terry Drive near West Park)* commemorates a treaty between white settlers and the Chickasaw Nation near here in 1783 which allocated much of the Cumberland basin to the settlers. Despite the friendliness of the Chickasaw, the settlers continued to battle with Cherokee and Creek Indians.

Nashville Toll Bridge *(site of Victory Memorial Bridge)* is where the Cherokee people passed through Nashville during their forced march, "Trail of Tears," to the Oklahoma Territories in 1838. About four thousand Indians died during the forced relocation. The Trail of Tears National Historic Trail (northern trail) starts in Calhoun, Georgia and ends in Oklahoma. In native Cherokee the trail is called nunna-da-ul-tsun-yi or "place where they cried."

Source: www.nativenashville.com, where much more information is available.

Wall Street of the South

- (8) Stahlman Building
- (9) Federal Reserve Building
- (10) Nashville Trust Building
- (11) American Trust Building

Between the Great War and the Great Depression, insurance, banking, and securities businesses made Nashville the "Wall Street of the South," and the nexus of that activity was Union Street at Third Avenue, not far from the City Square.

At the helm of this prosperity were Rogers Caldwell (1890-1968), known as the "J.P. Morgan of the South," and Luke Lea (1879-1945), a reformist politician and newspaper tycoon. Caldwell launched Caldwell and Company and the Bank of Tennessee, and invested in insurance, mills, oil firms, stores, and others. When the Depression hit, the collapse of Caldwell and Co. brought down 120 banks throughout the South. He retired to his 200-acre Brentwood Hall estate, which in 1961 became the headquarters for the state Department of Agriculture.

Lea was elected to the U.S. Senate in 1911 and raised the 114th Field Artillery Regiment during World War One. Following the armistice, Lea led a small band of men into Holland in an unsuccessful attempt to kidnap the exiled German Kaiser. During the 1920s he donated 868 acres of land in the affluent Belle Meade area of Nashville for Percy Warner Park, named after his father-in-law.

Four remarkable buildings can be seen at Union and Third, including the Stahlman Building, which was built in 1905-06 to house the Fourth National Bank. Its form follows the Classical Revival plan for skyscrapers, the entire building mimicking the form of a classical column. The three-story Doric columnade is the base; the shaft is represented by seven identical stories; and the top two stories form the capital. The architects were Carpenter and Blair, and Otto Eggers. Carpenter was Tennessee's first formally trained architect. He designed the Hermitage Hotel and Vanderbilt University's Joint University Library. He went on to design many apartment buildings on Manhattan's Upper East Side.

The building is named for Edward B. Stahlman (1843-1930), publisher of the Nashville *Banner* newspaper and owner of the Nashville Union Stockyards. It was Nashville's second skyscraper and the first to use modern elevators. The bank's original vault is still in the basement. Today it has been renovated into condominiums.

Next door, at 226 Third Avenue North, is the Federal Reserve Bank Building built in 1922. The building features Ionic columns supporting a massive classical pediment. It was designed by Ten Eyck Brown of Atlanta and Marr and Holman. The Federal Reserve is now situated on Eighth Avenue North.

Across the street is the Nashville Bank and Trust Co., built in 1925-26 and designed by Asmus and Clark. It features an ornate exterior in the Corinthian order and an opulent interior.

On the corner is the historic American Trust Building, which opened in 1926. The Classic Revival 15-story building features a four-story Ionic columnade. The architect was Henry C. Hibbs. The building has been renovated and converted into a luxury hotel.

12 Morris Memorial Building

Marker at 217 Fifth Avenue North

The Morris Memorial Building at Charlotte Avenue and 4th Avenue North was built in 1923-25 and designed by McKissack and McKissack, one of the nation's first African-American architectural firms. Founded in 1918 by Moses McKissack III, the company designed more than 2,000 buildings in the Mid-South.

The building was first occupied by the Citizens Savings Bank and Trust Co., formerly One Cent Savings Bank (1904), the second-oldest black-owned bank in the U.S. The bank was founded by attorney James C. Napier and publisher Richard H. Boyd. The building also housed the National Baptist Convention and the offices of McKissack & McKissack.

Architecturally, at the cornice level, carved stone swags are interspersed with a torch and wreath motif which is echoed in the stained-glass skylight in the lobby.

Today the building is occupied by the Sunday School Publishing Board of the National Baptist Convention, USA, Inc.

13 St. Mary's Church

St. Mary of the Seven Sorrows Catholic Church at 330 Fifth Avenue North was built in 1844-1847 as the first Catholic cathedral of the Diocese of Nashville under the first bishop, Richard Pius Miles. It is the oldest standing church building in Nashville. Bishop Miles died in 1860 and lies at rest in a tomb inside the church.

It is now believed that the architect was Adolphus Heiman although Capitol designer William Strickland was attributed to the design for many years. The building was notable at the time for its large freestanding sanctuary supported by horizontal stress beams.

During the Civil War the building was used as a military hospital, and more than 300 soldiers died there of wounds or disease. In 1914 the Cathedral of the Incarnation was built on West End Avenue and St. Mary's, now called "the old cathedral," became a parish church.

Today the westward-facing facade is stone covered, but originally the church was built entirely of brick. In 1926 the belfry was modified by enclosing the circular arcade with louvers.

In 1970 the church was placed on the National Register of Historic Places.

⑭ John Sevier State Office Building

The John Sevier State Office Building (1939-40) is located east of the Capitol at 500 Charlotte Avenue. The 108,349-square-foot edifice by Nashville architect Emmons Woolwine in the Streamlined Classical style is an example of the New Deal-era style of government buildings constructed during the 1930s. The building, which sits diagonally on its lot and faces the corner, is known for housing Tennessee historical murals by Dean Cornwell. The murals give the pictorial history of Tennessee starting with the first white men who stopped on the bluffs near Memphis. The art was completed in the 1940s. The bronze door artwork is by sculptor Rene Chambellan. The building is named for the state's first governor.

⑮ Musicians Hall of Fame and Museum

The Musicians Hall of Fame, located in the historic Nashville Municipal Auditorium at 401 Gay Street, is the only museum in the world that honors the talented musicians who actually played on the greatest recordings of all time. Some such as Jimi Hendrix are well known, while others such as L.A sessions drummer Hal Blaine are not as well known to the public, but these artists have played on hundreds of hit records from Elvis, Frank and Nancy Sinatra, The Byrds, The Mamas and The Papas, and The Beach Boys, just to name a very few. The Musicians Hall Of Fame And Museum has on exhibit the instruments that these musicians used to record many of these classic hits.

The Grammy Museum Gallery is an interactive facility that allows guests to explore the history of the Grammy Awards. With the privacy of headphones, visitors can play electric drums, keyboard, bass, and guitar, or sing along with Ray Charles and the Raelettes, the all-girl group who provided backing vocals for the legendary musician. For those interested in what goes on behind the scenes in the studio, exhibits for songwriting, engineering, and producing allow gallery attendees to get in the booth and see for themselves what it takes to cut a record. There are also interactive exhibits for singing, recording, and DJing, and a recording studio and rehearsal room for those who want the full recording experience.

The Musicians Hall of Fame and Museum ("Come See What You've Heard") is open Monday – Saturday 10-5. The last museum tour starts at 4:00 pm. Adult admission is $25; youth $15. Consult the website for latest changes at www.musicianshalloffame.com.

16) People of Tennessee Sculptures

Sculptures depicting the Tennessee people can be found on the west and north side of the Cordell Hull State Office Building at 436 Sixth Avenue North (directly east of the State Capitol).

The pieces were sculpted by Puryear Mims (1906-1975), a Vanderbilt University professor, in 1951-52.

From top to bottom are:
- The Equestrian Group
- The Industry or TVA Group
- The Farm Family
- The Mountain Group

⑰ Bicentennial Capitol Mall State Park

Bicentennial Capitol Mall State Park as seen looking north from Capitol Hill. In the forefront is the Capitol belvedere, or overlook, and James Robertson Parkway. In front of the white-painted railroad trestle is the large granite map of the state of Tennessee. Under the trestle to the right is the Visitors Center; to the left restroom facilities. At the far left, along 7th Avenue North is Farmers Market. In the park running parallel with the avenue is the Wall of History. Immediately behind the trestle in the center is the Greek-style amphitheater. The diagonal walkways in the park converge in the distance at the Court of Three Stars and the carillon towers. In the distance is the Germantown Historic District. The steeple near the water tower is that of the Church of the Assumption. Behind the church is the Werthan Mills building on Rosa Parks Boulevard. Time capsules are buried along the right side of the park.

The Bicentennial Capitol Mall State Park, located at 600 James Robertson Parkway just north of the State Capitol, is an urban history park dedicated in 1996 to commemorate the 200th anniversary of Tennessee statehood.

Admission to the 19-acre park is free, and so is parking along Sixth and Seventh avenues. The phone is (615) 741-5280. Interpretive history programs are provided by park rangers on weekdays. The park visitors center and gift shop are located under the east end of the train trestle and restrooms are under the west end.

The park is located at the historic salt lick and sulphur spring site (no longer visible), where the first French trading post was built.

The south entrance of the park features the 200-foot-long granite Tennessee map, which highlights the state's major roads, 95 counties, rivers, interesting geographic formations, and details of each county. Inlaid lighting illuminates the map at night.

Smaller granite maps nearby show the state's terrain, historic trails, music history, geology, and populations. The Zero Mile Marker is the point from which all state mile markers are measured.

Behind the train trestle, the Rivers of Tennessee Fountains consist of 31 vertical water fountains, one for each of the predominant waterways in Tennessee. The River Walk is accented with a bowed and arched granite wall with inscriptions describing Tennessee's waterways.

Along the west side of the park, a 1,400-foot-long Wall of History is engraved with historic events that have occurred over the past two centuries. A granite pylon marks each ten-year period along the wall. The wall breaks at the time of the Civil War to represent the divisive nature of the war on the state of Tennessee.

Also here is McNairy Spring, a monument and fountain representing the founding of Tennessee. The fountain sits on top of the sulphur spring that fed the Old French Lick Creek. A greenway trail has been built on top of the creek and winds from the park eastward to the Cumberland River.

At the 1940s pylon is perhaps the park's most distinctive feature: the World War Two Memorial and its giant granite globe floating on water. See the following pages for more details.

The east side of the park features the Walkway of Counties that contains a time capsule from each of Tennessee's 95 counties. These time capsules will be opened at the Tercentennial in 2096. This historical walkway highlights the topographical features of each region of the state, depicting the flat, mountainous, and rolling hills sections. Native trees,

Map of Bicentennial Capitol Mall State Park

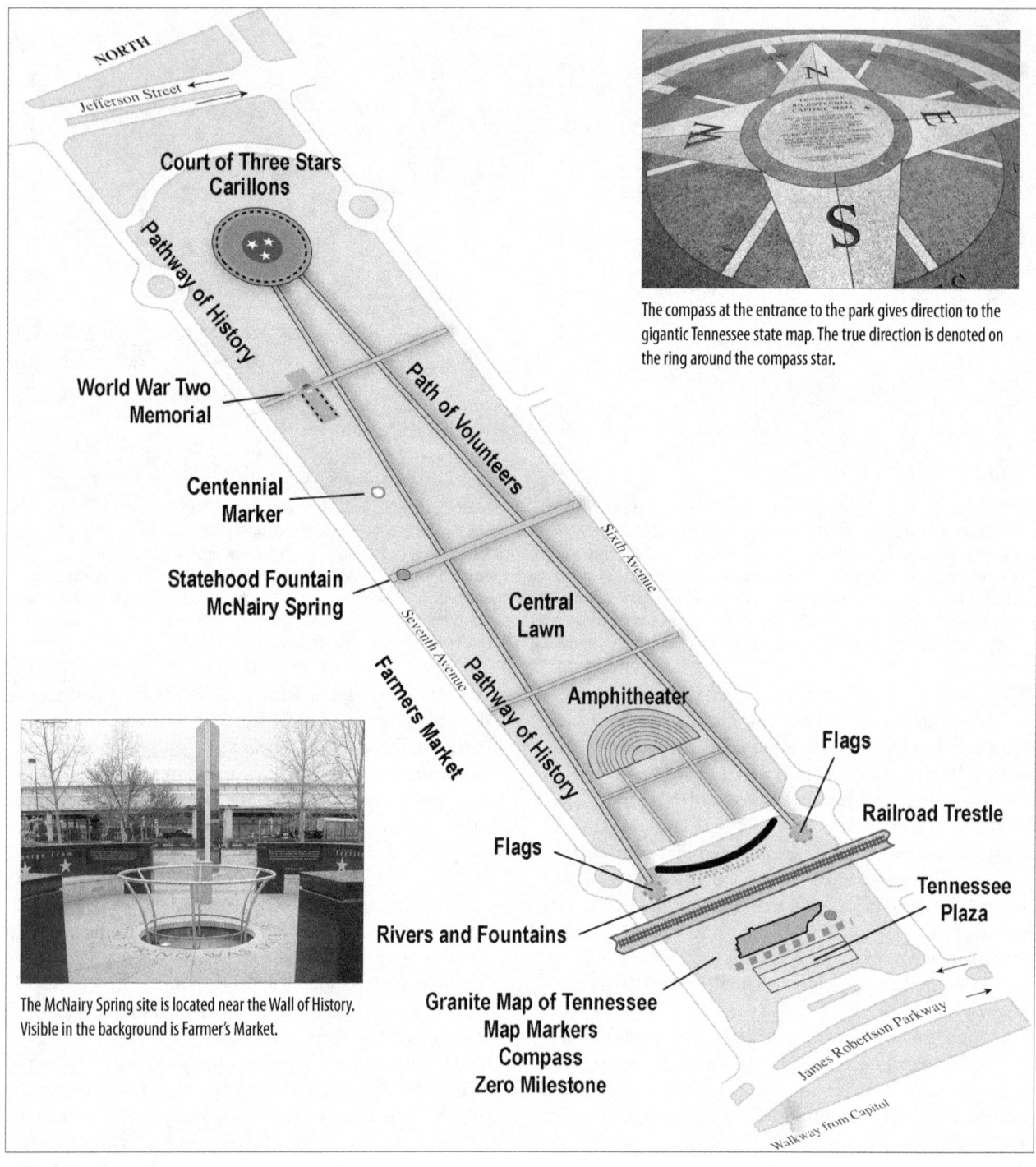

The compass at the entrance to the park gives direction to the gigantic Tennessee state map. The true direction is denoted on the ring around the compass star.

The McNairy Spring site is located near the Wall of History. Visible in the background is Farmer's Market.

Carillons at the Court of Three Stars

shrubs, ferns, grasses, and wildflowers along the walkway represent the diverse vegetation found across the state.

The center section of the park features a 2,000-seat amphitheater, composed of terraced lawns, and patterned after Greek amphitheaters, such as the one at Epidaurus.

Diagonal pathways lead to the north end of the park and the Court of Three Stars. Made of red, white and blue granite, this area represents the three grand divisions of the state—East, Middle, and West Tennessee. This is also the site of a 95-bell carillon representing Tennessee's musical heritage. The 95 bells represent the citizens of Tennessee's 95 counties. A 96th bell, known as the answer bell, is located on the elevated grounds of the State Capitol and rings in answer to the 95 bells, symbolizing government answering to the people. The carillons are the largest in the world.

Nearby is the Civilian Conservation Corps Memorial. CCC veterans and President Franklin Delano Roosevelt's grandson David dedicated the memorial in April 1998.

A fresh-water fountain on the French Lick Creek Greenway near the park at Sulphur Spring Bottom symbolizes the sulphur spring in north Nashville that first attracted wild animals, Indian hunters, European traders, and later white settlers.

According to greenway signage: "Fossils indicate that Pliocene mammals began drinking the salty sulphur spring water about 2.5 million years ago, These included giant camels, mastodons, wild horses, deer, ox-sized ground sloths, native American pigs, and saber-toothed tigers.

"The salt water rose from 1,000 feet below through Bigby Limestone made of marine creatures from an ancient sea (570 million years ago). The ratio of salt to sulphur has fluctuated over time."

Other free sources of this curative sulphur water were located at Morgan Park and at Werthan Packaging's spigot, which was turned off in 1994.

This area was also the site of the Sulphur Dell baseball field. Union soldiers occupying Nashville first played baseball here in 1862. Herman Sandhouse organized the first amateur team. By 1901 Nashville was a member of the professional Southern Association League. Nashvillian Newt Fisher managed the Nashville Americans (later the Fishermen and finally the Vols), who won the first of their nine league championships that inaugural season of 1901. The park was also occasionally used by the Negro National League's Nashville Elite Giants.

Bounded by Fourth and Fifth avenues north, Jackson Street, and the railroad spur, the park had several peculiarities, including a tendency to flood. The park was 22 feet below street level, and the outfield was inclined so that some fielders had to run 25 feet up a steep embankment to make a catch. The rightfield fence was only 262 feet from home plate. In 1908, famous Nashville sportswriter Grantland Rice gave the park its name, Sulphur Dell. When the park was closed in 1963, after 97 years of operation, Sulphur Dell was the oldest professional ballfield in America.

★ World War Two Memorial ★
Impressive Design Commemorates Greatest Generation

The World War Two Memorial honors the 360,000 Tennesseans who served in the armed forces and the 5,731 Tennesseans who lost their lives defending freedom. The memorial consists of a plaza bordered by ten large granite pylons which are engraved with illustrations and text about the conflict. The western row of five pylons commemorates the Pacific Theater with the titles of Outrage, Resolve, Valor, Fortitude, and Victory. The eastern row explains the war in Europe and North Africa with the titles Terror, Conviction, Courage, Triumph, and Gratitude.

The focal point is a nine-ton solid-granite globe—the largest of its type ever made—which rotates on a thin cushion of water. The vast distances that soldiers traveled from Tennessee are marked on the globe. (Due to icing problems, the globe does not float or rotate from December to March.)

The south end of the memorial lists the state's seven recipients of the Congressional Medal of Honor in WWII: Raymond Henry Cooley, Charles Henry Coolidge, Paul B. Huff, Elbert Luther Kinser, Charles L. McGaha, Vernon McGarity, and John Harlan Willis. Kinser and Willis were killed in action.

Inlaid glass gold stars are a reminder of the war's Gold Star Program in which survivors of the war dead hung gold star banners in the windows of their homes.

Nashville was a vital cog in the war machine. Nashville Bridge Co. produced approximately 14 anti-submarine vessels (sub chasers), two minesweepers, and 70 barges at its site on the east bank of the Cumberland River opposite downtown Nashville. Near the end of the war Nashville Bridge employed 900 workers for government contracts totaling $20.8 million.

Through innovation and initiative, the Tennessee Enamel Manufacturing Co., makers of gas heaters, obtained $20.5 million in contracts to build aircraft bombs. Its 700 employees could produce one million bombs every three months.

All in all, $226 million in defense contracts were awarded to 40 firms located in Nashville. More than 280,000 Tennesseans worked in war-related manufacturing.

In Oak Ridge, the Clinton Engineering Works was hastily built as part of the Manhattan Project, a closed and "secret city" whose huge industrial plants used both electro-magnetic separation and gaseous diffusion to produce enriched uranium for the first atomic bomb dropped over Hiroshima, Japan, bringing the war to an end.

Soldiers were trained at Camp Campbell and Camp Forrest, and pilots were trained at Smyrna Air Force Base near Nashville. Major General George Patton conducted tank maneuvers in Middle Tennessee in 1941.

Later, Middle Tennessee was the site of extensive war maneuvers by the U.S. Second Army involving 850,000 men prior to the invasion of France. The area was chosen in part due to its terrain resembling western Europe. Headquartered at Cumberland University in Lebanon, Red and Blue "armies" battled each other, learning tactics to be used during the invasion of Europe and generating $4 million in property-damage claims. On weekends, 100,000 enthusiastic military trainees flooded into Nashville looking for fun and recreation.

Detail from CONVICTION pylon: Shift change in 1945 at the Y-12 Plant at the Clinton Engineering Works (CEW) in the secret city of Oak Ridge, Tenn. as the work force, mostly young ladies who operated the calutrons, completes another day of work on "the device." The historic photo was taken by CEW photographer Ed Westcott.

⑱ Tennessee State Museum

5 Star Attraction

The new Tennessee State Museum, located at 1000 Rosa Parks Blvd. at Jefferson Street (near the northwest corner of Bicentennial Capitol Park), opened in late 2018 with permanent collections, including:

Natural History: Discover the origins of Tennessee's amazing landscapes as well as its diverse animal and plant life, and then see how fossils show examples of life from long ago. Learn about the incredible biodiversity – both plants and animals – of the Great Smoky Mountains National Park. Through a partnership with the Gray Fossil Site in Gray, Tennessee, learn about an animal like the red panda that lived in East Tennessee five million years ago. A media program explores the natural processes that continually shape Tennessee's land

First Peoples (13,000 BC to 1760 AD): The first peoples of Tennessee arrived at the end of the Ice Age. Groups adapted as the climate changed, shifting from small hunting and gathering bands to complex farming societies. In the 1500s, Spanish explorers became the first Europeans to encounter the native peoples living in Tennessee. Cultures collided as more Europeans continued coming into the area. Learn how the First Peoples of Tennessee lived, about their culture, and how they defended their homelands against the European encroachment.

Forging a Nation (1760 to 1860): The period from 1760 to 1860 was a time of almost unimaginable change. Through artifacts, film, and images, discover how settlers moved into the land that became the 16th state, and how Southeastern Indians resisted. Exhibits highlight the challenges and achievements of everyday Tennessee women and men, free and enslaved, who built communities across the Three Grand Divisions. This gallery also features artifacts that explore the lives of Tennessee leaders who shaped the future of the young United States, such as Andrew Jackson, James K. Polk, David Crockett, and Sam Houston. A rare 13-star United States flag is displayed with an exhibit on the role of Tennesseans in the Revolutionary War. War of 1812 artifacts include an American light artillery uniform coat, a sword that belonged to John Coffee who served as one of General Andrew Jackson's commanders, and a mold used by enslaved workers at a Dickson County iron furnace to make cannonballs for General Jackson's army.

Civil War and Reconstruction (1860 to 1870): The Civil War and Reconstruction were monumental times of conflict and

change for the people of Tennessee. Featured artifacts and stories in this exhibit document a period that forced Tennesseans to take sides and make sacrifices. Visitors will learn how Tennesseans determined to secede from the Union and how the state remained divided on the issue throughout the war. The major battles and personalities are featured including the experiences of common soldiers. African Americans are highlighted as they seek their own freedom, and some eventually fight for the Union.

Change and Challenge (1870 to 1945): Between 1870 and 1945, Tennesseans struggled to find ways forward through economic upheavals, social changes, and international conflicts. Featured artifacts document the tremendous changes that occurred in how people lived and worked. Exhibits highlight how African Americans resisted segregation, and women fought for the right to vote.

Tennessee Transforms (1945 to Present): After World War II, Tennesseans increasingly benefitted from new innovations in areas like business, technology, and education, ushering in an era of prosperity by the 1950s. Still, the Cold War, along with increasing social unrest, served as an uncomfortable backdrop. Featured artifacts and images document the struggle of Tennesseans to make sense of the changes brought about by these ironies. Exhibits highlight the impacts of post-war innovations on Tennesseans, the struggle of African-Americans to share in the new prosperity, the development of Tennessee's music industries and their importance in shaping how outsiders view Tennessee, and how today's Tennessee has emerged as a reflection of these dynamics. Through artifacts such as astronaut Barry "Butch" Wilmore's flight uniform, photos of Tennesseans involved in the modern Civil Rights Movement, and William Franklin "Frank" Lyell's posthumous Medal of Honor for his service in the Korean War, you will come away with an understanding of how Tennesseans navigated these times as a unique people who helped shape a national culture.

The 360 Interactive Theater features a cross-section of people, places, and events that have occurred across Tennessee from World War II to the present.

Children's Gallery: The Children's Gallery encourages children ages 3-8 to explore, play, and discover Tennessee's history and culture in a hands-on way. Take a tour of Tennessee by walking along a giant map of the state, stopping along the way to learn what makes Tennessee unique and extraordinary.

The museum's store offers handmade items from artisans across Tennessee in addition to history-related merchandise, books, and souvenirs. The museum also includes a digital learning center, a two-story grand hall, an assembly area, and educational classrooms.

Free parking can be used in the lot between the museum and the Farmers' Market. All of the museum's facilities are accessible to persons with disabilities.

Tours are available for groups of ten or more by calling (615) 741-0830.

The state museum's hours are:

Sunday: 1-5 pm

Monday: Closed

Tuesday and Wednesday: 10-5

Thursday: 10-8

Friday and Saturday: 10-5

Check the museum website at TNMuseum.org for latest changes. Phone (615) 741-2692 or (800) 407-4324

State Capitol Grounds and War Memorial Plaza

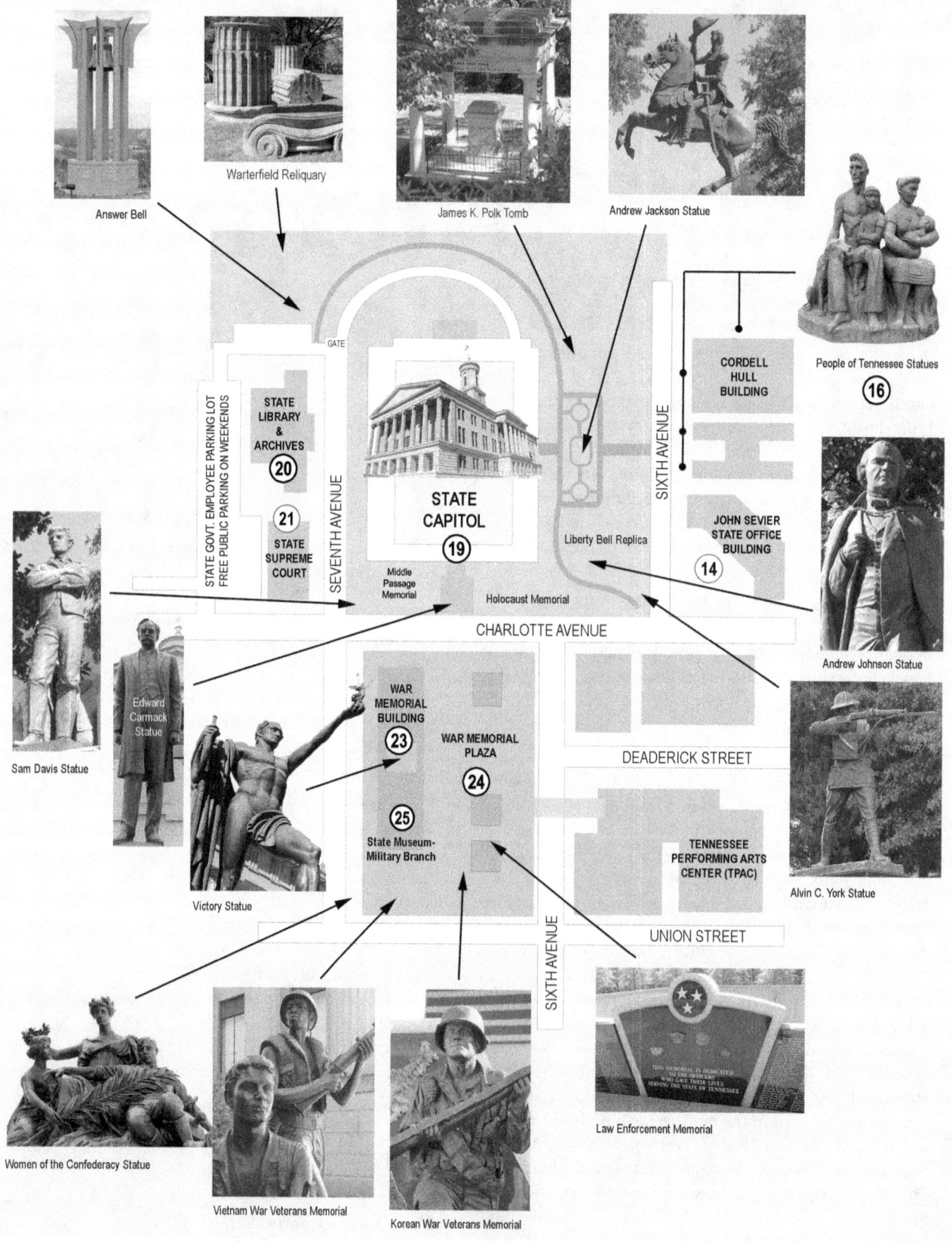

19 Tennessee State Capitol
National Historic Landmark Still In Use By Legislature

The Tennessee State Capitol, a hilltop temple of democracy on America's first frontier, was built in 1845-1859 and still serves as the seat of state government. The General Assembly meets there, the governor's office is located there, gala ceremonies are conducted there, and special-interest groups still protest there. Capitol Hill is designated a National Historic Landmark.

The Capitol is located in north-central downtown at 600 Charlotte Avenue, between Sixth and Seventh avenues.

On weekdays, visitors can enjoy free guided tours on the hour from 9 a.m. to 3 p.m. (except noon) beginning at the Information Desk on the first floor. Public entrance to the Capitol is on the west side, directly opposite the State Library and Archives. Groups of ten or more should make a reservation prior to their visit by calling the Public Programs Department at (615) 741-0830 or toll-free (800) 407-4324. Self-guided tours with an informational brochure can also be taken.

The Tennessee State Capitol is steeped in history, serving as a fort for Unionists during the Civil War, the backdrop for the naming of the American flag as Old Glory, the decisive battleground in securing women's right to vote, gunfire during Tennessee's readmission into the Union, at least one accidental

5 Star Attraction

death, and a virtual art gallery of sculptures and monuments to great men and women and their causes.

The Capitol's esteemed architect, William Strickland of Philadelphia, is buried within its walls, and President and Mrs. James K. Polk are buried on the grounds in a tomb designed by Strickland. The Chairman of the Capitol Commission, Samuel D. Morgan, the man most responsible for preserving the integrity of the building during its 16 years of construction, is also buried within its walls.

It is one of the few state capitols topped by a tower (forty others have domes). The Capitol is also a National Historic Civil Engineering Landmark for being the first to use structural iron roof trusses.

The State Capitol and grounds form the nucleus of a history-rich tourist district consisting of the War Memorial Plaza, War Memorial Building, State Museum and its Military Branch, and the Bicentennial Capitol Mall State Park to the north.

The Tennessee State Capitol, a Greek Revival temple by design, sits atop Campbell's Hill, 200 feet above the Cumberland

Tennessee State Capitol: National Historic Landmark

River, which flows six city blocks to its east. The four-acre site, originally known as Cedar Knob, was the home of attorney George W. Campbell. Although Tennessee became the 16th state in 1796, Nashville wasn't designated the permanent capital until 1843. Knoxville, Kingston, and Murfreesboro served at times as the state capital, and in Nashville the legislature met at the Davidson County Courthouse.

Representing the city, Mayor Powhattan Maxey bought the tract for $39,000 and offered it to the state for free, a major inducement for locating the capital in Nashville. Campbell's house was moved to south of Cedar Street (now Charlotte Avenue) and served as home to Military Governor Andrew Johnson during the Union occupation of Nashville during the Civil War. The house, along with many grand but dilapidated townhouses surrounding the Capitol, were torn down during 20th-Century construction and renewal projects.

Campbell had not been the only occupant on the hill. The Holy Rosary Cathedral was located at the northeast corner of the plot. According to the historical marker: "Near here in 1820 the first Catholic Church in Tennessee was built by Irish Catholic workers then building a bridge over the Cumberland River. In 1830 a brick structure known as Holy Rosary Cathedral succeeded the frame building. Here Bishop R.P. Miles, first Bishop of Tennessee, was installed Oct. 15, 1838. When St. Mary's Cathedral was built in 1847, Holy Rosary Church became St. John's Hospital and Orphanage. The site was sold to the state in 1857."

Philadelphia Notable Strickland Chosen Architect

It was with great and unprecedented fanfare, including elaborate Masonic ritual and political speechifying, that the cornerstone for the magnificent Tennessee State Capitol was laid on July 4, 1845. Tennessee's favorite son and national hero Andrew Jackson had died just a month before, while Old Hickory's protégé James Knox Polk had been inaugurated earlier that year as the eleventh U.S. President. At that time, Tennessee's third and future President, Andrew Johnson of East Tennessee, was serving in the U.S. House of Representatives.

Created by the General Assembly in 1844, the Tennessee Capitol Commission considered several architects before selecting Strickland. A native of New Jersey, Strickland was one of the young nation's most prestigious architects. As a teenager he apprenticed to Benjamin Latrobe, architect of the U.S. Capitol. He won a design competition for the Second Bank of the U.S. in Philadelphia. He supervised the restoration of the tower over Independence Hall. In 1832 he designed the Merchant Exchange in Philadelphia, which features a choragic tower. He designed the sarcophagus for George Washington's tomb at Mount Vernon. Several of his plans were rejected, however, including Washington monuments in Philadelphia and the District of Columbia and an enlargement of the U.S. Capitol.

The Story of Old Glory

The Tennessee State Capitol played a significant role in the story of the American flag becoming known as Old Glory. It happened in 1862 at the beginning of the Civil War.

Captain William Driver (1803-1886), a veteran merchant ship's captain from New England who had sailed around the world twice, retired to Nashville in 1837 after the death of his wife. In 1824 his wife had sewn a large 10 x 17 American flag to fly on her husband's ship. When he saw it for the first time he called it Old Glory.

In Nashville, Capt. Driver, a staunch Unionist, flew his beloved flag over the street at his home on holidays and his birthday, March 17. Originally it bore 24 stars but ten more were added in 1860, reflecting the growth of the nation, along with an anchor sewn on the canton. When the Confederates took over Nashville, he hid the flag within a quilt.

On Feb. 25, 1862, Union soldiers captured Nashville without firing a shot and marched up Cedar Street to the State Capitol. They raised the Stars and Stripes above the building. Driver uncovered his cherished flag and climbed above the east entrance and hoisted Old Glory up the flag mast. He remained to guard it all that night. Too fragile to fly for long, he retrieved it the next day. Soldiers and civilians then began to refer to the American flag as Old Glory, and the name stuck.

Although Driver strongly favored the Union, three of his sons fought for the Confederacy, and one was killed at the Battle of Perryville in Kentucky.

Captain Driver is buried at the City Cemetery in Nashville, where the American flag flies 24 hours a day by special Congressional approval.

Today the original Old Glory is stored at the National Museum of American History, Smithsonian Institution, Washington, D.C. although it is not normally on pubic display.

In 2006 the faded and fragile Old Glory returned to Nashville for the first time in 100 years for a temporary exhibition at the Tennessee State Museum.

At the invitation of the Capitol Commission, Strickland visited Nashville and submitted plans, which were accepted. On June 18, 1845, he signed a contract for the project at a salary of $2,500 a year.

Construction Brings Controversy

Strickland estimated the building would cost $340,000 ($90,000 less if convict labor was used) and take three years to construct. There is some evidence that Strickland intentionally low-balled the cost estimate. As it turned out, the construction lasted 16 years and cost three to four times the estimate.

Commissioners did not receive any compensation for their duties. During the 16 years of construction (1844-1859) one million dollars in legislative appropriations passed through

Tennessee State Capitol: National Historic Landmark

the Capitol Commission, and from all historical evidence the funds were expended honestly.

The meager annual appropriations from the legislature and the use of convict labor caused continuous controversy and frequent delays. Nevertheless, the project was one of the most ambitious of the era. The State of Ohio began its statehouse in 1839 and took 22 years to complete at cost of $1.3 million.

A Greek Monument Atop a Greek Temple

The Tennessee State Capitol is a Greek Ionic temple by design, 236 feet by 109 feet, with a unique tower bringing its height to 206 feet. The floor plan is somewhat deceiving from the exterior. The base is a rusticated vaulted stone crypt. The next level up was originally known as the basement; it now houses state offices. The next level up is the main level, housing the Senate and House chambers and the State Library Room. This high-ceilinged main level features two rows of windows, giving the illusion from the exterior that it is actually two stories. The building is surrounded by stone terraces.

There are porticoes at each of the four main facades. The east facade, facing the river, is the historic main entrance. The east and west porticoes each feature six Ionic stone columns. The larger north and south porticoes each feature eight columns. Each carved stone column is 36 feet tall and 4.5 feet in diameter.

The square rusticated base of the tower is 42 feet tall and the slender circular tower is 37 feet tall. The tower is based on the Choragic Monument built in Athens, Greece about 334 B.C. by Lysicrates, a great choral leader. The Tennessee tower is twice the size of the original Greek monument, also known as the Lantern of Diogenes. The columns of the tower are of the Corinthian order, with acanthus leaves. The cornice is topped by delicate acroteria. Strickland created a large wooden model of the tower during the construction phase which can be seen at the nearby State Museum.

Strickland also designed the Wilson County Courthouse (1848) in Lebanon with a choragic tower. This building does not survive. But Strickland could create other designs. In 1849 he designed the First Presbyterian Church in downtown Nashville in the Egyptian Revival style, very unusual for a Christian church of the period. This magnificent twin-towered brick church survives as the Downtown Presbyterian Church, and is designated a National Historic Landmark.

Although plans called for a magnificent stone building, it was not to be *too* elaborate. Cornerstone ceremony speaker Edwin Ewing stated that, "Plainess, durability, and convenience are to be studied as more in accordance with republican institutions." Capitol Commissioner John Bass wanted "nothing too elevated or grand for the State of Tennessee."

The Capitol was built entirely of stone. Efforts during construction to hold down costs by substituting brick interior work were rejected, probably at the insistence of Chairman Morgan. The interior walls and columns were made from East Tennessee marble. Architect Strickland noted that there are "no examples of any buildings in the United States, either public or private, in which the walls are constructed of rubbed or polished stones on the interior, indeed, there are very few buildings in Europe of this handsome and permanent class."

Capitol Artwork

The interior of the Capitol serves as a defacto art gallery. Portraits of Strickland, Morgan, and Presidents Jackson, Polk, and Johnson can be found on the first floor along with portraits of 20 former governors of Tennessee. Ceiling frescoes painted in 1858 by German immigrants John Schleicher and Theo Knoch depict Westward Expansion surrounded by Muses of Literature, Sculpture, Music and Painting; an American Eagle surrounded by 31 stars (the number of states at the time); Justice; Liberty; and the State Seal.

The Governor's reception room contains murals painted by Jirayr H. Zorthian during the 1938 remodeling—the First Tennesseans; Hernando de Soto; Fort Prudhomme 1682; Fort Loudoun 1756; Watauga Association 1772; Founding of Nashville 1779-80; Nashville 1855; Battle of the Bluffs at Fort Nashborough 1781; the State of Franklin 1784; and Agriculture and Commerce from the State Seal.

Behind the speaker's podium in the House chamber is the original Tennessee marble wallscreen with vertical Roman spears, signifying strength in unity. The columns in the House gallery are made of Nashville limestone nearly 22 feet tall.

The former State Library Room contains an ornate winding cast-iron staircase. Cast-iron portrait medallions on the railings depict William Shakespeare, Joseph Addison, Dante, U.S. Senator Ephraim Foster, Sir Walter Scott, Lord Byron, George Washington, Benjamin Franklin, Thomas Jefferson, Patrick Henry, Andrew Jackson, Daniel Webster, Henry Clay, John Milton, James K. Polk, Washington Irving, William Hickling Prescott, U.S. Sen. Felix Grundy, Gov. William Carroll, U.S. Sen. Hugh Lawson White, Joseph Story, John Bell, and John C. Calhoun.

Ceiling portraits painted by Schleicher and Knoch in 1859 depict Dr. Gerard Troost, Dr. Phillip Lindsley, James Kent, Dr. James Priestley, Rev. Charles Coffin, Henry Wadsworth Longfellow, Matthew Fontaine Maury, and William Hickling Prescott.

Busts on the main level portray Jackson, Polk, Johnson, John Sevier, Cordell Hull, Nathan Bedford Forrest, Admiral Albert Gleaves, Admiral David Farragut, Matthew Maury, Cherokee linguist Sequoyah, noted author Mary Murfree, and Sampson Keeble, a Nashville barber and first African-American to serve in the Tennessee Legislature, 1873-1874.

Tennessee State Capitol: National Historic Landmark

The tomb of President James K. Polk and Sarah Childress Polk is located on the Capitol grounds just north of the Jackson Garden. Polk died in 1849 only months after vacating the White House. A probable victim of cholera, Polk was first buried at City Cemetery. He was later moved to the tomb built at Polk Place, just blocks from the Capitol, and remained there until the death of Mrs. Polk, after which the tomb was moved to the Capitol grounds. The tomb was designed by Capitol architect William Strickland. Polk Place no longer stands.

Stonework Required Brute Force, Skilled Hands

The limestone for the Capitol was hauled from a quarry owned by Samuel Watkins less than a mile west of the hilltop site (where Charlotte Avenue now intersects with the interstate highway loop). The stone was described as "a stratified limestone, full of fossils, some of it very hard, of a slightly blueish-gray tint, with cloud-like markings." Unfortunately, this Tennessee limestone would prove to be relatively soft and filled with phosphate veins which would hold water, freeze in the wintertime, and crack the stone. Several extensive remodeling and renovation projects would be required over the years.

Located conveniently close to the state penitentiary, the quarry was worked by convict labor totaling about 120 men (convicts were not allowed to work at the building site). The commission deemed it necessary to hire on "15 able-bodied negro men" at $18 per month. Another one hundred men worked at the site and at other duties. The men worked six-day weeks extricating the stone from the quarry, cutting and rubbing stone, and sawing and rolling stone. Stonecutters were paid $2.50 a day; laborers $1 day.

To get started, eight thousand yards of stone and material were removed from the top of Campbell's Hill. The foundation of the Capitol was built of stone seven feet thick; the upper walls are 4.5 feet thick. Each stone weighed six to ten tons (20,000 pounds) and was moved by wooden derricks and block and tackle. The stones were so expertly cut and fitted that the averge mortar joint is less than 3/16ths of an inch.

More than two years after commencement, the Capitol building had risen only to the floor line of the main level. There were several problems and distractions during the construction phase.

In November 1847 Strickland complained: "There are many idle and mischievous boys and young men who indulge in writing pasquinades and vulgar words upon the walls of the State Capitol, and otherwise scarifying the building." (The word pasquinade refers to a statue in ancient Rome on which abusive Latin verses were posted.) In response, the legislature passed a law making it a misdemeanor "to deface the State House."

A cholera epidemic struck Nashville in 1849. Strickland moved to the boarding house of Mrs. Mary Ann Schaub at 924 Jefferson Street (the structure still stands). Strickland's dog Babe died at the time and was buried in the yard, noted by a marker. At the time, the boarding house was "out in the country" even though it could be seen from Capitol Hill.

The Capitol was roofed and enclosed during 1852. Three thousand sheets of copper weighing 27 tons were ordered from C.G. Hussey & Co. of Pittsburgh for the roof. The 210 tons of round and flat iron bars for the roof trusses were produced by Cumberland Iron Works of Stewart County, Tenn.

The Capitol Is Occupied by the Legislature

On Oct. 3, 1853, the General Assembly met in the new but far-from-finished building for the first time. Referring to the new structure, outgoing Governor William B. Campbell told the legislature: "May your proceedings be characterized by similar order, harmony, and dignity."

Historian and State Capitol Curator James Hoobler described the interior of the Capitol: "The interior included space on the ground floor for the governor's office, the State Archives, offices of the secretary of state, the treasurer, and the register of land, as well as the Tennessee Supreme Court, a federal district court, and the Repository of the Official Weights and Measures. The main floor contained the assembly halls for the House of Representatives and the Senate, legislative committee rooms, and the State Library, which is considered the finest room in the Capitol. The library features cast-iron stacks, surrounding galleries, and a cast-iron spiral staircase connecting the various stack levels. Wood & Perot Company provided the decorative iron work in the library, as well as the iron work for the staircases in the main building and the cupola tower." T.M. Brennan ironworks of Nashville produced the foliated ornamental iron on the tower.

The south crypt held furnaces and fuel while the north crypt was used as the State Arsenal and held 8,000 pieces of weaponry.

Lighting fixtures were provided by Cornelius and Baker of Philadelphia, which had provided fixtures for the U.S. Capitol and 11 state capitols. Four gasoliers were needed—one for each legislative chamber, one for the main hall, and one

Tennessee State Capitol: National Historic Landmark

Andrew Johnson (1808-1875) of East Tennessee served as the 17th President of the United States (1865-69) following the assassination of Abraham Lincoln. Although a Southern Democrat he had been elected as Lincoln's Vice-President on the Union Party ticket in November 1864. He went on to become the first President to be impeached; he avoided conviction in the U.S. Senate by one vote. He is the only President to later be elected to the U.S. Senate. At the time of the onset of hostilities he was the only Southern U.S. Senator to remain loyal to the Union (his native East Tennessee was strongly Unionist even though Tennessee was a Confederate state). In Nashville, during the Union occupation of the city, Johnson served as the military governor, tasked by Lincoln to bring Tennessee back into the Union fold. Johnson tried to force Union loyalty from the local populace, but most efforts failed. Johnson was not well liked in Nashville. He was shot in front of the State Capitol by a drunken Union soldier but only slightly wounded. During the war he ordered the Capitol fortified and protected by heavy guns. The statue of Johnson by sculptor Jim Gray was erected at the Capitol in 1995. Johnson is buried at the Andrew Johnson National Historic Site in Greeneville, Tenn.

The equestrian statue of General Andrew Jackson was dedicated in 1880 in a garden on the Capitol grounds just east of the building. The statue was sculpted by Clark Mills. Identical statues are found in Lafayette Park in Washington, D.C.; and Jackson Square in New Orleans. A copy is also found in Jacksonville, Fla.

for the library. The fanciful House gasolier featured 48 burners and bronze figures of Indians, American eagles, buffaloes, corn, tobacco leaves, and cotton blossoms. The Senate chamber gasolier had 30 burners. The gasoliers were converted to electricity in 1895.

Death of Strickland and Other Setbacks

On April 7, 1854, architect Strickland died unexpectedly at the City Hotel, where he was residing. The funeral conducted in the House chambers the next day drew 2,000 to 3,000 people. By his prior wishes, he was interred in a vault in the northeast corner of the Capitol. (The inscription on the vault is incorrect—he was age 66 when he died.)

Strickland's eldest son, Francis, age 36, was named architect. He had already been working with his father on the project for many months without compensation.

In March of 1855 a tornado caused $2,000 in damages to the roof (in 1998 a tornado blew out the center blue circle from the state flag atop the Capitol) and two weeks later a fire at the prison destroyed the stonecutters' shops. In that year the tower was installed and the Capitol was basically completed except for interior spaces and exterior terraces. Also in that year, Francis Strickland designed the new Davidson County Courthouse, which strongly resembled the State Capitol except for the absence of a tower.

In 1857 the state purchased the northeast corner of the plot once occupied by Holy Rosary Cathedral.

Francis Strickland was fired by the commission in 1857 after two years of disagreements. In December 1858 Harvey M. Akeroyd was hired to finish the work on the Capitol. He designed the elaborate State Library room, patterned after the library of Sir Walter Scott in Abbotsford, Scotland.

The Final Stone is Laid in 1859

On March 19, 1859, with no ceremony, the final stone was laid on the lower terrace. The Capitol grounds were still unfinished, described in one report as being "in a most chaotic state, a mere mass of huge broken rocks, together with various dilapidated out houses, altogether a disgrace to the State and city." A civil engineer was hired, and stabilization and landscaping plans adopted. Unfortunately, disaster struck again as the Civil War disrupted those plans. Chairman Morgan, a secessionist, was busy establishing a factory to make percussion caps for the Confederate army. Governor Isham Harris and the state legislature, meeting for several months as the govern-

Tennessee State Capitol: National Historic Landmark

ing body of a Confederate state, fled Nashville for Memphis as the Union army approached.

On Feb. 25, 1862, Nashville became the first capital of a Confederate state to fall to invading Union forces. After the mayor surrendered the city (no shots having been fired by either side), Union troops marched from the river up Cedar Street to hoist the Stars and Stripes atop the Capitol. Troops encamped on the rough grounds. Vandals broke into the State Library room in the Capitol and unwrapped the 3500-year-old Egyptian mummy displayed there, searching unsuccessfully for treasure. At least one of the Capitol's rooms was used as a military barracks.

The Capitol as Fortress

Andrew Johnson, a former governor of Tennessee, had been the only U.S. Senator from a Southern state not to resign after his state had seceded. He was named by President Lincoln as military governor of Tennessee. Fearful that Confederates would retake the city, Johnson ordered defensive works constructed and the Capitol fortified. A wooden stockade, turrets, and bales of cotton were assembled on the terraces. Parrott rifles, heavy seige artillery with rifled barrels, were positioned on the terraces pointing outward at the occupied city and its residents. The guns were never used in anger, but were fired several times in honor of Union victories or elections.

Like many buildings in Nashville the Capitol was temporarily used as a military hospital following the battle at Murfreesboro, Tenn., which ended on Jan. 2, 1863.

Post-War Improvements

After the war, in 1866, the legislature was ready to vote on the 14th Amendment, granting citizenship to blacks, when several opposing legislators attempted to flee and block passage by denying a quorum. Armed guards fired on the legislators, who halted and returned to the session. The legislation passed, paving the way for Tennessee to become the first Confederate state admitted back into the Union (it had been the last to leave). A sculpture off the main-level staircase commemorates this vote. The lower marble staircase railing is chipped from one of the bullets fired from the upper stairs.

Major Capitol Hill improvements were made in 1871-1877, with the building of an east terrace and the dumping of 35,000 cartloads of soil to accommodate landscaping. By the 1890s the cedar trees on the hill had given way to larger shade trees. In 1961 more than 600 trees were planted on Capitol Hill.

Famed Statue is Dedicated to Jackson

One of the biggest post-war events was the highlight of Nashville's Centennial—the unveiling on May 20, 1880 of the equestrian statue of General Andrew Jackson in the terraced garden on the east side of the Capitol grounds. The bronze statue by Clark Mills was the first equestrian statue in

Tomb of Capitol architect William Strickland

the U.S. and a bold design, considering that the entire sculpture is supported only by the horse's hind legs. It is the first of three castings and the artist's proof. Identical statues can be found in Jackson Square in New Orleans and Lafayette Park in Washington, D.C.

A month later, Capitol Commission Chairman Samuel D. Morgan—the driving force behind the construction and completion of the Tennessee State Capitol—died. On Christmas Eve 1881 his remains were interred in a tomb in the southeast corner of the Capitol.

By 1885 stone in parts of the building was "rapidly deteriorating and going to decay," but repair work was put off. However, the water closet located in the crypt was totally replaced at the cost of $2,000 after being described as producing "a stench in the nostrils of decency" and deemed a nuisance by the State Board of Health.

In 1890, a civilian died after falling from an upper portico at the Capitol, prompting the installation of safety railings.

The turn of the century saw the building of a south stonework entrance and a major repair effort. Stone on the building was scrubbed with wire brushes and covered with a mixture of boiling paraffin wax and linseed oil. Surfaces were patched with "granitoid," made from Portland cement concrete. The entire building was electrified.

In 1909 a statue of Sam Davis, the "Boy Hero of the Confederacy," by sculptor George J. Zolnay was erected at the southwest corner of the Capitol grounds. Before being hanged as an alleged spy by Union troops in 1863 because he would not name his accomplices, Davis spoke his last words, "I would die a thousand deaths before I would betray a friend."

Encroachment and a Need for More Space

In 1916, Mrs. John (Elizabeth) Akins and Mrs. Robert (Margaret) Weakley created the Tennessee Capitol Association to protect and enhance property around the Capitol. Mrs. Eakin

Tennessee State Capitol: National Historic Landmark

bought parcels around Capitol Hill for the next five years to prevent encroaching commercialization. In 1921 the legislature voted funds to purchase plots around the Capitol and to reimburse Mrs. Eakin.

By 1917 the state needed additional office space, already renting four additional downtown buildings. Architect Harry Frahn drew up plans for a massive 10-story addition atop the Capitol building. The design looked so ungainly it was not seriously considered.

Later the Capitol would be flanked on the east by new massive state office buildings and on the west by the new State Supreme Court Building (1936) and the new State Library and Archives (1953).

Statue to "Martyr of Political Assassination"

In 1925 a life-size statue of Edward Ward Carmack by Nancy Cox McCormack was erected on the south steps overlooking Charlotte Avenue. A former U.S. Congressman and editor of the Nashville *Tennessean,* Carmack was killed in a gunfight with political enemy Duncan Cooper and his son Robin Cooper at the corner of Seventh and Union on Nov. 9, 1908. Liquor prohibitionists claimed the killing was a "political assassination" and made Carmack a martyr to their cause. Two months after the shooting, Tennessee outlawed the sale, manufacture, and consumption of alcohol, years ahead of national prohibition. The Coopers were tried and convicted, but the elder Cooper was pardoned by his friend, Governor Malcolm Patterson. The younger Cooper was granted a new trial and released.

At the turn of the century Marathon Motors of Nashville produced newfangled horseless carriages. To prove how rugged the vehicles were made, the company conducted a public demonstration by driving a motorcoach up the steps on Capitol Hill. The stunt was successful.

Statue of Edward Ward Carmack.

Women Win the Right to Vote

The final dramatic showdown over the 19th Amendment giving women the right to vote played out in 1920 in the Tennessee State Capitol. Both sides had established headquarters and handed out propaganda literature. Suffragists, identified by wearing yellow roses, needed one more state to ratify the amendment and Tennessee was their last chance. The Senate approved, but the vote in the House was thought to be evenly split. Henry Burn, the youngest legislator, was against ratification and wore a red rose until he received a note from his mother urging him to vote in the affirmative. His "yea" for the amendment was the deciding vote.

Urban Renewal Changes the Landscape

Following World War Two, Nashville became the first city in the nation to receive federal funds for "urban renewal." The subsequent Capitol Hill Redevelopment Plan resulted in the relocation of 600 families and 140 businesses as hundreds of shacks, outdoor privies, and dilapidated 19th-century townhouses were torn down. Capitol Hill was drastically reshaped with the building of James Robertson Parkway partially encircling it to the north. The Capitol Hill Redevelopment Plan ended in 1966 at the cost of $9.6 million. Twenty-five new structures were built to the north of the Capitol.

Extensive Remodeling Finally Tackled

By the 1950s the Capitol building itself was in need of extensive repair and restoration. The original exterior Bigby limestone was replaced with 90,000 cubic feet of Oolitic limestone from Indiana during a four-year project. All of the terrace stonework was replaced, as well as all 28 Ionic columns and the entire entablature, including the pediments and parapets of the porticoes. A 50-ton guy derrick mounted on a steel tower was used to renovate the Capitol's lantern tower. The copper roof and all doors and windows were replaced.

In 1957 interior work was performed. The crypt level was excavated and transformed into offices. Limestone floors were replaced with marble from Carthage, Mo. New heating, air conditioning and electrical systems were installed. The 300-foot-long Motlow Tunnel was built beneath the south side of Capitol, offering convenient access from Charlotte Avenue.

In 1974 Legislative Plaza was completed, with a subterranean state office building beneath a large urban plaza.

Interior Restored to Former Grandeur

In 1984, James Hoobler, director of the Tennessee Historical Society, reported to state officials deteriorating conditions inside the Capitol. The leaking roof and exterior stonework were repaired. The State Library and Supreme Court chambers were restored to their original state of elegance. The project was finished four years later.

The Charles Warterfield Reliquary was created at the northwest corner of Capitol Hill in 1995 honoring the young assistant architect from the 1950s renovation of the Capitol who had also worked on the grounds again in the 1990s.

Tennessee State Capitol: National Historic Landmark
A Most Unlikely War Hero — Sgt. Alvin C. York

Sgt. Alvin C. York (1887-1964) of Tennessee was the most celebrated enlisted soldier of the Great War, earning the Congressional Medal of Honor and national fame. On October 8, 1918, as a corporal, York and 16 other soldiers found themselves behind enemy lines in the Meuse-Argonne sector of France and confronted by superior numbers of German soldiers and multiple hillside machine-gun nests overlooking the scene. York, acting on orders from two other corporals who had been placed in command after the unit's sergeant was hit 17 times, subdued the machine-gunners, killing 25 of the enemy and taking 132 German prisoners. Eight other Americans participated in the action.

York had entered the war as a 30-year-old conscientious objector who wrote "Dont want to fight" on his draft card. A rowdy youngster raised on a subsistence farm in rural Pall Mall, Tenn., York experienced a religious conversion during a revival in 1914. York stopped drinking, gambling, and fighting. Like many rural youth, he became an excellent marksman. It was only after weeks of debate and soul-searching that York agreed with his company commander that the war was moral and ordained by God.

After the war, York was honored as a hero but he turned down offers from Hollywood, Broadway, and advertisers. York raised funds to create the York Institute, dedicated to educating the young people of his native Fentress County. As another European war loomed in the 1930s York adopted an isolationist stance. Yet when the biographical film *Sergeant York* was produced and released with his cooperation in July 1941, the reluctant warrior once again came to believe that war was justified. Actor Gary Cooper won the Academy Award for his portrayal of York. York attempted to re-enlist in the Army but was rejected due to his age.

In 1954 a stroke confined him to bed rest. Three years previously the IRS had accused York of tax evasion on profits from the movie. After ten years of haggling, the IRS was ordered by President John Kennedy to resolve the tax matter, which he termed a disgrace. York died in 1964 and is buried in the cemetery of the Wolf River Methodist Church. A state park in Pall Mall interprets his life.

The statue of Sgt. York at the southeast corner of the State Capitol grounds was sculpted by Felix de Weldon, who also sculpted the Iwo Jima Marine Corps Memorial in Arlington, Va. The York statue was dedicated on Dec. 13, 1968.

York's Medal of Honor and uniform can be viewed at the State Museum's Military Branch.

20 State Library and Archives

The Tennessee State Library and Archives (TSLA) is located at 403 Seventh Avenue North, just west of the State Capitol. The phone is (615) 741-2764. The building was designed by Clinton Parrent, built in 1952-53, and features a central structure fronted by a Greek Ionic colonnade, flanked by wings. The state library was founded in 1854, five years after the creation of the Tennessee Historical Society. In 1919 the library was joined with the state archives under John Trotwood Moore, the first State Librarian and Archivist. Originally the library was housed in the State Capitol. The TSLA holds more than one million items, plus 27 million official records and 4.8 million manuscripts. The staff includes more than 90 archivists, librarians, assistants, and specialists in microfilming, photography, and computer networking.

21 State Supreme Court Building

The Tennessee Supreme Court Building, located at 401 Seventh Avenue North, adjacent to the State Capitol, exemplifies a Greek Doric design that was very modern for its time. Built of Tennessee marble at a cost of $750,000, the Tennessee Supreme Court Building was dedicated on Dec. 4, 1937. The Tennessee Supreme Court Historical Society was formed in the 1990s. In 2002 the group published the first comprehensive history of the State Supreme Court. Another major project, with the financial assistance of the Frist Foundation, was the dedication of tablets honoring all Appellate Court judges in Tennessee's history from 1796 to date. The black marble tablets were dedicated in December 2003 in the rotunda of the Supreme Court Building.

22 Tennessee Tower

The Tennessee Tower, which contains state government offices, is a 31-story skyscraper occupying the block between Union Street and Charlotte Avenue, from Seventh to Eighth avenues. The structure, once the tallest in Nashville, was built in 1969-70 and was designed by Skidmore, Owings & Merrill of Chicago. Built at a cost of $15 million, it encloses 831,665 square feet of space.

The tower is built of reinforced concrete in the form of two rectangular load-bearing tubes, one within the other. Italian Travertine marble on the outer tube forms the exterior wall. The inner tube surrounds the core service area. The bronze glass windows are floor-to-ceiling. High-speed programmable elevators were installed, as were escalators. At night, lights in the building can be programmed to spell out messages or form an image, like a giant billboard.

The tower originally housed the headquarters for the National Life and Accident Insurance Company, founded in 1901, and was later known as the American General Center (1982). A twin tower was planned but never built. National Life created a radio station, WSM (We Shield Millions), which later hosted a musical program called the Grand Ole Opry. The original downtown National Life building, where the Opry was first staged, no longer stands.

23) War Memorial Building

The War Memorial Building, stretching between Union Street and Charlotte Avenue between Sixth and Seventh avenues, was built by the state, county, and city in 1925 to honor the 131,000 Tennesseans who served in World War One, especially the 3,836 Tennesseans who gave their lives in the Great War. The names of the war dead are listed on ten bronze plaques on the north and west sides of the atrium. The designer for this project was Nashville architect Edward Dougherty, affiliated as an associate with McKim, Mead, and White of New York. The granite and marble building in Greek Doric style has a large, open memorial courtyard with the massive statue Victory holding aloft the goddess Nike, created by Belle Kinney (1890-1959) and husband Leopold F. Scholz. Two wings extend from the open court housing government offices, a 2,200-seat auditorium and the Tennessee State Museum's Military Branch. At one time, the auditorium served as the home of the Grand Ole Opry. As many as 131,000 Tennesseans participated in the armed services in 1917-18 (the war began in 1914 but the United States did not enter until 1917). Many volunteered, some served as part of the state's National Guard, and others were drafted. Six Tennesseans received the Congressional Medal of Honor for duty in World War One: Joseph B. Adkinson, James E. Karnes, Milo Lemert, Edward R. Talley, Calvin John Ward, and Alvin C. York. The 30th Division, nicknamed the Old Hickory Division, played a decisive role in breaking through the Hindenburg Line in the final phases of the war.

(24) War Memorial Plaza

The **Korean War Veterans Memorial**, titled "The Korean War (1950-1953) Where Communistic Military Aggression was Defeated," was dedicated on July 4, 1992 by the Tennessee Korean War Memorial Association in cooperation with the State of Tennessee. Russell Faxon of Bell Buckle, Tenn. is the sculptor of the bronze statue, which features a relief map of Korea. The American death toll in the so-called "forgotten war" totaled 33,629. A quarter-million South Koreans lost their lives; North Koreans twice that number. Chinese deaths totaled in the millions. Ten thousand five hundred Tennesseans served in the armed forces during the war; 843 Tennesseans were killed in combat. Thirty thousand American soldiers are still stationed in South Korea to enforce the armistice.

The **Vietnam Veterans Park** was opened in 1985, with the bronze statue unveiled on Memorial Day, 1986. The sculpture of three soldiers was designed by Alan LeQuire. The park is located in the southwest corner of War Memorial Plaza near the entrance to the Tennessee State Museum-Military Branch. The memory wall contains the names of the 1,289 Tennesseans who were killed in Southeast Asia from 1961-1975. More than 49,000 Tennesseans served in the war and 6,000 were wounded. The first name on the Vietnam Memorial in Washington, D.C. is that of a Tennessean.

Inscription: "During America's longest war, they served with distinction and valor, but often without recognition. We, who cherish freedom, dedicate this memorial to their unselfish sacrifice."

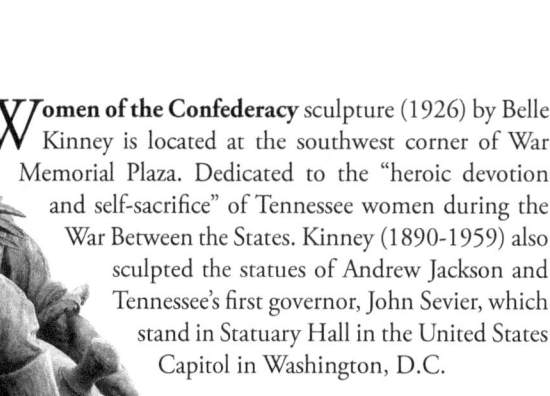

Women of the Confederacy sculpture (1926) by Belle Kinney is located at the southwest corner of War Memorial Plaza. Dedicated to the "heroic devotion and self-sacrifice" of Tennessee women during the War Between the States. Kinney (1890-1959) also sculpted the statues of Andrew Jackson and Tennessee's first governor, John Sevier, which stand in Statuary Hall in the United States Capitol in Washington, D.C.

Historical Markers at War Memorial Plaza

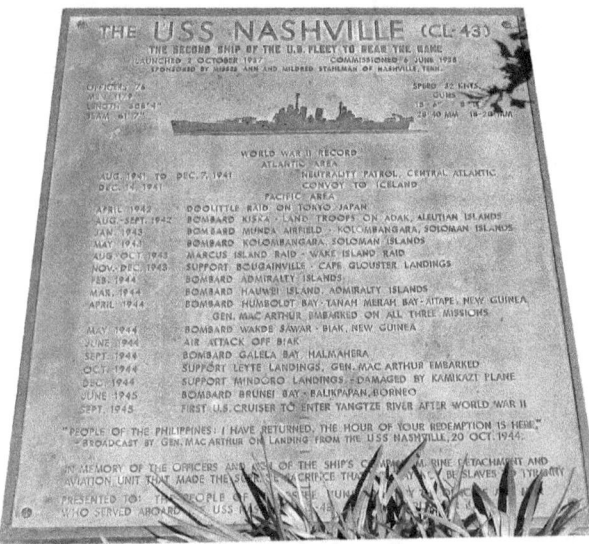

The *U.S.S. Nashville* served in the Pacific Theater during World War Two, participating in the Doolittle B-25 raid on Tokyo, the Leyte Gulf landings, and bringing General Douglas MacArthur back to The Philippines. The ship suffered and recovered from a deadly Kamikazi aircraft attack, and was the first U.S. cruiser on the Chinese Yangtze River following the war.

▶ A plaque by the American Merchant Marine Veterans, Mid-South Chapter, Nashville, Tenn., July 1999, honors the American merchant seamen who served in all wars since 1775. During World War Two, 833 merchant ships were sunk by enemy action, including 33 that vanished without a trace. More than 6,000 seamen lost their lives.

Memorial to all Law Enforcement Officers in Tennessee who have given their lives in the line of duty. 470 Tennessee officers have died protecting the public safety, according to the National Law Enforcement Officers Memorial Fund.

▶ Still on Patrol: U.S. Navy submarines paid heavily for their success in World War II. A total of 374 officers and 3,131 men are on board these 52 U.S. submarines still on patrol. In the Pacific U.S. submarines sank 30 percent of the Japanese navy and 60 percent of their merchant marine vessels.

On July 23, 1950, thirty-one young Nashville Air Guardsmen boarded a C-46 transport plane at Myrtle Beach Air Force Base, S.C., bound for home after summer camp. Seven minutes after takeoff the plane crashed; there were no survivors. The crash was one of the worst National Guard accidents in history.

25) State Museum-Military Branch

The Military Branch of the Tennessee State Museum is housed in the War Memorial Building, with the entrance on the south side. This museum covers the Spanish-American War, the World Wars, and military actions through the Vietnam War. Special artifacts include Sgt. Alvin York's Medal of Honor and the deck gun from the *USS Nashville* that fired the first shot of the Spanish-American War. Numerous ship models, flags, posters, and weapons can also be examined. Admission is free; donations are accepted. Hours are 10 a.m. to 5 p.m., Tuesday through Saturday.

The Hotchkiss Gun from the *USS Nashville* that fired the first shot of the Spanish-American War against the merchant ship *Buena Vista*. The 1895 model fires a 37mm shell. Later in the war 26 crewmen of the *USS Nashville* received the Medal of Honor for cutting Spain's undersea telegraph cable from Cuba to Europe.

▲▲ Patriotic posters helped persuade citizens to buy bonds to fund the war.

▲ A poison-gas mask from World War One.

◄ Silver service from the *USS Tennessee* presented by citizens to the newly commissioned armored cruiser in 1906. It was used to entertain foreign dignitaries at ports of call. In 1920 the silver was transferred to the new *USS Tennessee* battleship and was aboard on Dec. 7, 1941 when the ship was attacked by Japanese aircraft at Pearl Harbor. The ship returned to active duty in 1942.

An exhibit for Medal of Honor recipient Corporal William F. Lyell of Hickman County, Tenn. He was mortally wounded on Aug. 31, 1951 near Chup'a-ri, Korea, when his platoon leader was killed and he took command, personally and successfully attacking with a recoilless rifle and grenades three enemy bunkers while under heavy fire. His "extraordinary heroism, indomitable courage, and aggressive leadership reflect great credit on himself and are in keeping with the highest traditions of the military service." He is buried at Nashville National Cemetery.

Chet Atkins Statue

Picking his trademark Gibson Chet Atkins Country Gentleman guitar is a life-sized bronze likeness of the guitar man himself, Chet Atkins (1924-2001), at the corner of Union Street and Fifth Avenue North (Bank of America Branch). The incredibly detailed sculpture, which includes an empty stool for aspiring pickers to have their picture taken with Atkins, was sculpted by Russ Faxon and dedicated in 2000. Atkins made his first appearance on the Grand Ole Opry in 1946 and during the 1950s and 1960s he helped create the "Nashville Sound," a combination of pop and country music influences. He designed guitars for Gibson and Gretsch. Atkins earned numerous awards, including eleven Grammy Awards and nine CMA Instrumentalist of the Year honors, as well as a Lifetime Achievement Award from NARAS. He died of cancer in 2001.

Hermitage Hotel

The Hermitage Hotel at 231 Sixth Avenue North was designed by Tennessee architect J. Edwin Carpenter (1867-1932) in the Beaux Arts style and built between 1908 and 1910. It was the city's first million-dollar hotel. Noteworthy is the polychromed terra-cotta exterior detailing. The lobby centers on a huge stained-glass skylight.

Over the years the Hermitage Hotel served as a center for the social and political life of Nashville, providing accommodations for six U.S. Presidents (LBJ, JFK, Nixon, FDR, Taft, and Wilson), visiting celebrities such as Al Capone, Helen Hayes, and Al Jolson, and foreign dignitaries.

On the lower level hangs an autographed photograph of Gene Autry visiting the Hermitage Hotel dressed in full cowboy garb. The famous billiards player Minnesota Fats resided at the Hermitage Hotel for many years.

The Hermitage Hotel was the headquarters for the Tennessee Democratic Party and for both factions in the battle to ratify women's suffrage in 1920. Francis Craig and his orchestra performed there from 1929 to 1945, part of that time producing a broadcast of a radio show featuring their music.

The hotel closed in the late 1970s, but was renovated and reopened in 1980. It underwent further renovation in 1994-1995. Today the luxury five-star hotel features 123 rooms and suites. The phone is (888) 888-9414.

28 Doctors Building

The Doctors Building at the corner of Church Street and Polk Street is a six-story steel-frame structure built to provide office space for doctors and dentists. The first three stories were built in 1916 and the second three stories in 1921. The architects were Dougherty and Gardner. The Italian Renaissance exterior features ornamental designs to include wreaths, garlands of fruit, floral motifs, winged cherubs, lion's heads, and zigzag banding. The building was renovated in the 1980s and sold to a hotel developer in 2006.

29 Bennie-Dillon Building

This 12-story building at 702 Church Street, one of Nashville's first skyscrapers, was constructed in 1925-27 and named after its builders—wholesale merchandise company president George Bennie and real estate developer William Dillon. The local firm of Asmus and Clark designed the Renaissance Revival-style building in the Louis Sullivan three-part scheme in which tall buildings mimick the elements of a classical column—base, shaft, and cornice. Foster and Creighton were the contractors. Especially interesting are the glazed terra cotta exterior designs. A renovation in 1999 converted the office building into apartments.

30 James Robertson Hotel

The James Robertson Apartment Hotel located at Seventh Avenue North and Commerce Street was dubbed "The South's Finest" when it opened and was named after one of Nashville's founding pioneers. The architecture of the structure is in the Art Deco style. Completed in 1929, this building served as the base hotel for the Grand Ole Opry stars performing at the Ryman Auditorium. Today the building is used as income-restricted apartments.

31 Castner-Knott Building

The Castner-Knott Building at 616-618 Church Street was built in 1906 to house the Castner-Knott Dry Goods Company, one of the first commercial establishments to move into this historically residential area. The company had been established in 1898 by Charles Castner and William Knott. The original five-story Classical Revival building on Church St. expanded in 1911 to include the Italianate Armstrong building at Church and Capitol Boulevard. In 1958-59 all levels of the buildings were connected, the storefront windows were covered in polished granite panels, a corner entry was added, and interiors were designed with Art Moderne details. A 1999 renovation uncovered many of the building's historic details.

32 Nashville Public Library

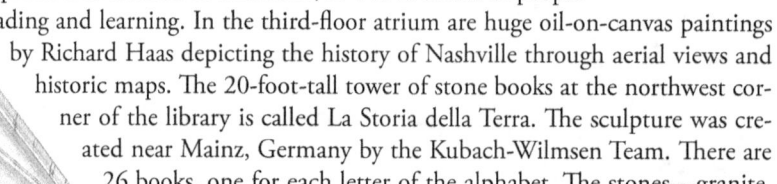

The Nashville Public Library at 615 Church Street opened in 2001 in its new modern-classical 300,000-sq.-ft. main building designed by Robert A.M. Stern Architects of New York. The structure includes a 4500-sq.-ft. Grand Reading Room and an integrated courtyard. The building is faced with Alabama limestone and features Ionic columns, echoing the State Capitol visible down Capitol Boulevard. The bronze doors at the main entrance were created by sculptor Alan LeQuire and depict native plants and animals of Tennessee, as well as scenes of people reading and learning. In the third-floor atrium are huge oil-on-canvas paintings by Richard Haas depicting the history of Nashville through aerial views and historic maps. The 20-foot-tall tower of stone books at the northwest corner of the library is called La Storia della Terra. The sculpture was created near Mainz, Germany by the Kubach-Wilmsen Team. There are 26 books, one for each letter of the alphabet. The stones—granite, marble, and quartz—come from all over the world. Each continent is represented.

Docent-led tours of the library can be arranged by appointment. Reduced-priced parking is offered in the Library Parking Garage, with entrances on Sixth and Seventh Avenues between Church and Commerce. The phone number is (615) 862-5800.

The Carnegie Library opened downtown in 1904 at Eighth Avenue and Union Street. In 1965 this building was replaced by the Ben West Library, which has recently been used as temporary city hall offices during the county courthouse renovation. Two of the 20 branch libraries located throughout Davidson County are the original Carnegie libraries, located at 206 Gallatin Pike in East Nashville and at 1001 Monroe Street in North Nashville.

33 McKendree Methodist Church

McKendree Methodist Church at 523 Church Street was named for Bishop William McKendree, the first American bishop. This is the fourth McKendree Methodist Church building to occupy this site. The first building was completed in 1833 and hosted the funeral of President James K. Polk. It also hosted the 1850 Convention on Southern Secession. In 1876, a new larger Gothic building was erected. Three years later it burned, and a third building was erected in 1882. This building was also destroyed by fire in 1905. The present church was dedicated in October 1912. Additions to this marble, neo-classical structure were made in 1966.

34 Saint Cloud Corner

The buildings on the corner at Church Street are the cornerstone of the Fifth Avenue Historic District, which contains several examples of Victorian and Art Deco commercial architecture. This area became the city's retail center following the Civil War. St. Cloud Corner at 201 Fifth Avenue was built in 1869. The French Piano Company Building at 240-242 Fifth Avenue was built in 1889 and has a sheet-metal facade featuring floral decoration, scallops, garlands, and stylized human faces. During the 1960s this street was the center of the civil rights demonstrations, peaceful sit-ins at retail counters which became the model for similar protests throughout the South.

35) Kress Building

Part of the Fifth Avenue Historic District, the S.H. Kress Building at 237-239 Fifth Avenue is an outstanding example of the Art Deco style. Built in 1935 to replace an older store, this building features multi-colored terra cotta floral decoration. This was one of two 5&10-Cent stores operated in Nashville by Samuel H. Kress. The new Fifth Avenue store was described as "the finest type of mercantile building known to modern engineering." Kress stores operated in the U.S. from 1896-1981. The structure has been renovated for use as residential condominiums.

36) Fifth Third Bank Building

Built in 1983-86 as the Third National Financial Center, this tall skyscraper is Nashville's first PostModern office tower. The building was designed by Kohn Pederson Fox. Topped by a Colonial-style gabled roofline the building employs sloping columns and curved cornices to reflect the architecture of the Downtown Presbyterian Church across the street. The building is now occupied by Fifth Third Bank.

37) Downtown Presbyterian Church

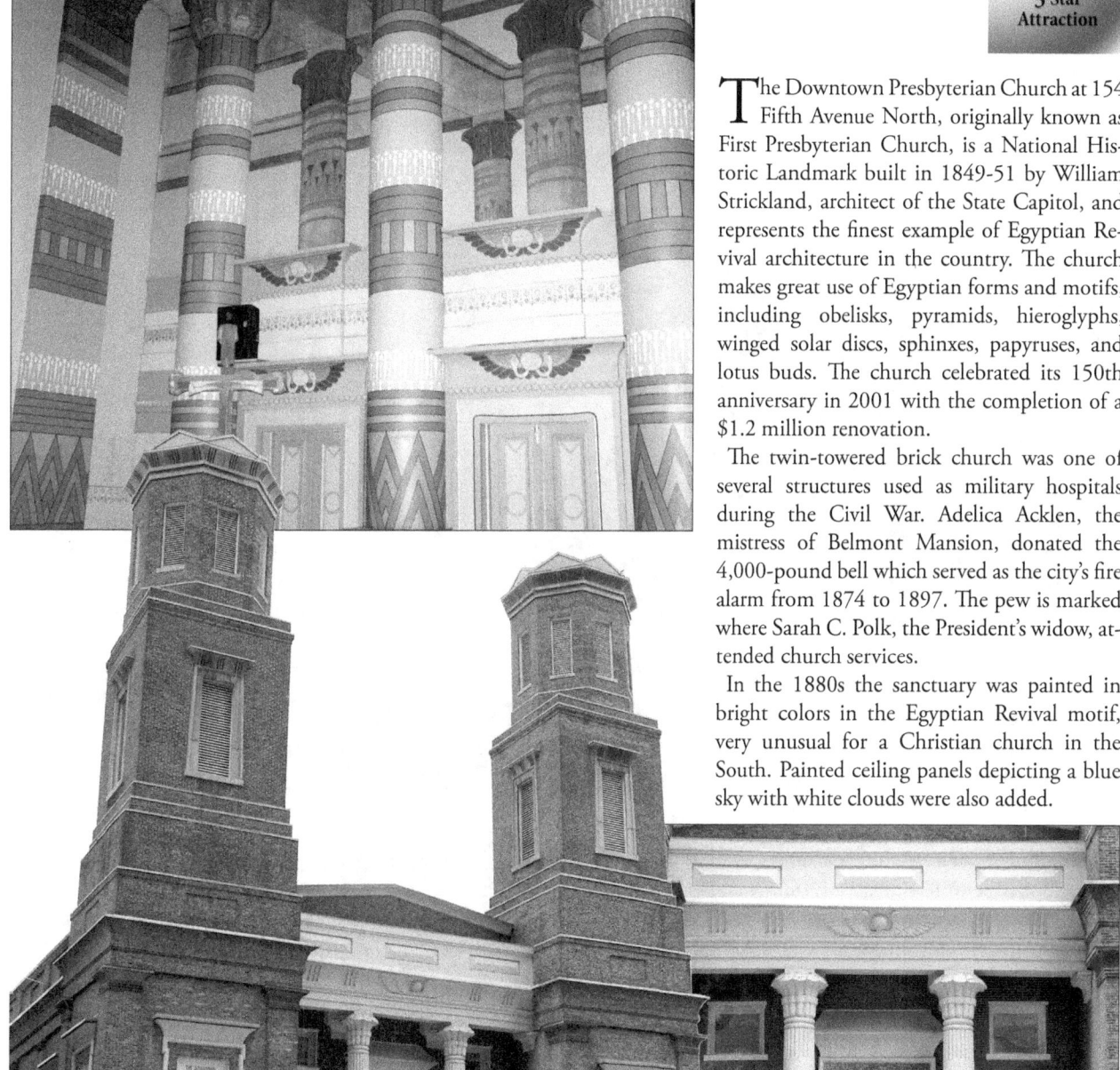

5 Star Attraction

The Downtown Presbyterian Church at 154 Fifth Avenue North, originally known as First Presbyterian Church, is a National Historic Landmark built in 1849-51 by William Strickland, architect of the State Capitol, and represents the finest example of Egyptian Revival architecture in the country. The church makes great use of Egyptian forms and motifs, including obelisks, pyramids, hieroglyphs, winged solar discs, sphinxes, papyruses, and lotus buds. The church celebrated its 150th anniversary in 2001 with the completion of a $1.2 million renovation.

The twin-towered brick church was one of several structures used as military hospitals during the Civil War. Adelica Acklen, the mistress of Belmont Mansion, donated the 4,000-pound bell which served as the city's fire alarm from 1874 to 1897. The pew is marked where Sarah C. Polk, the President's widow, attended church services.

In the 1880s the sanctuary was painted in bright colors in the Egyptian Revival motif, very unusual for a Christian church in the South. Painted ceiling panels depicting a blue sky with white clouds were also added.

⟨38⟩ Cohen Building

Meyer Cohen, a successful pawnbroker and jeweler, set up shop in 1890 in the Renaissance Revival-style building at 421 Church Street. The top two floors served as the residence for he and his wife George-Etta Brinkley Cohen. The building was one of the first in Nashville to feature an elevator. Mrs. Cohen furnished the residence with a carved oak mantelpiece, stained-glass windows, and a grand staircase.

Known as a man-about-town and a socialite, Meyer Cohen died in 1915, and the building has housed several businesses since then, including a business that manufactured custom-made military uniforms, a sign company, glass company, and printing company. The top two floors have been vacant since the 1950s, and the last tenant moved out in December 2000.

Recently the commercial facade was removed to reveal the two-story white glazed-brick arch and balustraded loggia with bay windows.

The building is now used for office space.

⟨39⟩ L&C Tower

This 31-story tower built in 1956-57 for the Life & Casualty Insurance Company at the southwest corner of Church Street and Fourth Avenue North was Nashville's first modern (post-World War II) skyscraper and the tallest building in the South until the mid-1960s. The building was designed by Edwin A. Keeble, whose placement of windows and vertical aluminum fins resulted in substantial energy savings, years before environmentalism became fashionable. The curved, glazed four-story entrance lobby is reminiscent of Miami Beach architecture.

An observation deck 364 feet above street level provided views reaching 26 miles. The deck was closed to the public in 1995 after a young woman jumped from the balcony to her death.

At the top of the building are 25-foot-high "L&C" letters which flashed weather conditions in code: red for rain or snow; blue for clear skies; pink for cloudy skies; rippling lights downward for falling temperatures, and so on. Radio station WRLT leases the top floor of the structure.

On the 60th anniversary of the company in 1963, Becker's Bakery constructed an 18-foot-tall, 540-layer cake weighing three tons—an exact scale model of the L&C Tower.

40 Old First National Bank Building

This 12-story building constructed in 1905 by banker Frank Overton Watts at the corner of Fourth Avenue North and Church Street was Nashville's first skyscraper. Over the years it has been known as the First National Bank Building, the Independent Life Building, the Third National Bank Building, the J.C. Bradford Building, and since 1999 the Courtyard by Marriott Hotel. Third National Bank acquired the site in 1938 and doubled the size with an addition to the east. New Art Deco exterior details replaced the original neo-classical decoration. The building was also known for its giant movable iron screen in the lobby which featured circular medallions of polished brass, each with a sign of the zodiac. The artwork was done by Rene Chambellan.

41 Noel Hotel Building

The former Noel Hotel is located at 200 Fourth Avenue North at the corner of Church Street. The property had been in the Noel family since 1854, at which time a huge spring flowed here, furnishing most of the water for residents living along the Cumberland River.

The 250-room hotel was built by John and Oscar Noel. It was designed by Marr, Holman Architects, with Nicholson Company as general contractors. The hotel opened on Jan. 6, 1930. It was considered a luxury hotel and over the years was host to local residents at the "Kaffee Klatsch," where businessmen gathered to share coffee and business as well as for celebrity guests, including Eleanor Roosevelt, Babe Ruth, Roy Rogers, and Jayne Mansfield.

A freak elevator accident here during the Second World War resulted in the decapitation of a visiting serviceman.

The Noel closed as a hotel in September 1972 when it was bought by Hamilton Bank. Today the building is headquarters for First Bank.

㊷ The Men's Quarter

In the late 1800s entrepreneurs opened several new saloons between Cherry (Fourth Avenue) and Front Street (First Avenue) featuring Victorian ornamentation. This notorious section of town became known as the Men's Quarter. The Maxwell House Hotel at the corner of Church and Fourth had to install a separate entrance on Church Street so that respectable women would not have to be seen on Fourth Avenue. Three buildings of that era survive, although not in their original functions—the Southern Turf (left) at 212 Fourth Avenue North, the Climax Saloon (bottom left) at 210 and the Utopia Hotel (below) at 206. Marcus Cartwright, reportedly a nationally famous bookmaker, opened the Southern Turf in 1895. He filled it with mirrors, bronze statues, rare paintings, and mahogany furnishings. The manager, Ike Johnson, sold choice domestic and imported liquors and wines and expensive cigars.

43 The Arcade

The Arcade opened in 1902 as Nashville's first shopping center, built in Overton Alley between Fourth and Fifth avenues north. The two-story design is 360 feet long and 75 feet wide and open only to pedestrian traffic. Among the many small shops is a U.S. Post Office branch. The indoor mall was conceived by Daniel Bunton, who formed a corporation to build the structure. It originally housed about 52 shops on two levels. It is said he patterned the design after a galleria in Milan, Italy.

The Arcade was designed by Thompson, Gibel, and Asmus and constructed by Nashville Manufacturing Co. The pitched roof of wire-reinforced glass is supported by a rolled steel bracing system. The original mall has been modified by several renovations. In 1973 it was added to the National Register of Historic Places.

44 Printers Alley

Both an entertainment district and historic district, Printers Alley runs from Church Street to Union Street between Third and Fourth Avenues. By the turn of the 20th Century this district became the center of Nashville's printing industry, with 13 publishers and ten printers in the area serviced by the alley. At one time Nashville's two largest newspapers, *The Tennessean* and the Nashville *Banner* (now defunct), had their offices here. The street contained hotels, restaurants, and saloons, which became speakeasies during Prohibition (which began in 1909 in Tennessee). Nightclubs opened here in the 1940s. Among the many stars who performed here were Boots Randolph, Chet Atkins, Waylon Jennings, Dottie West, The Supremes, Hank Williams, Barbara Mandrell, and Jimi Hendrix. Today, the district remains a lively nighttime destination.

One of the more colorful entertainers at Printers Alley during the 1970s was Heaven Lee, a native Cuban and exotic dancer who once rode nude (she actually wore a bodystocking) on horseback down James Robertson Parkway to protest environmental pollution.

㊻ Market Street Historic District

Market Street (now Second Avenue North) features historic storefronts that now house nightclubs, restaurants, taverns, and tourist attractions. The buildings in the block between Market Street and Front Street (now First Avenue North) were used as warehouses for all the goods brought to Nashville's Cumberland River wharf by steamboat. The Victorian warehouses handled bulk quantities of dry goods, hardware, and groceries, which were retailed from the storefronts on Market Street. The buildings fell into disrepair but were renovated during the 1970s. The Victorian architectural details and fenestration are most prevalent one story and more above street level.

Washington Manufacturing Co. (1870s) at 214-216 Second Ave. North

T.M. DeMoss & Sons (1879) 126 Second Ave. North

㊻ Silver Dollar Saloon

Victor E. "Manny" Shwab, a German immigrant and business partner of whisky maker George Dickel, built the red brick Silver Dollar Saloon at the corner of Broadway and Market (Second Avenue) in 1893. It was designed by Nashvillian J.G. Zwicker. The name refers to the silver dollars which were embedded in every other floor tile. The saloon, which also featured fine cigars, catered to the rough and tumble riverboat trade until it was shut down by statewide prohibition in 1910. At one time it housed the Metro Historical Commission. It now serves as a gift shop for the nearby Hard Rock Cafe.

(47) Broadway Historic District

The Broadway Historic District between Second and Fifth Avenues is a stretch of honky tonk bars, retail houses, and tourist attractions better known as Lower Broad. At one time, Lower Broad was a seedy red-light district of beer joints, pool halls, and X-rated movie theaters. Today the re-developed district is Nashville's premier entertainment destination. The old Merchants Hotel (below) at 401-403 Broadway (now a restaurant) is a three-story Victorian building completed in 1892 with a turret and elaborate brickwork. Broadway is the main downtown street connecting the waterfront with the West End.

Lower Broadway is home to various historic architectural styles and modern usages. The old stone American National Bank Branch at 301 Broadway, a neo-Classical design, now houses a tattoo parlor.

48 Schermerhorn Symphony Center

The magnificent Schermerhorn Symphony Center, home of the Nashville Symphony, opened at Fourth Avenue South and Demonbreun Street in September 2006. It is named for the late Kenneth Schermerhorn, who directed the symphony for 22 years. The Laura Turner Concert Hall seats 1,860 and features natural interior light through 30 special soundproof windows. An automatic convertible seating system can be configured for any type of musical setting. The hall features a concert organ made by Schoenstein & Co. of San Francisco, composed of 47 voices, 64 ranks, and 3,617 pipes with three 32-foot stops. The building also features a public garden and cafe enclosed by a colonnade, which is open to the public during the day and during concerts. Free guided tours are available to the public. The phone number is (615) 687-6500.

(49) Country Music Hall of Fame and Museum

The country's busiest popular museum, the Country Music Hall of Fame and Museum at 222 Fifth Avenue South, tells the story of how Nashville became Music City USA. The museum, operated by the Country Music Foundation, is self-guided; a thorough visit will take two hours. Also offered is a 70-minute audio tour. Admission is charged.

The museum's permanent exhibit, "Sing Me Back Home: A Journey Through Country Music," tells the story of country music using artifacts, photos, original recordings, archival video, films, and interactive media. The intimate Ford Theater holds 213 spectators for special live performances. Special exhibits have focused on the lives of Hank Williams, Chet Atkins, Brenda Lee, Kitty Wells, Marty Robbins, Earl Scruggs, and many other stars. Some of the historic musical instruments on display include Maybelle Carter's 1928 Gibson L-5 guitar, Bill Monroe's 1923 Gibson F-5 mandolin, Emmylou Harris' 1955 Gibson J-200 guitar with rose inlay, Chet Atkins' D'Angelico Excel, and Hank Williams' Martin D-28 guitar. Significant artifacts include Elvis Presley's 1960 Cadillac limousine, Carl Perkins' blue suede shoes, a cocktail gown worn by Patsy Cline, Ray Price's stage jacket created by Nudie the Rodeo Tailor, and Hank Williams Jr.'s boots with signature phoenix logo.

Country Music Hall of Fame members are presented on bronze plaques in the unique Rotunda. The first three inductees in 1961 were Jimmie Rodgers, Hank Williams, and Fred Rose. The inductees in 2012 were Garth Brooks, Hargus "Pig" Robbins, and Connie Smith.

Tours of Historic RCA Studio B on Music Row depart on a regular schedule from the museum. Also run by the CMF is Hatch Show Print on Lower Broad. Dining is available at the Two Twenty-Two Grill. Gifts are available for purchase at the museum gift shop. The museum phone is (615) 416-2001.

The $37 million downtown museum opened in May 2001 with its striking symbolic architecture, replacing the original museum on Music Row built in 1967. The architects and designers were Tuck Hinton Architects and Ralph Appelbaum Associates. With a subsequent expansion, the museum boasts 350,000 square feet of space.

The Music City Walk of Fame is located in Hall of Fame Park in front of the museum. The inductees include Reba McEntire, Ronnie Milsap, Roy Orbison, Boudleaux and Felice Bryant, the Fisk Jubilee Singers, The Crickets, John Hiatt, Wynonna Judd, Emmylou Harris, Kenneth Schermerhorn, Francis Preston, Michael W. Smith, Buddy Killen, Barbara Mandrell, Vince Gill, Bob DiPiero, Rodney Crowell, and Jimi Hendrix.

5 Star Attraction

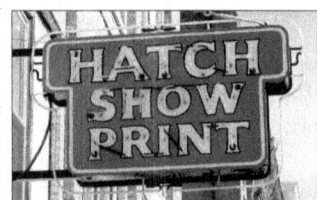

Hatch Show Print, now located at the museum, is one of the oldest surviving show poster printers. The shop is a working museum of wall posters, mechanical presses, wooden type and art blocks, and the smell of multi-colored ink. Visitors can browse for free and purchase a variety of historic posters.

Founded in 1879 by two brothers, Herbert Hatch and Charles Hatch, the shop supplied promotional handbills and posters for performers throughout the Southeast and events such as minstrel shows, vaudeville acts, and circuses. Posters at Hatch Show Print are made with the letterpress process, much as they were one hundred years ago. In fact, the process is basically the same as Johann Gutenberg used in 1455. Designs carved into wooden blocks are combined with moveable type in a lockable frame, and positioned upside down and backwards. The frame is inked with rollers and pressed with paper to produce a positive image. Each color requires a separate woodblock design and/or type. Typically, Hatch uses two or three different colors for their posters. Hatch Show Print's posters are of a very distinctive design and are still widely used today.

50 Nashville Visitors Center

The Nashville Visitors Center is located at the Bridgestone Arena, Fifth Avenue South and Broadway, in the bottom floor of the tall glass and metal tower. The phone is (615) 259-4747. The center features free tourist information, brochures and maps, special ticket offers, a coffee cafe with wireless service, and a gift shop. Also on display is Nashville's saber-tooth tiger (see below).

There is another Visitors Center located in the lower level of the US Bank Building at Fourth Avenue North and Commerce. The phone is (615) 259-4730. Hours are Monday to Friday, 8-5.

The arena, built in 1996, is home to the NHL Nashville Predators hockey team and also hosts numerous concerts and special events.

Located inside is the 7200-sq.-ft. **Tennessee Sports Hall of Fame Museum,** which chronicles professional and amateur sports teams and stars of the Volunteer State. Hours are Monday through Saturday, 10-5. Admission is charged. The phone is (615) 242-4750.

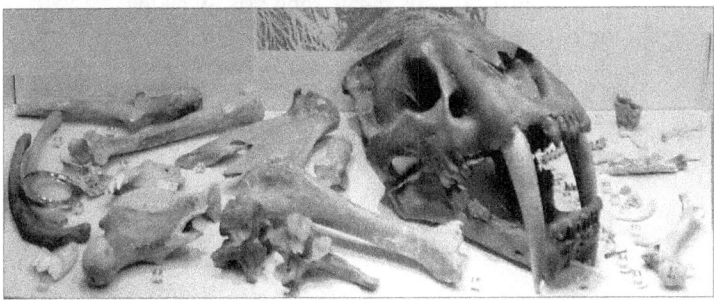

In the summer of 1971 workmen discovered a cave about 33 feet down at the site of the First American National Bank in the block of Third and Fourth avenues, Union and Deaderick streets. Archaeologists found the remains of a saber-toothed tiger (smilodon). Bones of various other prehistoric animals were also found. The tiger has been found infrequently in the eastern U.S. The Nashville cat is one of the largest specimens ever recorded, perhaps the largest. The animal lived here about 9,500 years ago, according to carbon dating. Previously it had been believed that the smilodon became extinct 14,000 years ago. The saber-toothed tiger was larger than the African lion, with heavier forequarters, lighter hindquarters, and a bobtail. It preyed on mastodon, giant beaver, and giant bison. The mascot of Nashville's NHL Predators hockey team, Gnash, is a saber-toothed tiger.

Nashville Songwriters Hall of Fame

Induction into the Nashville Songwriters Hall of Fame (NaSHOF) is one of the nation's highest songwriting achievements. Since 1970, the hall has enshrined some of the greatest writers ever to put words to music in Music City. Operated by the non-profit Nashville Songwriters Foundation, the Hall of Fame is dedicated to honoring Nashville's rich songwriting legacy. In 2013, NaSHOF realized a long-held dream with the opening of its Hall of Fame Gallery, located on the first floor of the Music City Center (201 5th Avenue South), directly across the street from the Country Music Hall of Fame and Bridgestone Arena.

51. Underground Railroad House

The brick house at 104 Fifth Avenue South (near the corner of Lower Broad) is considered the oldest residential building in downtown Nashville, built in 1820. The adjoining building at 106 Fifth Avenue was built around 1880. Reportedly the older house was used by the "underground railroad" prior to the Civil War to help runaway slaves escape to the North. A 1980s renovation revealed an 18-inch layer of silt and sand in a sealed-off basement, evidence that the Cumberland River had flooded as far up Broadway as Fifth Avenue in the early 1800s.

52. Ernest Tubb Record Shop

The Ernest Tubb Record Shop at 417 Broadway was the site of the second-longest running radio show in history, the Midnight Jamboree, played following performances of the Grand Ole Opry at the Ryman Auditorium down the street. Singer Ernest Tubb (1914-1984), known as the Texas Troubadour, opened the store and mail-order business in 1947 and moved to this location in 1951. His theme song was "Walking the Floor Over You." Tubb played the Grand Ole Opry from 1943 to 1984. A segment of the movie *Coal-Miner's Daughter*, the biography of Loretta Lynn, was filmed here.

The Midnight Jamboree continues its broadcasts on WSM 650-AM from the Texas Troubadour Theatre, an affiliated outlet in Music Valley Village, across from Opryland USA and the Opryhouse.

(53) Ryman Auditorium: Mother Church of Country Music

The Ryman Auditorium in downtown Nashville, affectionately known as the Mother Church of Country Music for hosting the *Grand Ole Opry,* was built by a riverboat captain and an evangelist as a tabernacle for religious revivals, but the venerable structure also hosted a who's who of 20th Century American entertainment.

5 Star Attraction

Known foremost as the former home of the *Grand Ole Opry,* the Ryman Auditorium underwent its own revival and now hosts a multitude of musical acts (some as far from country music as one can get) and has earned the reputation as one of the most acoustically perfect music settings in the world. It is also known as the birthplace of a uniquely American art form—bluegrass music.

The *Grand Ole Opry* radio/TV show has now occupied its spacious modern OpryHouse venue at the Gaylord Entertainment complex upriver from downtown Nashville longer than its former tenure at the Ryman. The first act at the new OpryHouse in 1974 was Marty Robbins (he was also the last regular *GOO* act at the Ryman) and the special guest for the night was President Richard Nixon (who failed on stage to successfully work a yo-yo despite instruction by master yo-yo'er Roy Acuff). A six-foot circle of dark oak planking was cut from the old Ryman stage and inlaid at the new OpryHouse stage so that a little piece of the Ryman will remind performers of the show's heritage. It was Acuff singing "The Great Speckled Bird" that inaugurated the *Opry* at the Ryman back during World War Two.

The *Opry* was created in 1925 by the National Life and Accident Insurance Company as a barn dance show on 1000-watt radio station WSM (We Shield Millions) as a promotion to sell life insurance. Originally the radio show featured classical music, string quartets, and dance music. George Hay, former MC at Chicago's WLS barn dance began airing some old-time music. The first performer was fiddler Uncle Jimmy Thompson, and the response from the listening audience was enthusiastic. Soon the station was broadcasting with 5,000 watts of power and reaching most of the South and Midwest. Hay, who called himself the Old Judge despite being only 30 years old, is credited with naming the musical segment the *Grand Old Opry,* later changed to *Grand Ole Opry.*

In 1932, WSM built a new radio tower, the tallest in the nation at 878 feet, which transmitted at a powerful 50,000 watts.

The *Opry* soon grew out of its fifth-floor radio station studio (500 capacity) at the National Life and Accident Insurance Co. building at Seventh and Union. The show moved to the Hillsboro Theater, then to the Dixie Tabernacle in East Nashville, then to the War Memorial Building downtown, and finally to the Ryman Auditorium. (In 2010-2011, the *Opry* was staged at six different locations after the Opryhouse was closed by the Great Nashville Flood of May 2010.)

It was on the stage at the Ryman in 1954 that a gyrating Elvis Presley was met with a cool reception (he never appeared on the *Opry* again). Electrified instruments and drums were at first forbidden and then only reluctantly accepted as legitimate. Hank Williams set the place on fire when he debutted on June 11, 1949 but later was told not to come back after he indulged too much in drugs and alcohol. Same for Johnny Cash, but only temporarily. Cash ended up videotaping his highly successful 1960s television show from the Ryman.

The statue of steamboat captain Thomas Ryman is located at the modern visitors entrance on Fourth Avenue North. The sculptor is Steve Shields.

Ryman Auditorium: Mother Church of Country Music

After its abandonment in 1974, the old auditorium risked demolition until Emmy Lou Harris and her Nash Ramblers performed a series of concerts there and recorded an album. The Ryman opened again as a music venue in 1994 and has been going strong ever since (although some purists might cringe at the thought of heavy metal bands shaking the rafters there). But even before Harris, another performer dedicated a song to the Ryman's preservation—John Hartford, who besides being an innovative modern musician was also a certified riverboat captain.

At the east end of the Ryman property stands a prominent statue of a riverboat captain standing at the wheel of his ship. The likeness is that of Captain Thomas Ryman, who owned and operated a successful steamship line (35 vessels) on the Cumberland River in the latter 1800s. In 1885 Ryman built a new home for his family on College Hill overlooking the river. The Queen Anne-style house had seven gables, two turrets, a slate roof, and extensive landscaping. It was that same year that Ryman attended a religious tent revival meeting led by the fiery orator the Reverend Sam Jones. The preacher was said to have given 1,000 sermons to three million people across the U.S. in one year. A former drinker, he became an ardent prohibitionist.

Legend has it that Ryman and a bunch of his rowdy rivermen went to the revival to heckle and taunt Jones, but Ryman ended up converted. He then ceased selling liquor on his riverboats and personally supervised the dumping of barrels of whiskey into the river.

In reality, Ryman attended the revival with his wife and six children, ages four to 14, and was converted to Christianity, according to descendant and author Charmaine Gossett. He joined the Elm Street Methodist Church. Over time, Ryman allowed the contracts of the concessionaires who sold liquor on his boats to expire and then refused to sell liquor on his boats anymore.

Ryman brought the idea of a community auditorium to Rev. Jones, who enthusiastically endorsed the concept. Enough money was raised by 1888, and the construction of the Union Gospel Tabernacle was completed in 1892 with a seating capacity of 3,000 and at a cost of $100,000. The designer was leading Nashville architect Hugh Cathcart Thompson. The Gothic Revival brick and stone building is 120 feet wide by 178 feet long. One of the more notable features of the old tabernacle are the pinewood church benches or pews furnished by the Indiana Church Finishing Co., which remain to this day.

Five years after completion, a balcony was added which doubled the capacity in anticipation of the Confederate Veterans convention during the Tennessee Centennial Exposition. The balcony has been called the Confederate Gallery ever since. This addition made the tabernacle the largest assembly hall in the South. A proper stage was finally built in 1901 to accommodate the appearance of the New York Metropolitan Opera in Nashville.

"There is not a life in this city from the highest to the lowest that the life of Captain Ryman did not touch."

Nashville had boasted of several other auditoriums, the first theater opening in 1818. The antebellum Adelphi Theater opened in 1850 and hosted P.T. Barnum and operatic singer Jenny Lind, the Swedish Nightingale. During the Civil War, prominent actor John Wilkes Booth performed numerous plays in Nashville.

Ryman died in 1904 and at his funeral at the Union Gospel Tabernacle on Christmas Day, the Rev. Jones suggested the building be renamed in his honor. "There is not a life in this city," said Jones, "from the highest to the lowest that the life of Captain Ryman did not touch. It is fitting on a Christmas Day, on a Sabbath Christmas day, that we should meet to mingle our sympathy, our tears, and our love." Two years later, funeral services were held at the Ryman for the Reverend Jones.

Eleven years later, Ryman's son, also a steamboat captain, was shot to death on the *Jo Horton Fall* on the Cumberland River in Wilson County by a disgruntled former employee. He was shot seven times and died instantly. The gunman was tried but no verdict could be reached; he was acquitted of first-degree murder at the second trial.

Many years later, the Ryman would serve as the venue for special memorial services and funeral services for entertainers such as Patsy Cline, Johnny Cash, Waylon Jennings, Bill Monroe, Owen Bradley, Tammy Wynette, Chet Atkins, and Harlan Howard.

Religious revivals were also held at the Ryman by prominent evangelists Dwight L. Moody, a publisher and founder of the Moody Bible Institute; and Billy Sunday, a former professional baseball player who preached to millions.

In the following decades, the tabernacle would be host to some of the grandest performances in American history, including grand opera, Shakespearean plays, symphonic concerts, lectures, vaudeville and comedic acts, passion plays, dance recitals, Broadway musicals, Golden Gloves boxing, and an Old-Time Fiddlers Contest.

Paul Ryman, another son of the captain, would perform at the auditorium, singing tenor. So did the great Irish tenor John McCormack.

In 1893, Lieutenant Robert Peary presented his lecture on Arctic exploration, especially the exploration of Greenland. He would return 17 years later to explain how he had reached the North Pole in 1909. Years later, Norwegian Captain Roald Amundsen would lecture about his explorations at the South Pole.

William Jennings Bryan, the Great Commoner who had lost the Presidential election the previous year and who would proceed to lose two other such elections, filled the whole building

Ryman Auditorium: Mother Church of Country Music

with his "golden voice" in 1897. Bryan would become best-known for his role as a prosecuting lawyer in the 1925 Scopes monkey trial in Dayton, Tenn.

The New York Metropolitan Opera Company performed *Carmen, The Barber of Seville,* and *Faust* in 1901 after a special stage was built to accommodate the performances. The New York Symphony Orchestra performed on stage as did the Chicago Orchestra, Edward Strauss and the Vienna Orchestra, and Victor Herbert and the Pittsburgh Symphony.

In 1904, a newly widowed woman by the name of Lula Clay Naff, known as L.C., began booking acts into the Ryman as an employee of the DeLong Rice Lyceum Bureau. In 1920, she was hired as the director of the Ryman and worked diligently to bring entertainment to Nashville until her retirement in 1955. Described as "tough, determined, shrewd, and capable," she reportedly kept the receipts from performances in a shoebox.

Surely, one of her proudest bookings was that of President Teddy Roosevelt in 1907, who used the Ryman stage as a bully pulpit and lectured to a large audience during his famous one-day visit to Nashville.

Operatic singer Adelina Patti, the most celebrated soprano in the world, performed at the Ryman, as did the French Grand Opera Company of New Orleans. Madame Nellie Melba, for whom melba toast and peach melba are named, also performed there, as did the Divine Sarah Bernhardt, who performed in *Camille,* a year after losing her right leg to gangrene.

The Walter Hampden Shakespeare Company performed for Nashville audiences, and *Madame Butterfly* was presented by the San Carlo Opera Company.

Not all performers were human. Beautiful Jim Key, the smartest horse in the world, performed his stunts on stage, reading, writing, spelling, and arithmetic, as trained by his owner, Dr. William Key, a former slave and self-taught veterinarian.

Famous civil rights activist Booker T. Washington lectured from the stage as did General William Booth, founder of the Salvation Army, and Sir Robert Baden Powell, founder of the Boy Scouts.

John Phillip Souza, the March King and composer of the *Stars and Stripes Forever,* put the audience in a martial mood with his brazen band of musicians.

Vaudeville came to the Ryman with famous Scottish comedian Harry Lauder, author of *Roamin' in the Gloamin',* who often performed in full Highland regalia.

In 1915, the Fisk University Jubilee Singers performed onstage to celebrate the 50th anniversary of their famous historically black college. The original singers had toured the world raising funds for Fisk and in the process popularized Negro spirituals as an art form. Many years later in 1941, also gracing the stage was Miriam Anderson with her vibrant contralto singing. Anderson had performed in 1939 at the Lincoln Memorial after being banned by the DAR from performing at Constitution Hall due to segregation policies. Eleanor Roosevelt resigned from the DAR over the Anderson incident.

During World War One, the king of movies, Francis X. Bushman, appeared in support of war bonds, as did silent-movie stars Charlie Chaplin, Douglas Fairbanks Jr., and Mary Pickford.

Enrico Caruso, the renown Italian operatic tenor and one of the first performers to record his performances, visited the Ryman a year before his retirement in 1920, possibly while he was wooing a 25-year-old New York socialite.

The magnificent but nervous soprano Rosa Ponselle made her appearance two years after debuting at the Metropolitan Opera.

In 1907 President Teddy Roosevelt used the Ryman Auditorium as a bully pulpit during his famous one-day visit to Nashville.

Clownish DeWolf Hopper presented his comedic *Casey at the Bat* routine. Bald from birth, he wore wigs on stage and his complexion was bluish from medications he took. A skirt chaser, he had six wives and countless young mistresses.

Isadora Duncan, creator of modern dance, partnered with silent-picture hearthrob Rudolph Valentino, the "Latin Lover," on the Ryman stage, her long scarves flowing.

Eccentric Vladimir de Pachman, one of the greatest pianists in the world, performed Chopin in a farewell concert, gesturing, muttering, and addressing the audience.

Veteran inebriate W.C. Fields went onstage mumbling his sarcastic asides and probably yelling, "Who put pineapple juice in my pineapple juice!" Reportedly, no children were kicked.

The Spike Jones Orchestra and his Musical Depreciation Revue featuring the City Slickers performed their manic magic.

Basil Rathbone, known for his portrayals of Sherlock Holmes; Orson Welles, instigator of the *War of the Worlds* radio-show hoax; and Katharine Cornell, First Lady of the Theater, starred in *The Barretts of Wimpole Street,* a melodrama performed on a nationwide tour during the Depression.

Helen Hayes, the First Lady of the American Theater, performed twice at the Ryman, depicting Mary of Scotland in 1934 and Victoria Regina in 1938. In 1941, Katharine Hepburn performed in *The Philadelphia Story* and Tallulah Bankhead in *Reflected Glory.* Bela Lugosi, best known for his portrayal of Count Dracula, performed in *Arsenic and Old Lace.*

Also performing at the Ryman Auditorium were Bob Hope, Doris Day, Martha Graham, Harpo Marx, Roy Rogers and Dale Evans, Mae West, and Gene Autry.

The Ryman Auditorium was featured in several movies, including the controversial *Nashville!* (1970), *Coal Miner's Daughter* (1980), *Honky Tonk Man* (1982), *Sweet Dreams: The Patsy Cline Story* (1985), and *Big Dreams and Broken Hearts: The Dottie West Story* (1995).

54 AT&T Building

The AT&T Building (formerly the BellSouth Building and South Central Bell Building) is the tallest skyscraper in Tennessee, soaring 617 feet above downtown Nashville. The 33-story skyscraper at 333 Commerce Street is affectionately known by locals as the Bat Tower or Batman Building due to the resemblence to Batman's mask.

The tower is the regional headquarters of AT&T Southeast (BellSouth's successor), and also served as the temporary headquarters for Nissan North America, while its new offices were being constructed in nearby Franklin, Tenn.

The tower was completed in 1994, designed by Earl Swensson Associates. The building's styling is similar to the Melbourne Central Tower in Melbourne, Australia.

The tower does not feature a public observation deck. Atop the western spire are two video cameras operated by a local TV station which provide spectacular video footage of the surrounding area.

55 Gruhn Guitar

Gruhn Guitar was started in 1970 by George Gruhn and associates at Lower Broad and Fourth Avenue North and today represents the world's finest collection of vintage and used instruments, including acoustic and electric guitars, mandolins, basses, and banjos. Many famous performers, while in Nashville, stop by to browse and add to their collections.

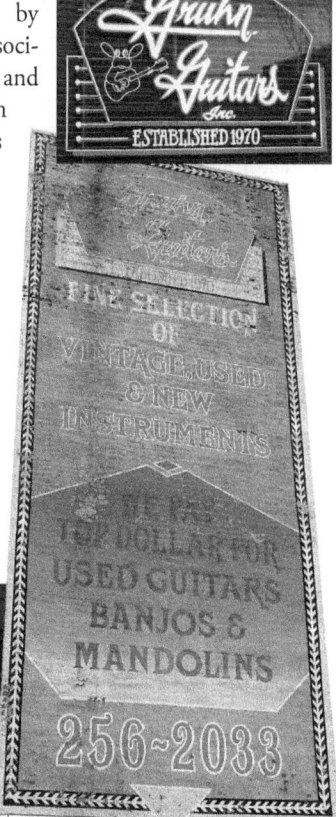

56 Tootsie's Orchid Lounge

The premier honky tonk in Nashville is Tootsies Orchid Lounge, located at 422 Broadway, across an alley from the Ryman Auditorium. The proprietor from 1960 to 1978 was Hattie Louise "Tootsie" Bess, who bought the lounge called Mom's and named it after herself. According to tradition, the exterior was painted orchid purple by mistake but never changed. Struggling artists such as Willie Nelson and Kris Kristofferson frequented the lounge, as did performers on break during Grand Ole Opry performances at the Ryman. The walls of the lounge are called Tootsie's Hall of Fame.

57 Masonic Grand Lodge

The Masonic Grand Lodge is located at 100 Seventh Avenue North at Broadway. The Scottish Rite Temple was built in 1925 of Bedford limestone in the Greek Revival Ionic style. The building, which houses the offices of the Freemasons, features a 1,500-seat auditorium, a ceremonial lodge, and a Freemasonry museum, open and free to the public.

58 First Baptist Church

The tall steeple marks the First Baptist Church, the de facto mother church of the Southern Baptist Convention, at the southeast corner of 7th Avenue and Broadway. The church was organized in 1820. Members met for services in the county courthouse. The congregation met in two different church buildings before occupying the current location at 615 Broadway in 1886. During a building project from October 1967 to 1970 the original Victorian Gothic church building designed by Thompson and Zwicker was torn down. The taller of the two old steeple towers was retained and incorporated into the new larger church building designed by Edwin A. Keeble & Associates.

The three-stage brick tower with stone trim has offset buttresses, an open belfry, and a tall spire clad in green copper. The architectural style of the main building is American Gothic, with a variety of arches. The foundation and exterior walls are brick. The stained-glass windows are by Nashville portraitist Goode Davis. The structural engineer, Ross Bryan, designed a roof framing system for the 2,000-seat sanctuary that consists of two hollow five-sided post-tensioned concrete box beams. Modern construction was by J.B. Regen and Son at a cost of $2 million, including a 59-rank Aolian-Skinner organ.

⑤⑨ U.S. Customs House

The gargantuan Victorian Gothic stone building at 701 Broadway is the historic U.S. Customs House, the first federal building in Nashville. In 1877, President Rutherford B. Hayes helped lay the cornerstone with a golden trowel. It was completed in 1882. The east and west wings were added in 1918. The Customs House, as federal buildings were known at the time, was a symbol of the end of Reconstruction in the South. The building housed the Nashville Post Office, federal courtrooms, and the currency exchange.

The granite and limestone Federal Office Building features a clock tower 190 feet tall and a deeply recessed triple-arch entrance. The building was designed by U.S. Treasury architect William Appleton Potter.

The Post Office moved to new quarters on Broadway in 1934. In 1952 most of the federal offices were moved to a new federal building and courthouse across Eighth Avenue.

In 1972 the building was declared surplus property and in 1979 the city obtained the property and leased it for redevelopment. Today it houses the U.S. Bankruptcy Court and business offices.

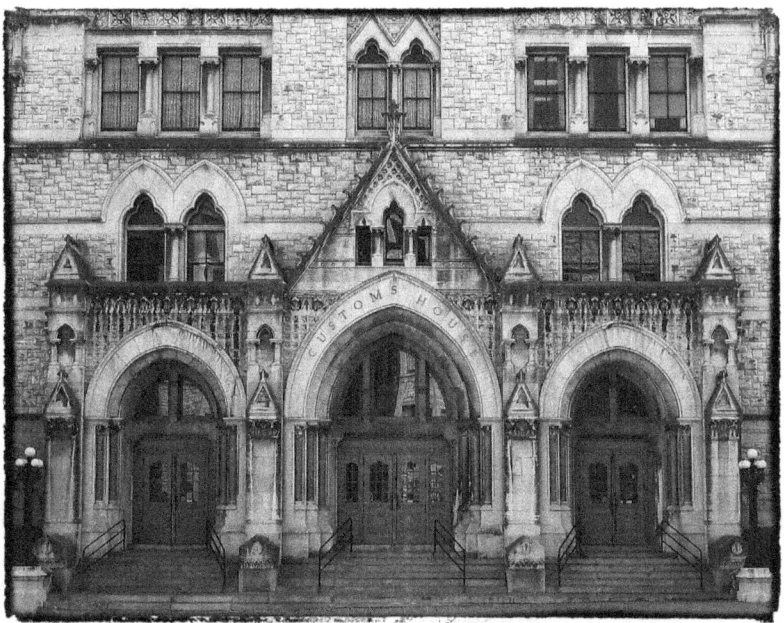

60 Hume-Fogg High School

Hume-Fogg Magnet School at 700 Broadway and Rosa Parks Boulevard (Eighth Avenue) sits on the site of Nashville's first public school, Hume School, built in 1855 and honoring David Hume, an early advocate of public education. In 1875 Fogg High School was built, honoring Frances Fogg, an attorney and member of the city's first public board of education. In 1912 the two schools were consolidated in this four-story, stone-clad building designed by William Ittner of St. Louis in the Norman Gothic style with Tudor Gothic details. Originally the building was asymetrical; the right (east) wing was added later. Over the main entrance are stone-cut figures symbolizing the classical curriculum taught at the school until the 1930s. Today the school attracts gifted students and a highly educated faculty.

61 Frost Building

The Frost Building at 161 Rosa Parks Blvd. (Eighth Avenue North) was built in 1913 to house the Baptist Sunday School Board, now known as Lifeway Christian Resources. The building was designed by Hart Gardner Architects of Nashville and named for Dr. J.M. Frost, the first chief executive officer of the Southern Baptist Convention's Sunday School Board. The building, known as the Executive Building until 1955, is one of the finest examples of Classical Revival commercial architecture in the city.

62 The Standard at Smith House

This 1840s Italianate-style 20,000-sq.-ft. mansion at 167 Rosa Parks Blvd. (Eighth Avenue North) is the oldest remaining townhouse residence in downtown Nashville and now houses The Standard at Smith House restaurant.

The three-story dark-red brick building was built in the 1840s by Mary Claiborne as a boarding house and later occupied by Dr. Giles C. Savage, a Vanderbilt University professor of opthalmology, and his family from 1898 to 1975 and used both as an office and residence. In 1883 the Standard Club built a ballroom with ornate tin ceiling at the rear of the building and added Nashville's first bowling alley underneath. The fireplace mantle in the ballroom once stood in another nearby home; Andrew and Rachel Jackson took their marriage vows in front of it. Several of the mirrors and lamps are from the old Maxwell House Hotel. In the 1980s and 1990s the popular Gaslight Lounge was used as the setting for many music videos.

In 2005, Joshua Smith and parents Sharon and Jerry Smith, bought the residence and renovated it into a upscale historic restaurant.

63 Berger Building

The Berger Building at 164 Rosa Parks Blvd. (Eighth Avenue North) was constructed in the 1920s by Samuel Berger, a leading merchant, and is a fine example of an ornate commercial building. It was designed by architect O.J. Billis, who also designed many Nashville apartments and residences. The ornate features include green and white-glazed terra cotta decorations, lion's heads and floral designs, and an elliptical cornice inscribed with "Berger Building, 1926" on terra cotta panels.

64 Old Methodist Publishing House

The Methodist Episcopal Church, South constructed this building in 1906 to house their publishing operations, which they had moved from Philadelphia to Nashville in 1854. This five-story neo-classical structure used steel-frame construction to accommodate heavy printing equipment. The pronounced cornice and carved limestone entrance are unique. The Methodists moved their publishing operations to other quarters in 1957.

65 Christ Church Cathedral

Christ Church Cathedral at 900 Broadway is a fine example of Gothic Revival architecture, built in 1887-92 of Sewanee sandstone, a gift from the University of the South at Sewanee, Tenn. The church serves as the cathedral of the Episcopal Diocese of Tennessee and has sent eight rectors to ordination as bishops.

The original church was built in 1830 at the corner of Sixth Avenue and Church Street. In 1890 the church was sold and a new lot was purchased for the church on Broad and McLemore (Ninth Avenue).

The present structure was designed by Francis Hatch Kimball of New York. The tower, although originally planned, was not built until 1947 under the supervision of local architect Russell Hart. Stone gargoyles, rare in Nashville, can be seen perched on the tower.

The complex gabled and hipped roof is composed of slate shingles. Bowling Green gray stone was used for the trim and in the tower. The interior of the church has a distinct early-English ambience, known for its handcarved woodwork and stained glass windows, two groups of which were designed by Louis Comfort Tiffany.

Guided public tours of Christ Church Cathedral are conducted; call (615) 255-7729 for details.

66 Frist Center for the Visual Arts

5 Star Attraction

The Frist Center for the Visual Arts is housed in the former United States Post Office building on Broadway, between 9th and 10th avenues south. It was designed by the Nashville architectural firm of Marr and Holman (Thomas Scott Marr and Joseph W. Holman) and constructed in 1933-34 with funds allocated by Congress during the Hoover administration. The front of the building is classical in style, while the interior is Art Deco. It was listed on the National Register of Historic Sites in 1984. The structure served as the main U.S. Post Office for Nashville until 1986. It continued as a downtown branch of the post office after that time. The building was transferred to the City of Nashville in 1998 in preparation for its use as home to the Frist Center for the Visual Arts. The Frist Center opened in 2001. The lobby of the Frist has been restored to the 1934 design, with the exception of glass doors leading to exhibit galleries and Art Deco style benches that are not original. Thomas F. Frist Jr., M.D. and his family, through the charitable Frist Foundation, committed to lead the effort to create the center, which required a public/private partnership to acquire the historic building and land as the new home for an art center. The Frist features 24,000 sq. ft. of permanent and temporary fine-art exhibits. The center features a gift shop, cafe, children's ArtQuest room, and memberships. The phone number is (615) 244-3340.

67 Union Station

Union Station at 1001 Broadway, originally built in 1898-1900 as the depot for the Louisville & Nashville Railroad, has been restored and now functions as one of Nashville's finest hotels. The Richardson Romanesque-style building was designed by Richard Montfort, the railway's architect, and built of rusticated limestone and marble. The 220-foot-tall tower was originally topped by a bronze statue of the Roman god Mercury, but a storm toppled it in 1951. The statue had originally graced the Commerce Building at the 1897 Tennessee Centennial Exposition. The tower originally contained an early mechanical digital clock; when replacement French silk drive belts proved unavailable during World War I, it was replaced by a traditional analog clock.

The three-story lobby, a 67-foot-tall barrel-vaulted light well, once featured two alligator ponds. Decorations include bas-relief artwork by Chicago sculptor M.J. Donner, arched doorways, colorful paintwork, and ornate fixtures. Original brass and wrought-iron railings are still in use.

The station reached its peak of usage during World War Two, when thousands of servicemen passed through on their way to the war fronts. A USO canteen was stationed here. Eventually, in 1975, the building was closed and allowed to deteriorate. It was restored and opened as a hotel in 1986.

Behind the station stood the unique train shed, an unusually large single-span, gable roof structure listed as a National Historic Landmark. Unfortunately the structure could not be saved and was demolished in 2000.

Today the station is a Wyndham Historic Hotel and has undergone extensive renovations. The phone is (615) 726-1001.

5 Star Attraction

68 Cummins Station

Cummins Station at 209 Tenth Avenue South was the first reinforced-concrete building in Nashville and reportedly the largest such building in the world when constructed in 1906-07 by William J. Cummins and the Wholesale Merchants Warehouse Company. The five-story warehouse building measures 132 by 500 feet and contains 480,000 square feet. The structure is located south of the Union Station complex along the railroad "gulch." Renovations in the 1990s converted the warehouse into modern offices and retail outlets.

Historic Sites of West, North, South, and East Nashville
Table of Contents

MAPS:
Downtown Nashville and Surrounding Area .... Page 72
Davidson County 72
West End 73
Southwestern Davidson County 74
Extreme Southwestern Davidson County 75
North Nashville, Germantown 76
South Nashville 77
Southern Davidson County 78
Goodlettsville, Inglewood and Madison 79
Edgefield and East Nashville 80
Donelson, Hermitage, Old Hickory, Airport Area 81

HISTORIC SITES:
Music Row USA .... Page 82
Vanderbilt University 84
Feature: Gladiators of the Gridiron 85
Scarritt-Bennett Center 86
Cathedral of the Incarnation 86
Centennial Park and Map 87
James Robertson Monument / House 88
The Parthenon 89
Athena Parthenos 90
Gold Star (World War I) Statue 91
U.S.S. Nashville Monument 92
Feature: Tennessee Centennial Exposition 93
Belle Meade Plantation 97
Cheekwood Gardens and Art Museum 98
Newsom's Mill 99
Germantown Historic District 100
Church of the Assumption 100
Marathon Village 101
Fisk University and Jubilee Hall 102
Old State Penitentiary 103
African-American Historic Sites 104
Belmont Mansion 106
Western Military Institute 107
Rutledge House 107
Geddes Fire Hall 108
Litterer Laboratories 108
Elm Street Methodist Church 109
Lindsley Avenue Church of Christ 109
St. Patrick's Church 110
Holy Trinity Episcopal Church 110
Fort Negley 111
Battle of Nashville Monument 113
Confederate Redoubt No. 1 113
Shy's Hill 113

Travellers Rest Plantation and Museum .... Page 114
Tennessee Agricultural Museum 115
Edgefield Historic District 116
Tulip Street Methodist Church 116
Carnegie Library 117
Holly Street Fire Hall 117
Woodland Presbyterian Church 117
Two Rivers Mansion 118
The Hermitage: Home of President Andrew Jackson 119
Amqui Station and Visitors Center 123
Old Stone Bridge 123
Bowen-Campbell House 124
Historic Mansker's Station Frontier Life Center 125
George Peabody College 127
Disciples of Christ Historical Society 127
Upper Room Chapel and Museum 127
McConnell Field Site 127
Percy Warner and Edwin Warner Parks 127
Dutchman's Curve 127
Kelley's Point Battlefield 127
Stock-Yard Building 127
Werthan Building 129
Old Schaub House 129
Isaac Litton High School 129
Idlewild Mansion 129
Edgehill Polar Bear Plaza 129
Fall School 129
Grassmere Historic Farm 129
Lane Motor Museum 131
Sunnyside Mansion 131
David Lipscomb University 131
Stewart's Stone Wall 131
Battle at the Barricade 131
Old Hillsboro Pike Fire Hall 131
Cane Ridge Cumberland Presbyterian Church 131
Brentwood Hall 131
Edgefield Baptist Church 133
Old Warner Public School 133
Old East High School 133
Old Gallatin Road Fire Hall 133
Tennessee Central Railway Museum 133
Jere Baxter Statue 133
Cloverbottom Mansion 133
Buchanan Log House 135
Colemere Mansion 135
J. Percy Priest Dam 135
Old Hickory Lock and Dam 135
Old Hickory Village 135

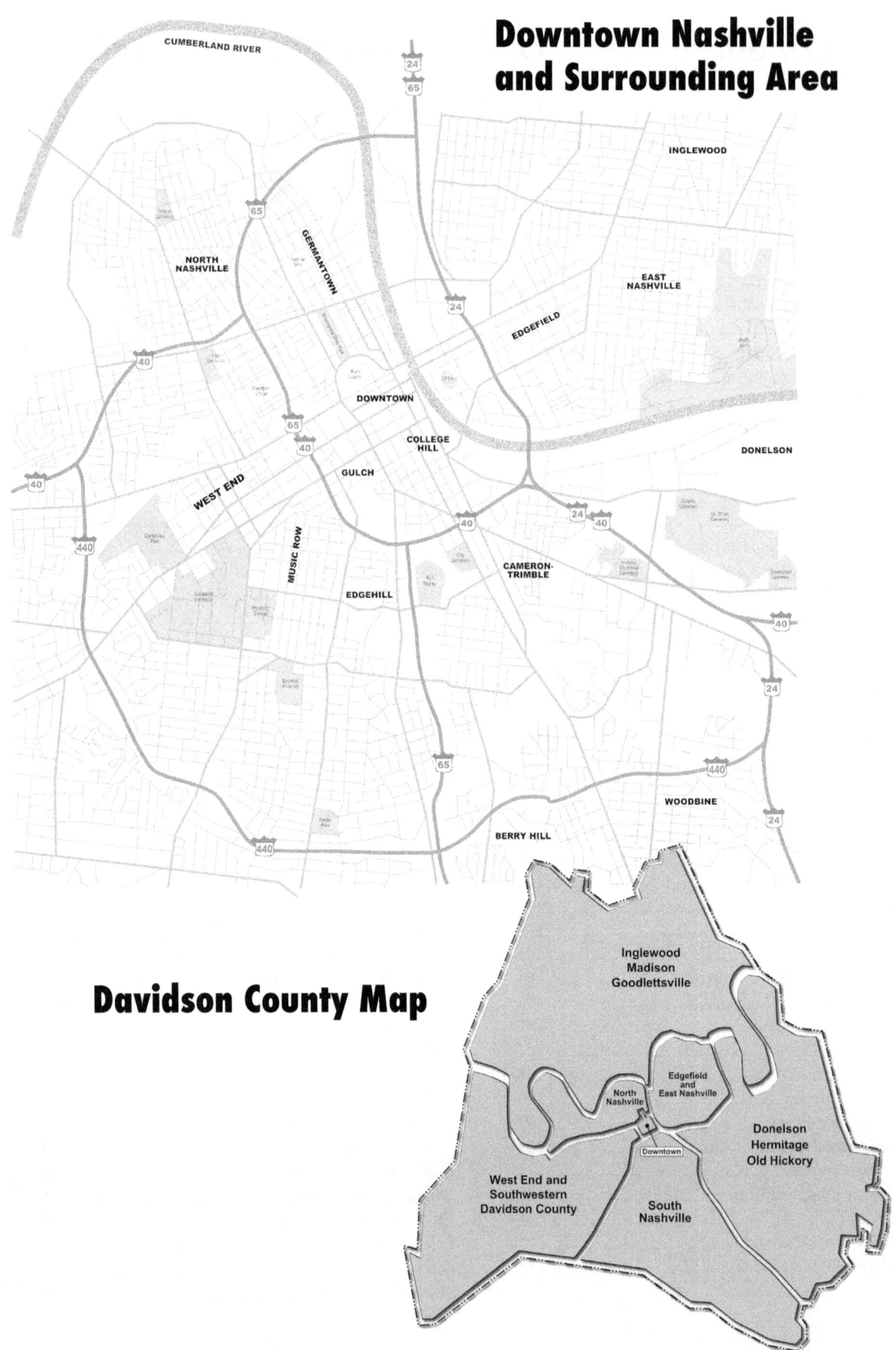

West End Map

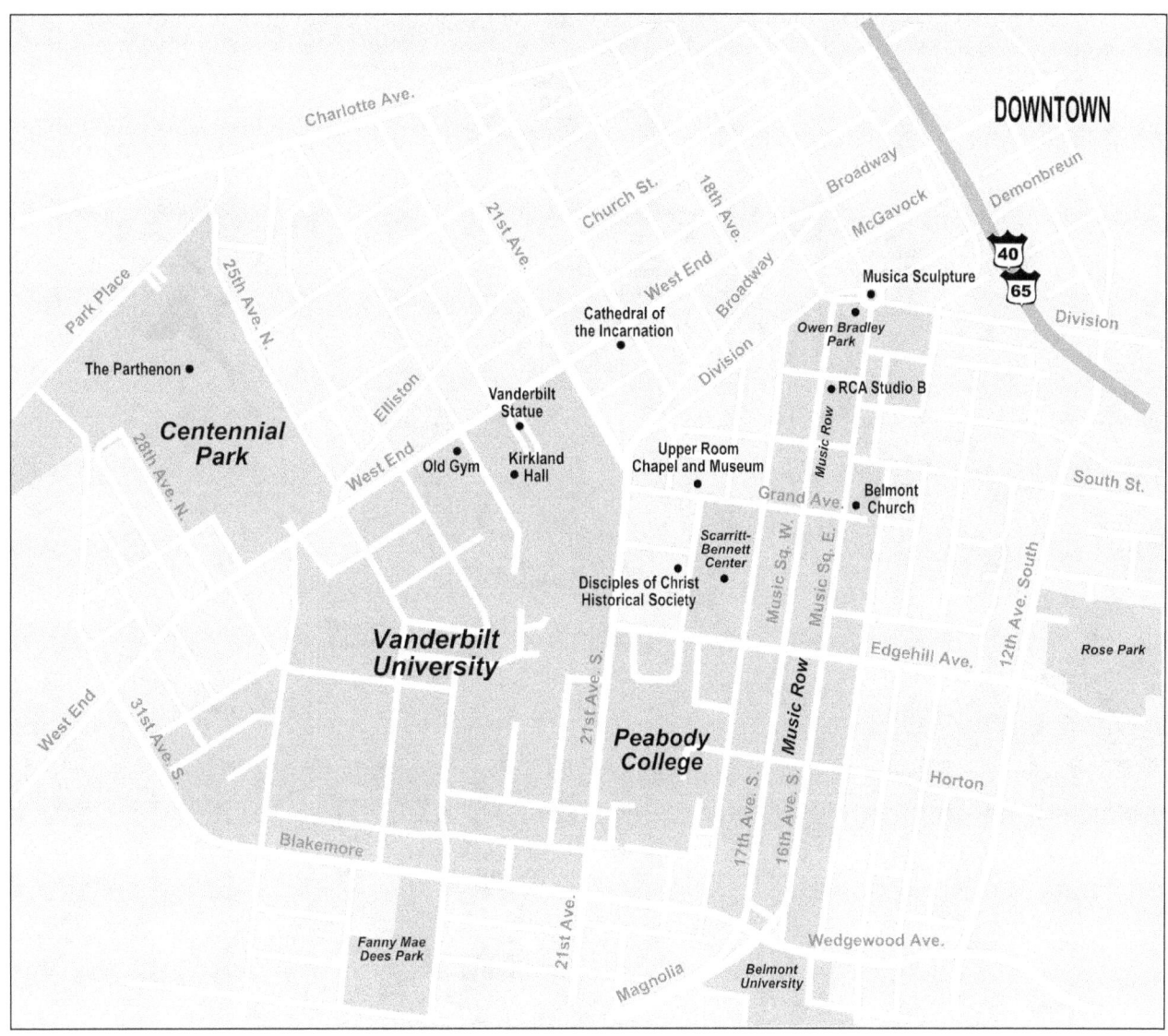

Map of Southwestern Davidson County

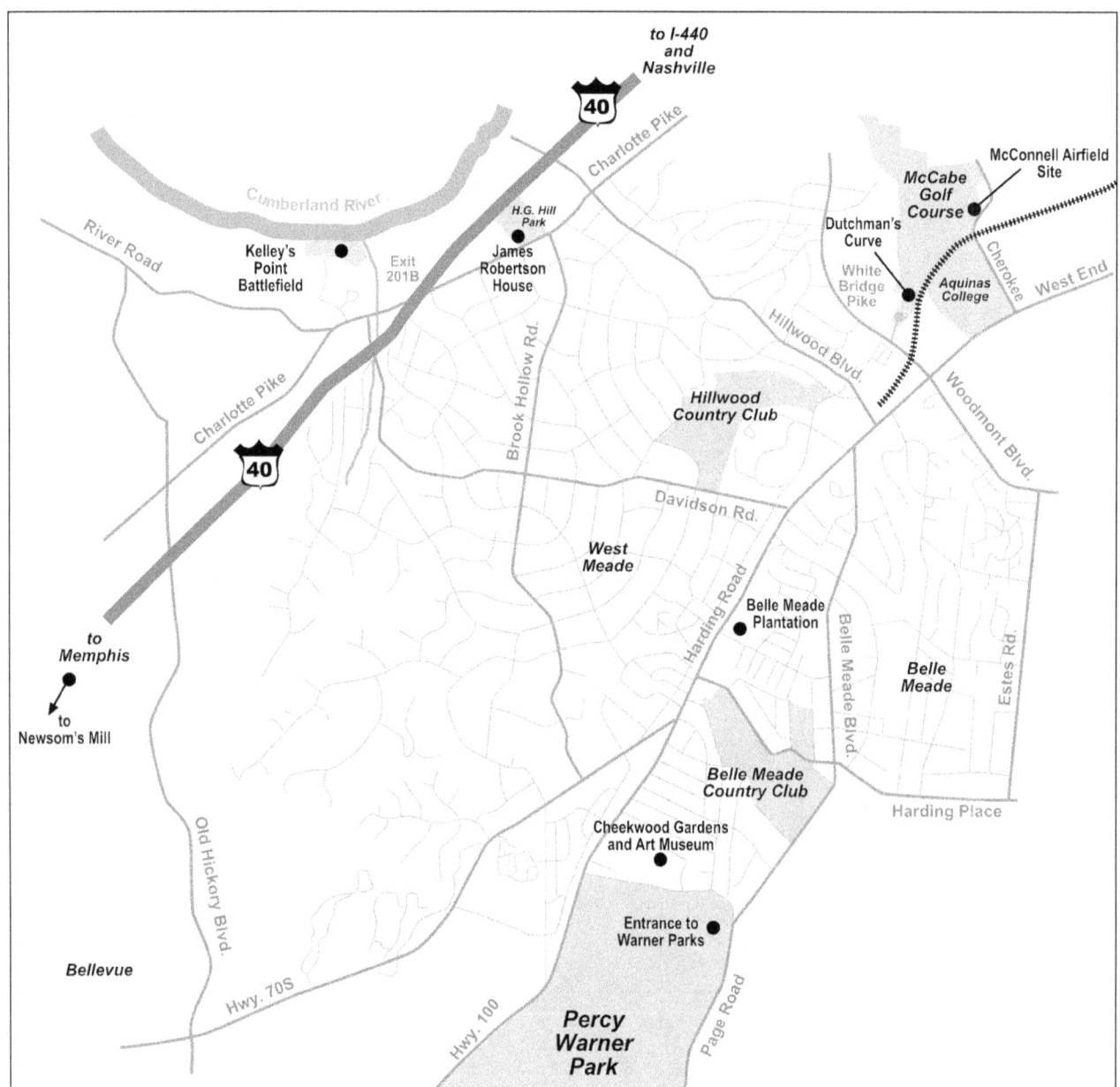

Map of Extreme Southwestern Davidson County

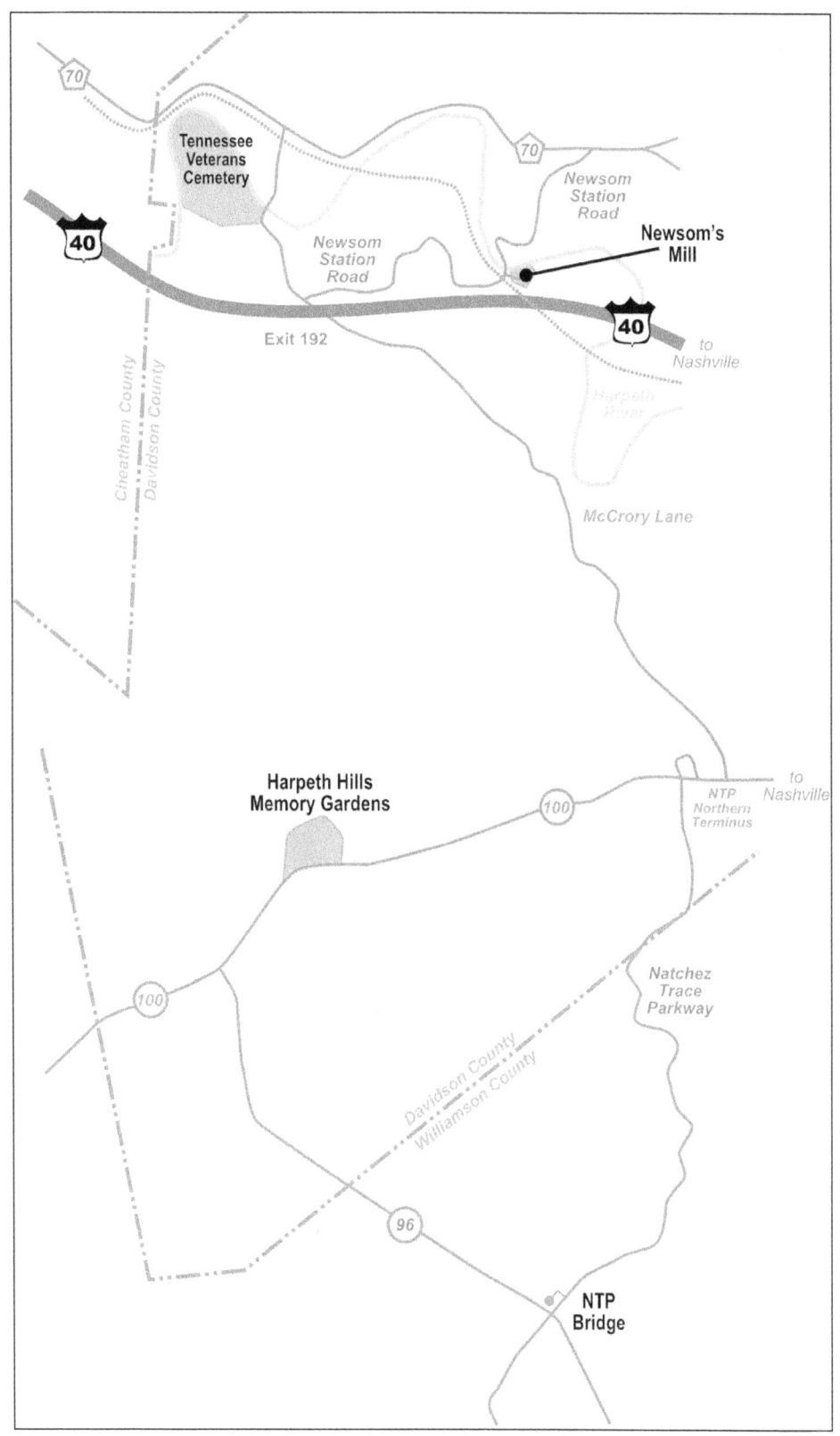

Map of North Nashville, Germantown

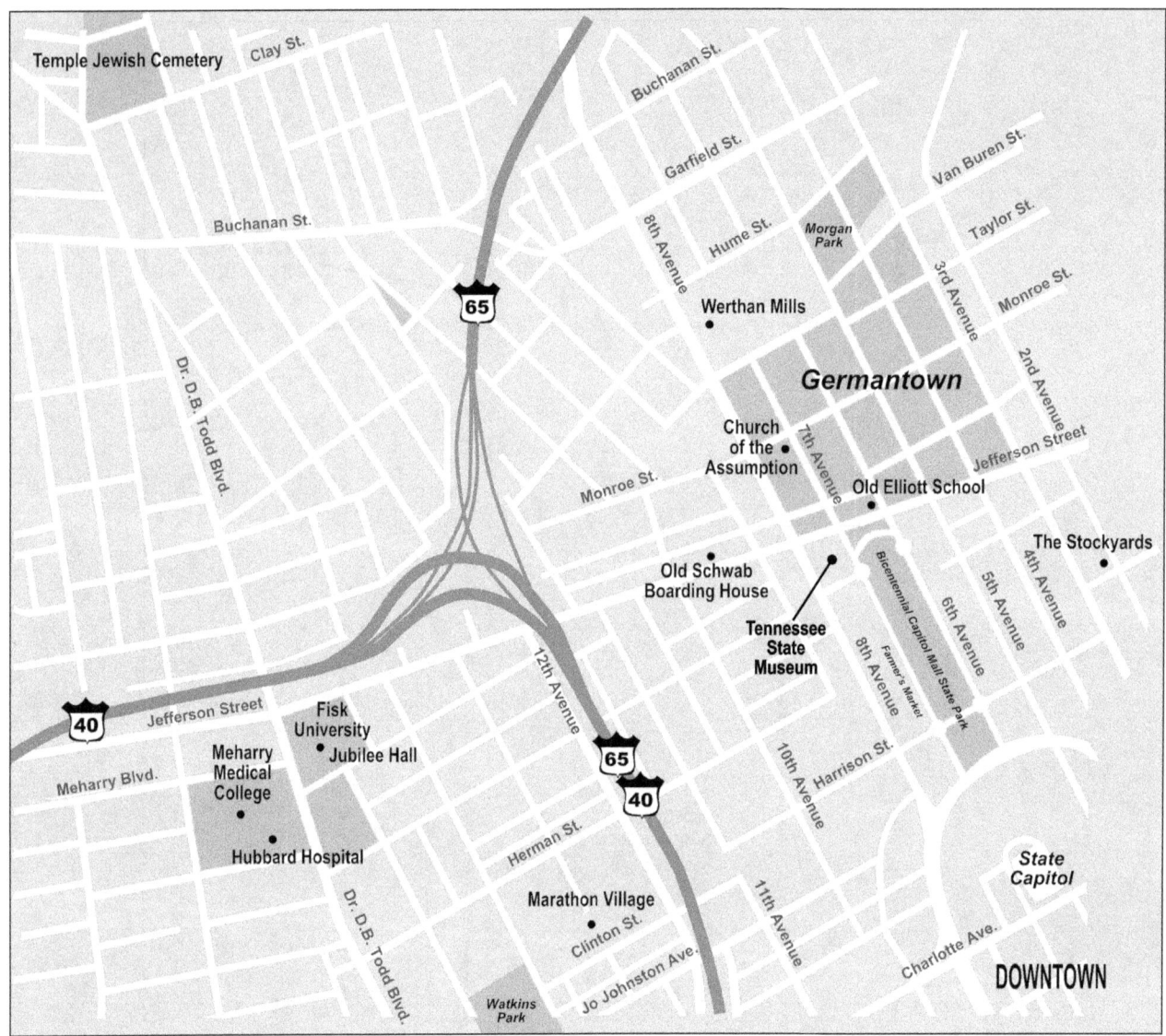

Map of South Nashville

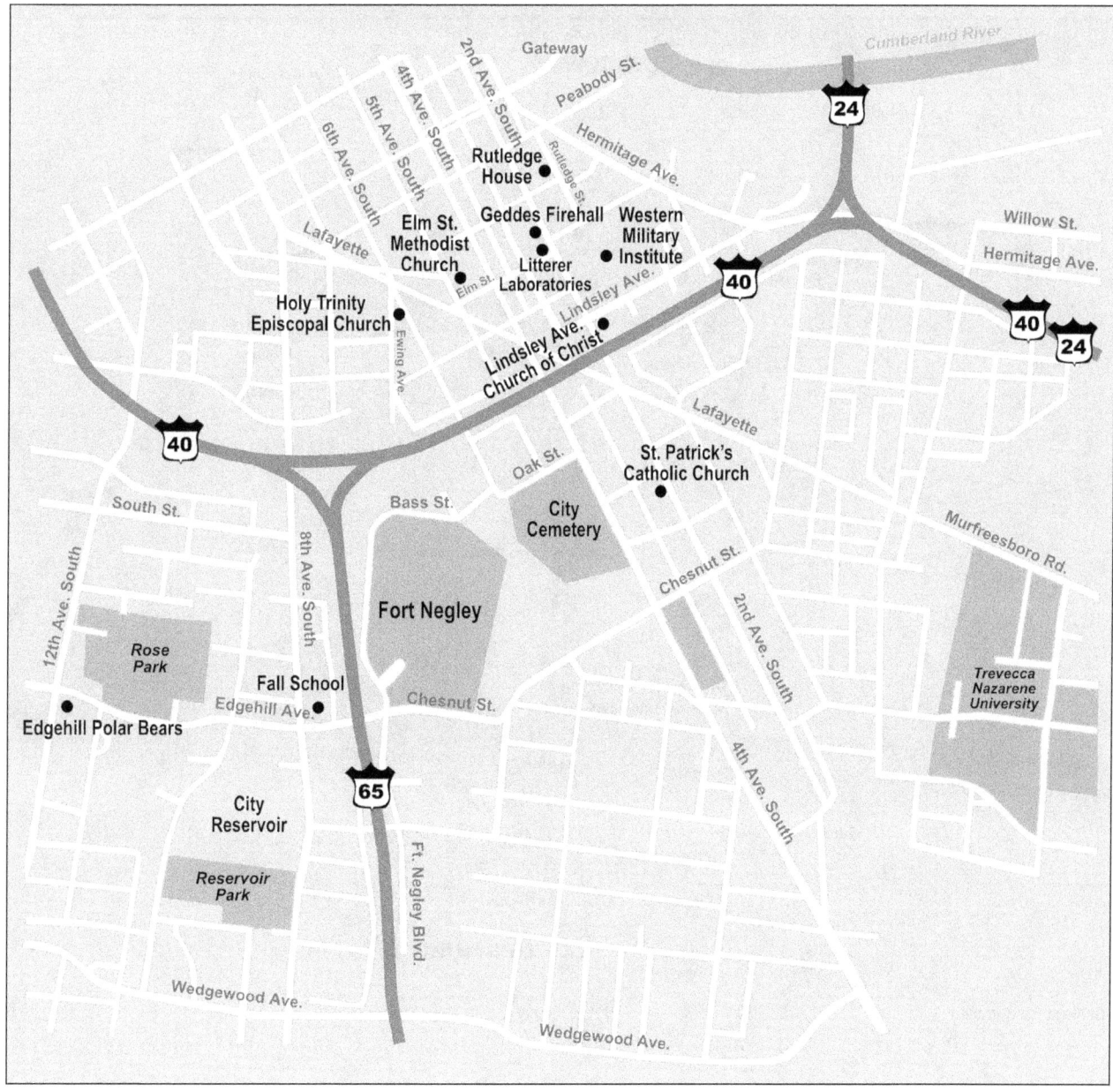

Map of Southern Davidson County

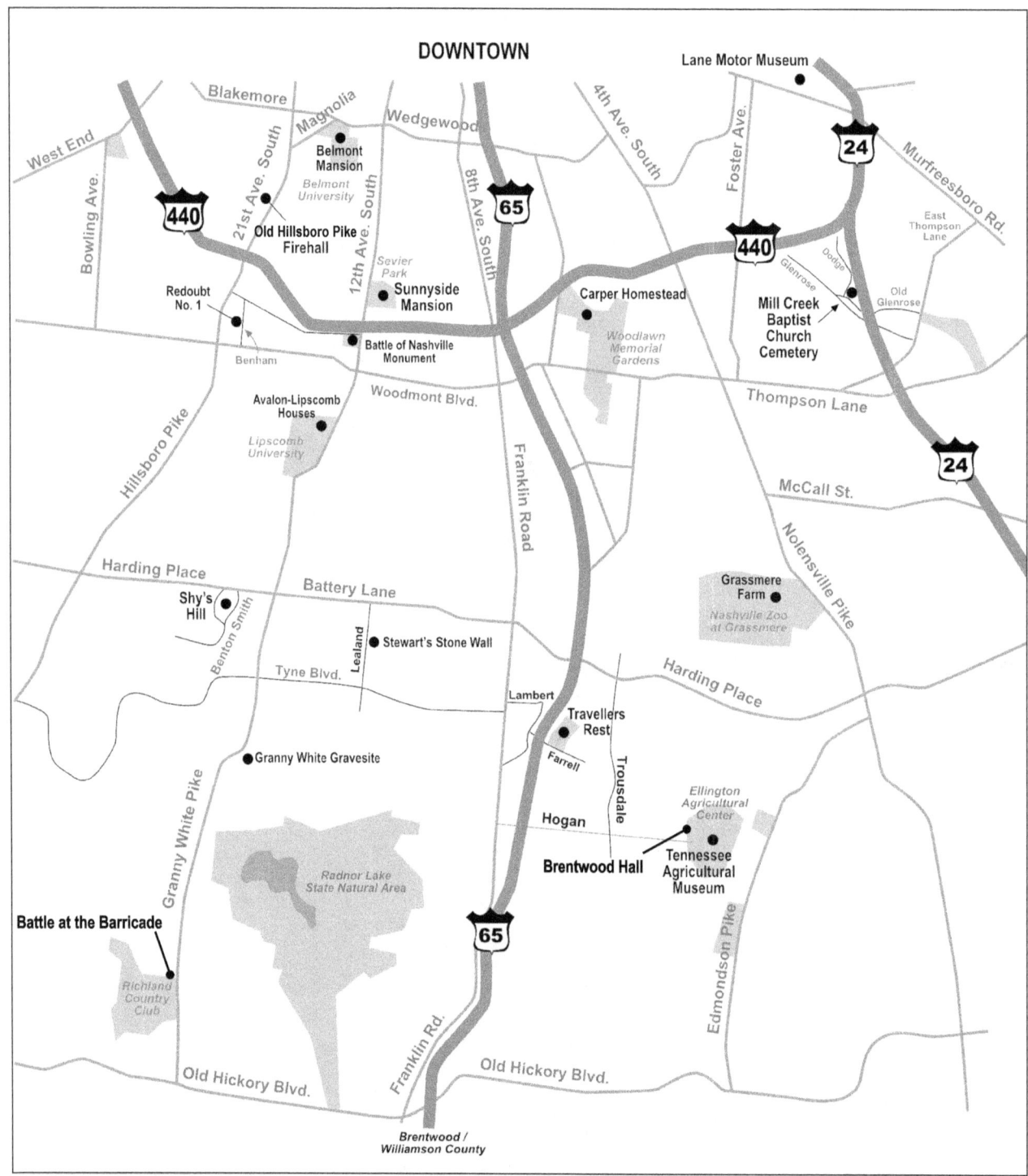

Historic Sites of West, North, South, and East Nashville

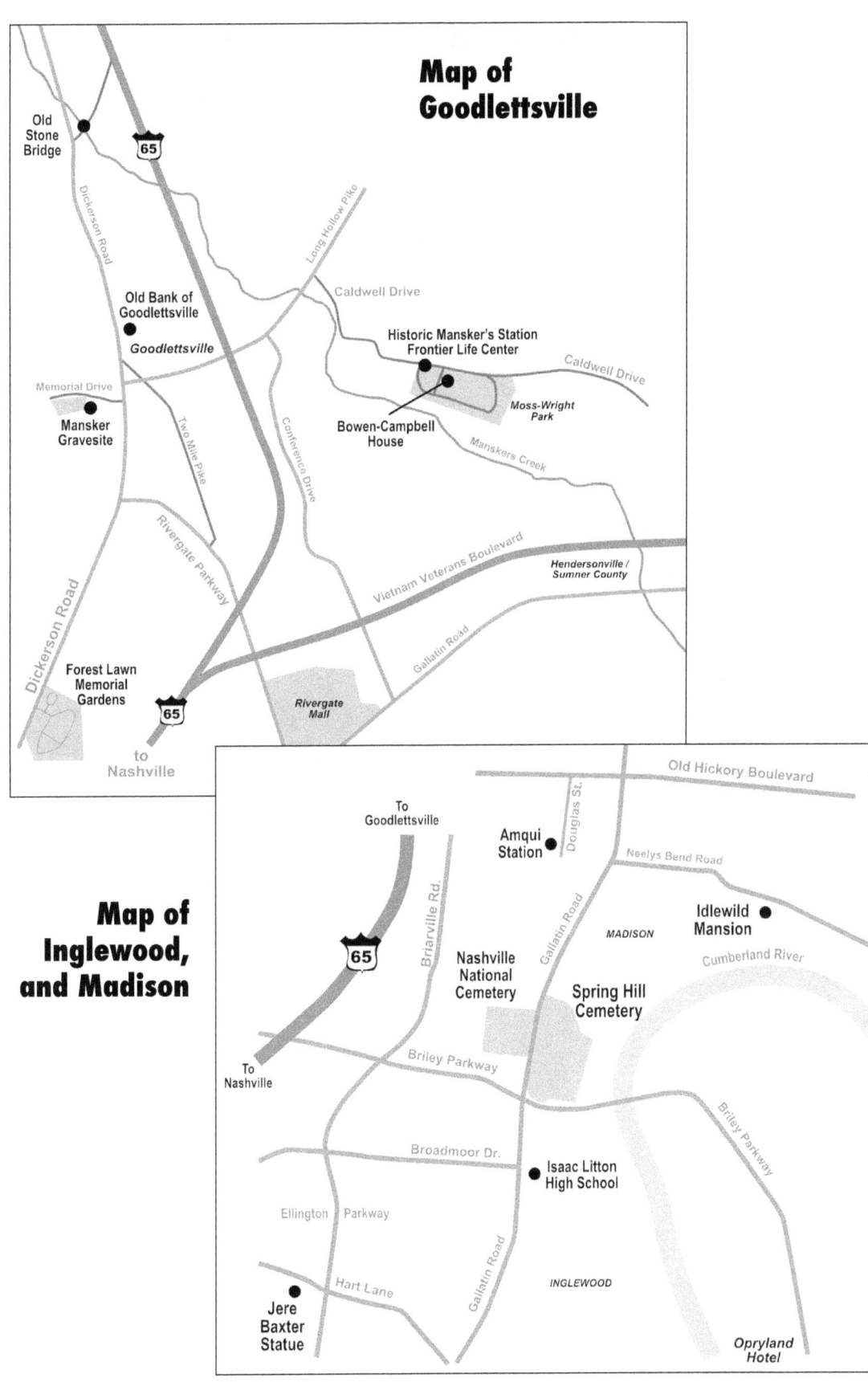

Map of Edgefield, East Nashville

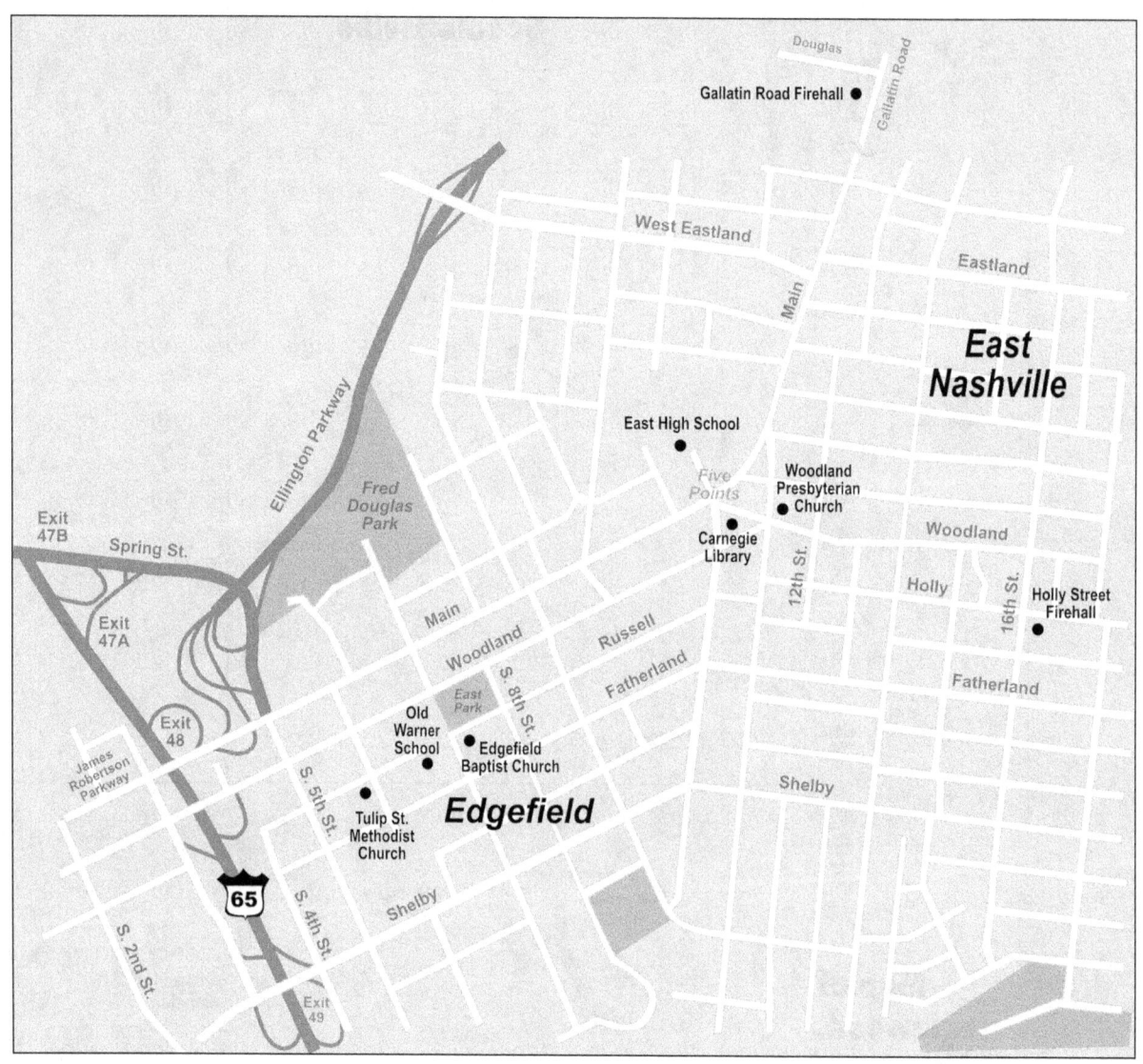

Historic Sites of West, North, South, and East Nashville 81

Map of Donelson, Hermitage, Old Hickory, Airport Area

Music Row USA

Music Row, a section of 16th and 17th avenues, is home to dozens of recording studios, music publishers, record labels, and performing rights organizations. This is the business hub of Music City Nashville. This industry, however, had humble beginnings.

In 1945 three WSM radio engineers opened Castle Studio, the first recording studio in Nashville, in the downtown Tulane Hotel. WSM, home of the *Grand Ole Opry*, called itself the "Air Castle of the South." The first recording was a jingle for local jewelers by Snooky Lanson, who later appeared on the network TV show *Your Hit Parade*. Owen and Harold Bradley accompanied on piano and guitar respectively.

Among those performing at the Castle were the Everly Brothers, folk singer Burl Ives, country star Kitty Wells, rockabilly artist Jimmie Logsdon, and Red Foley.

Owen Bradley began recording music in 1956 in a small house in what would become the Music Row section of town. He and brother Harold purchased a metal war-surplus Quonset hut designed for military use during World War Two and soundproofed it with old curtains, wooden louvers, and raw insulation covered with burlap. The rest, as they sing, is history.

OWEN BRADLEY PARK features a bronze sculpture by Gary Ernest Smith of "Nashville Sound" pioneer Owen Bradley seated at a piano. In 1954 Bradley and his brother Harold built a recording studio in a military-surplus Quonset hut at 804 Sixteenth Avenue and recorded songs performed by Hank Williams, Kitty Wells, Webb Pierce, and Red Foley. Together with Chet Atkins, Bradley is credited with producing the unique crossover Nashville Sound of the 1960s.

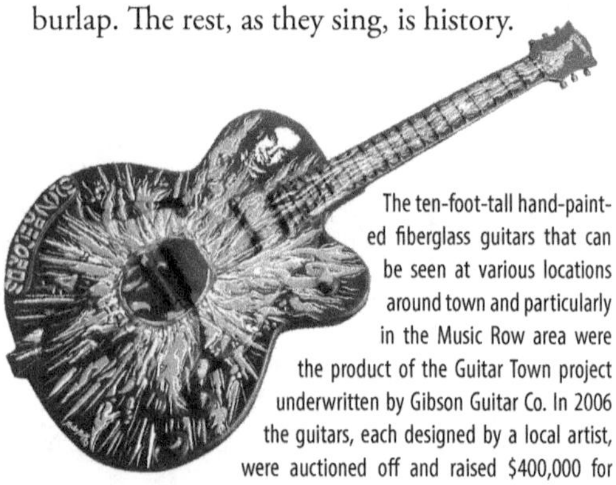

The ten-foot-tall hand-painted fiberglass guitars that can be seen at various locations around town and particularly in the Music Row area were the product of the Guitar Town project underwritten by Gibson Guitar Co. In 2006 the guitars, each designed by a local artist, were auctioned off and raised $400,000 for charity.

The octagonal nine-story Artists Building, formerly known as the United Artists Tower, at 50 Music Square West, now features residential, retail, and office units, as well as two recording studios.

Historic Sites of West, North, South, and East Nashville 83

Tours of historic **RCA STUDIO B** on Music Row depart from the Country Music Hall of Fame and Museum downtown and are available only with museum admission. Built by Dan Maddox in 1957, Studio B was the incubator for the smooth 1960s "Nashville Sound" of Chet Atkins, Eddy Arnold, Jim Reeves, and others. Elvis Presley recorded "It's Now or Never" here in 1960 and used the facility until 1971. Skeeter Davis recorded "The End of the World" here as did Roy Orbison with "Only the Lonely." More than 35,000 songs were recorded here. In 1964 RCA built a larger studio called "A" and the original studio was then known as Studio B. The studio closed in 1977, but in 2002 the studio became a learning laboratory for students through the cooperative efforts of the Curb Family Foundation and Belmont University.

Music Row is anchored by the traffic roundabout, Owen Bradley Park, and *MUSICA*, a 40-foot-high bronze statue of nine nude dancers sculpted by noted artist Alan LeQuire. The $1.5 million sculpture was unveiled in October 2003 and has stirred Bible Belt controversy ever since. The anatomically correct dancers, twice life-size, represent the importance of music—all styles of music—to Nashville in that dance is the physical expression of music. The sculpture weighs ten tons and was created in Wyoming and shipped to Nashville.

BELMONT CHURCH at 68 Music Square East (Sixteenth Avenue South) was organized as a Church of Christ by R.V. Cawthon in 1911. The original Greek Revival building, now used as a conference center, was built in 1915. During the 1970s the "Revolution at 16th and Grand" sparked by Don Finto introduced instrumental music into worship, contrary to the orthodox Churches of Christ, and was a factor in the church's movement to denominational independence. The Koinonia Coffee House across the street serves as a venue for aspiring Christian music performers, having helped spark the career of popular singer Amy Grant, among others.

Vanderbilt University

Old Gymnasium

Kirkland Hall

Vanderbilt University on West End Avenue was made possible in 1873 through a $1 million gift from Commodore Cornelius Vanderbilt (1794-1877), a shipping and rail tycoon in New York. Vanderbilt's hope in supporting a university in the South was that it would "contribute to strengthening the ties which should exist between all sections of our common country."

The original campus consisted of the Main Building, an astronomical observatory, and houses for professors. In 1905 a fire destroyed the Main Building; it was rebuilt as Kirkland Hall in honor of the school's longest-serving Chancellor, James H. Kirkland. Kirkland guided the rebuilding process and also navigated the university through its separation from the Methodist Church.

Today Kirkland Hall houses the administration offices. The building and the statue of Cornelius Vanderbilt can be seen at the West End Avenue main entrance. The statue was sculpted by Giuseppe Moretti and first stood at the 1897 Tennessee Centennial Exposition. Vanderbilt himself never visited the campus named for him.

The Fine Arts Gallery is housed in the Old Gymnasium at 23rd Avenue and West End Avenue. The brick gymnasium was designed by Peter Williamson and built in 1880 in Victorian Gothic style. Funds were donated by William Vanderbilt, the eldest son of the Commodore. The gym featured "rowing machines, chest expanders, parallel and horizontal ladders, springboards, and Indian clubs."

◀ In Bishops Corner, northwest of the Divinity School, is the tomb of Methodist Bishop Holland N. McTyeire. He went to New York City in 1873 for medical treatment and stayed with the Vanderbilt family (he was a cousin of Cornelius Vanderbilt's second wife). McTyeire convinced Vanderbilt to fund a university in the South. Vanderbilt choose McTyeire to select the site of the school and supervise the construction.

Vanderbilt University consists of 330 acres and 233 buildings and has been designated a national arboretum. One walking tour features 63 labeled trees, and a shorter tour features 46. The oldest tree on campus is the bicentennial oak, located between Rand and Garland halls, which stood during the Revolutionary War.

See Map on Page 73

Gladiators of the Gridiron: When Vanderbilt Was A Powerhouse

On Nov. 19, 2005 at Neyland Stadium in Knoxville, Tenn., the Vanderbilt Commodores football team beat their arch-enemy, the Tennessee Volunteers, 28-24, for the first time in 23 years. It took a last-minute touchdown pass from Jay Cutler to Earl Bennett and a last-second pass interception to accomplish. The game was the 101st meeting between the intrastate schools. The last time Vanderbilt beat UT two years in a row Calvin Coolidge was President. The all-time rivalry record in 2005 was 67 Tennessee wins, 28 Vandy wins, and five ties.

Vanderbilt is the Southeastern Conference's only private school, sometimes known as "the Harvard of the South." Vanderbilt's all-time football record lies below .500 (they've lost more games than they've won). They have not won a conference championship since 1923 (Southern Conference). They have played in only five post-season bowl games. Their highest final season ranking was 12th in 1948. Since 1959, the Commodores have enjoyed only four winning seasons. But it wasn't always that way.

In fact, Tennessee's most famous coach, General Robert Neyland, one of the winningest coaches in college football history, was hired in 1926 with only one goal in mind—Beat Vanderbilt!

Vandy and UT first locked horns in 1892, playing twice, Vandy winning both games, the latter one in a snowstorm. Vanderbilt played the first college football game in Tennessee in 1890, beating the University of Nashville. Four years later, it was one of the seven founders of the Southern Intercollegiate Athletic Association. In the first three years of the 20th Century, Vandy went 20-3-2.

In 1904, Vanderbilt hired Dan McGugin from Michigan, where he had played guard for two years and served a year as assistant coach. His first Vanderbilt team won all nine games by outscoring their opponents 474 to 4. He was the only coach in history to win his first three games by 60 points in each. McGugin would coach the Commodores through 1934 (with 1918 off to serve in World War One) and compiled a record of 197-55-19 (.762). He had one losing season, in 1914. Over his Vanderbilt coaching career, his team outscored their opponents 4-to-1. They scored one hundred or more points in three games.

Quarterback Irby "Rabbit" Curry, also known as the "Bachelor of Ugliness," guided the team in 1914 to 1916 but was shot down over France as an Allied fighter pilot. McGugin kept a portrait of his beloved player on his law office wall for the rest of his life.

In a famous game in 1922 in Nashville against his Michigan alma mater, McGugin told his players before the game that they were going to play against Yankees whose grandfathers had fought and killed their grandfathers in the Civil War. They didn't know that McGugin's father had been an officer in the Union Army. The game ended in a scoreless tie. This game was in dedication to Vandy's newly built football stadium—the first football-only stadium built in the South.

Vandy won ten conference championships 1904-1923, including two undefeated seasons. They played Michigan, Ohio State, Navy, Harvard, and Yale. They played Texas at the Texas State Fair in Dallas seven times in the Roaring Twenties and won five of them. In 21 games with the Tennessee Volunteers, Vanderbilt under McGugin won 18 and tied once.

One of their players was Grantland Rice, who went on to become one of America's greatest sportswriters ("It's not whether you won or lost, but how you played the game"). Another was quarterback Ray Morrison, who is credited with inventing the "Statue of Liberty" play in 1910, and as a coach at SMU popularized the passing play. Three other Hall of Famers became celebrated coaches—Wallace Wade at Alabama and Duke; Jess Neely at Clemson and Rice; and Red Sanders at Vanderbilt and UCLA.

One of the most successful collegiate teams in Tennessee are the **TIGERS OF TENNESSEE STATE UNIVERSITY**, a historically black college in Nashville. A powerhouse from its beginnings in 1912, the team won national championships in 1946, 1947, and 1954 under Coach Henry Arthur Kean (TSU record of 93-16-3). TSU was coached by Hall of Famer John Merritt from 1963 to 1983. He compiled a record of 174-35-7 (.806), twenty straight winning seasons, five undefeated seasons, and eight black college football titles. The Big Blue won the Ohio Valley Conference Championships in 1998 and 1999 under Coach L.C. Cole. Among the many fine football players produced by TSU were Ed "Too Tall" Jones, picked No. 1 in the 1974 NFL draft by the Dallas Cowboys; quarterback Joe Gilliam Jr., who was the first starting black quarterback in the NFL for the Pittsburgh Steelers; and Dominique-Rodgers Cromartie, who helped lead the Arizona Cardinals to their first Super Bowl appearance. The TSU marching band, "The Aristocrat of Bands," has played at many bowl games, NFL games, and marched in President John F. Kennedy's inaugural parade.

Scarritt-Bennett Center

Scarritt-Bennett Center at 1008 Nineteenth Avenue South is a conference, retreat, and educational center. Belle H. Bennett had initially urged the building of a missionary training school in 1887. The Scarritt College for Christian Workers moved to Nashville in 1923 as a United Methodist training school for missionaries. Architect Henry C. Hibbs built the structures with Tennessee Crab Orchard stone and Indiana limestone in the Gothic Collegiate style. Wrightman Hall with its 115-foot-tall Gothic tower was the tallest building in Nashville at the time. In 1929 the campus design received a gold medal from the American Institute of Architects. In the 1980s the name and mission of the facility changed.

Cathedral of the Incarnation

The Cathedral of the Incarnation at 2015 West End Avenue was built in 1907-14 under the supervision of Bishop Thomas Sebastian Byrne, bishop of Nashville from 1894 to 1923. The designers were Asmus and Norton. The Catholic mother church of the Nashville Diocese is modeled after San Martino of the Hill in Rome. The yellow-brick Renaissance-style church features a red terra cotta tile roof supported by 32 columns and pilasters, beamed gold-leaf ceiling, and water fonts that are miniatures of those by Michaelangelo in St. Peter's in Rome. Rising 100 feet above the Cathedral is the campanile, or tower, which is a replica of the tower at the famous Roman church, St. Damase. The bell rings each day at 6 a.m., noon, and 6 p.m. The main ceiling is a central feature of the cathedral's interior. It is believed to be the first of its kind in the United States, made of an ornamental plaster called Rigalico. The rectory, a representation of the Farnese Palace in Rome, and the three-story school, St. Albert Hall, were completed on the site in 1908. Major renovations took place in 1937, 1987, and 2007.

Centennial Park: *Nashville's Premier Urban Park*

Centennial Park on West End Avenue is Nashville's outstanding urban park and the site of The Parthenon, symbol of Nashville's reputation as "The Athens of the South." The 132-acre park was formerly known as West Side Park and used for horseracing before being chosen as the site of the 1897 Tennessee Centennial Exposition. After the exposition, Centennial Park formed the foundation of the city's new park system. Surviving the exposition was the Parthenon (the current permanent structure was built in the 1930s), Lake Watauga, and the sunken gardens. Today the park boasts an art gallery, bandshell, various historical monuments and statues, a jet fighter airplane, a steam locomotive, and much more.

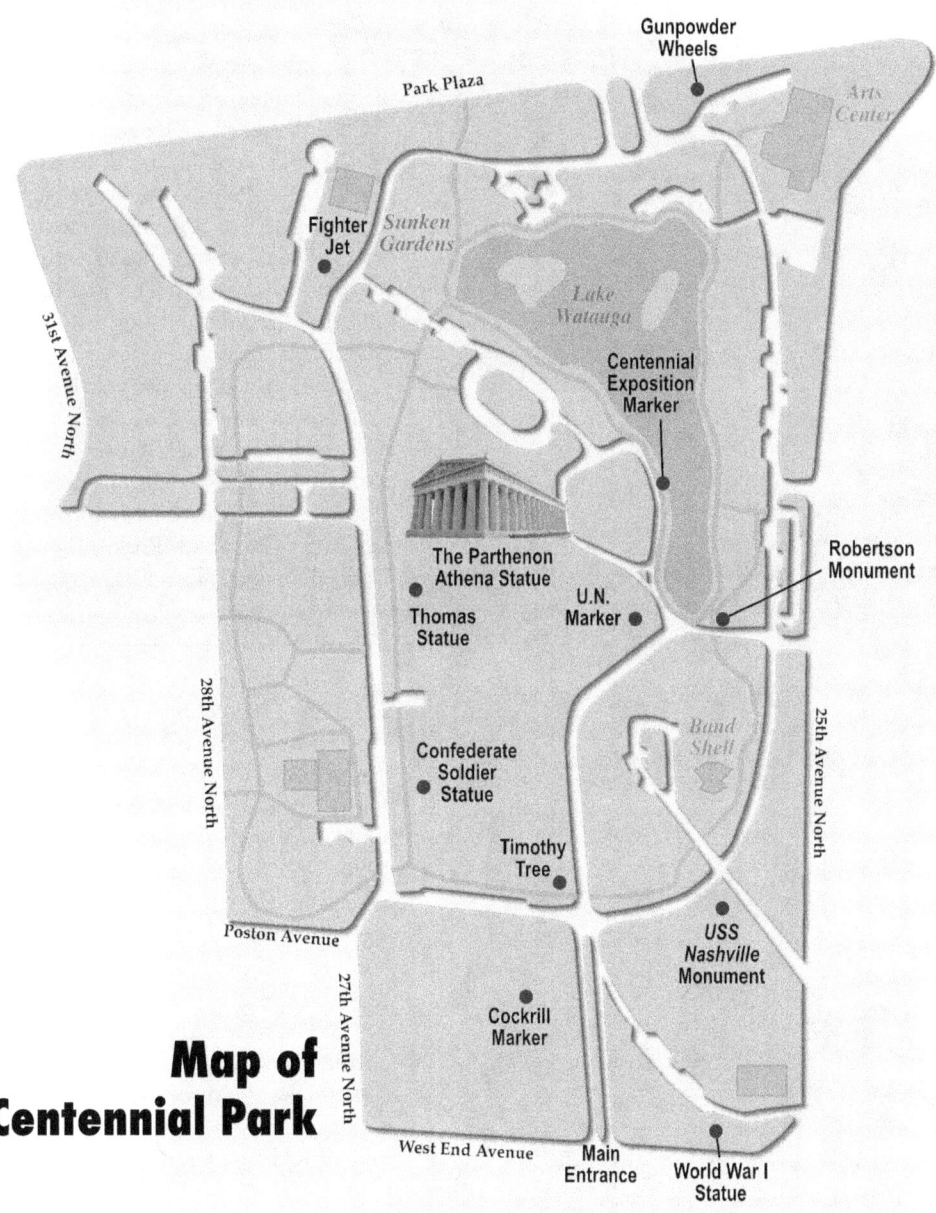

Map of Centennial Park

James Robertson Monument and James Robertson House

The monument to General James Robertson, the "Father of Middle Tennessee," sits in view of the Parthenon at the southern end of Lake Watauga in Centennial Park. Dedicated on Oct. 11, 1903, this 50-foot-tall granite shaft was quarried at Stone Mountain, Ga. and shipped to Nashville for display in the Mineral and Forestry Building at the 1897 Tennessee Centennial Exposition. During transport, part of the shaft broke off. After the exposition closed down, the permanent monument, which weighs more than 52 tons, was suggested by Major Eugene Lewis, newspaper owner, civil engineer, and director general of the exposition.

In 1972, descendants of the Robertsons gathered at the monument for "James Robertson Day." Among those attending was Dickson Wharton Robertson, who as a three-year-old toddler had pulled the string in 1903 to unveil the monument dedicated to his great-great-grandfather.

Robertson and his party arrived overland at the Nashville site in 1779 as the first permanent white settlers. In his book *Winning of the West*, Teddy Roosevelt called Robertson's trek "being equal in importance to the settlement of Jamestown or the landing at Plymouth Rock." The monument is inscribed on four sides with biographical information about Robertson and his wife Charlotte.

A replica of General James Robertson's House, a 1779-1784 double-log dogtrot design, was constructed by the West Nashville Founders Museum, Inc. in H.G. Hill Park, 6730 Charlotte Pike, in West Nashville near the West Sector Police Station. The replica was built during the state's bicentennial in 1996. Robertson's first residence was a one-room cabin constructed of hand-hewn poplar and cedar logs in early 1779 during his three-month exploration of the Cumberland country. It was located on Richland Creek, at present-day 23rd and Park streets, west of James Avenue and north of Robertson Road. That locale is about 1.2 miles northeast of H.G. Hill Park, where the reconstructed Robertson House is located. When the Robertsons permanently moved to their Richland Creek land in October 1784, they resided in the log cabin while their new home—the first brick house in Middle Tennessee—was under construction (at present-day 5904 Robertson Road) inside Robertson's Station. After the Robertsons moved into their brick home in 1787, Scottish schoolmaster David Hood lived in the expanded log structure. The brick mansion was renamed Richland in 1816 (it burned in 1902).

See Map on Page 74

The Parthenon: *"Athens of the South"*

The centerpiece of Nashville's Centennial Park is the exact replica of the Parthenon of ancient Athens, Greece, built in 1896-97 for the Tennessee Centennial Exposition. The Parthenon is owned by the city and serves as the city's art gallery, home to the James Cowan Collection of paintings. Admission is charged. The museum is a self-guided tour with brochures available. There is a museum gift shop.

The 1897 exposition celebrated the 100th anniversary of statehood (held a year late due to funding problems) and Nashville's reputation as the "Athens of the South." The site selected for the Exposition was the West Side Race Track and Park, located on the old fairgrounds surrounding the historic Cockrill Springs area at the end of Church Street and the terminus of the West End Avenue streetcar line.

The two men most responsible for supervising the extravaganza were Major Eugene C. Lewis, owner of the *Nashville American* newspaper and a consulting civil engineer, and John W. Thomas, president of the Nashville, Chattanooga & St. Louis Railroad. The railroad interests were a major financial supporter of the exposition.

The Centennial Exposition was held May 1 through October 30, 1897, featured 12 large buildings of exhibits, drew 1.8 million attendees, and met all expenses. After the Exposition closed, all buildings except the Parthenon were torn down and removed. The site was developed into a city park, the beginnings of Nashville's public park system. In 1921-31 the crumbling Parthenon was reconstructed of more durable materials—brick, stone, reinforced concrete, and cast concrete aggregate.

The design of the Parthenon is intricate. All horizontal architectural elements arch slightly in the center. This means there are no true straight horizontal lines in the Parthenon. These architectural refinements make the Parthenon look alive and flawless to the human eye.

The peristyle consists of 46 Doric columns, 17 on each side, 6 on each end (not counting the corner columns twice). All of the exterior columns incline slightly inward. The corner columns are diagonally inclined; that is, they are angled toward both sides. The columns of the building differ in diameter from the ones beside them and are all spaced slightly differently. All of the columns share a refinement called entasis, a slight bulge or convex curvature of the shaft. Thus, although the shaft tapers, the largest diameter is about one-third of the way up rather than at the base.

The four bronze doors weigh 7.5 tons each, making them the largest set of matching bronze doors in the world. They are 24 feet tall, seven feet wide, and one foot thick.

The Parthenon was the site of the Harvey's (Department Store) Nativity Scene in front of the structure every Christmas from 1954-1967. The scene was 280 feet long, 75 feet deep, and flooded with colorful lights.

Athena Parthenos

The statue of Athena Parthenos inside Nashville's Parthenon is the largest indoor sculpture in the Western World, standing at 42 feet tall. Crafted by Nashville sculptor Alan LeQuire over an eight-year period, the 12-ton statue was dedicated in 1990. Twelve years later the plain white statue was painted and gilded with gold. The plumes in Athena's helmet are supported by a sphinx in the center and a pegasus on either side. Athena holds in her hand a six-foot-tall statue of Nike, the goddess of victory. In the center of Athena's breastplate is the head of Medusa, the gorgon who has snakes for hair. The large snake between Athena and her shield is probably Ericthonios, a legendary king of Athens. The shield is carved with scenes of the battle between the Greeks and the Amazons. The original Athena Parthenos was sculpted by Phidias and consisted of ivory and gold on a wooden frame. The statue epitomized the golden age of Athens under the rule of Pericles. The statue was lost in the 5th Century, 900 years after its creation.

Gold Star Statue
"I gave my best to make a better world."
1917-1918

This emotive monument to the soldiers of World War One was erected in 1923 by the Nashville Kiwanis Club. The sculptor is George J. Zolnay. More than 3,836 Tennesseans gave their lives overseas during the war. A Veteran's Day service is held at the statue every November 11 at 11:00 a.m., usually attended by 50 to 75 club members. The armistice to end the Great War was signed in 1918 at the eleventh hour of the eleventh day of the eleventh month. The sculpture is located in the southeast corner of the park.

> **A bronze plaque at the base of a tree in Centennial Park reads:**
> This tree was planted May 24, 1919 by the Catholic Children of Nashville in grateful memory of Lieutenant James Simmons Timothy of the 80th Company, 6th Regiment, U.S.M.C. who was killed in action at Belleau Wood, France, June 14, 1918, aged 25 years.
> He was first wounded while serving with the French in the Verdun sector, Mar. 22, 1918. On the day of his death he took his company of two hundred men "over the top" and returned with only five. Later in the day he was killed by an enemy shell. Lieutenant Timothy was the first Tennessee officer to make the supreme sacrifice in the Great War for justice and humanity. His last words were,
> "Into Thy hand, O Lord, I commend my soul."
> Strong in faith, no fear he knew,
> This gallant knight of God so true:
> Pure, courageous, grand was he
> Our hero son of Tennessee.

USS Nashville Monument

The first *USS Nashville* was a gunboat built in Norfolk, Va. in 1897. She participated in the blockade of Cuban ports during the Spanish-American War and fired the first shot of the war, capturing a Spanish steamer. The deck gun is on display at the State Museum-Military Branch. She also served as a flagship in Manilla Bay during the subsequent Philippine Insurrection. She visited several Chinese ports during the Boxer Rebellion. During World War One the ship protected convoys in the Caribbean and patrolled for submarines near Gibralter. She was decommissioned in 1918.

The second *USS Nashville* was a light cruiser of the Brooklyn class commissioned in 1938. She carried $25 million in gold bullion from England to New York. During World War Two she accompanied the *USS Hornet* aircraft carrier during the Doolittle retaliatory raid on Tokyo. In 1944 she led the attack on the Philippine Islands with General Douglas MacArthur aboard. She then joined the Battle of Leyte Gulf.

In December 1944 a Kamikaze aircraft with two bombs struck the ship near the bridge and created massive fires and explosions. Courageous sailors brought the massive fires under control in 20 minutes. The attack killed 133 sailors and wounded 190. The *USS Nashville* then made two trans-Atlantic cruises, bringing 1,300 soldiers home from Europe. She was decommissioned in 1946.

The latest *USS Nashville* (LPD-13), an Amphibious Transport Dock ship, was built in Seattle, Wash. and commissioned in 1970. She has served in the Caribbean, Persian Gulf, and North Atlantic. Her mission was to transport a landing force ashore. She could support up to 515 Navy crewmembers and 964 Marines. Her insignia is a blue field of 13 stars (for the 13 Colonies and the fact that she is the 13th ship in her class) surrounded by the Seal of the Metro Government of Nashville. Also inscribed on the ship's banner are the words of the city's namesake Gen. Francis Nash, "From the first dawn of the Revolution I have ever been on the side of liberty and my country." The *USS Nashville* (LPD-13) was decommissioned in Sept. 2009.

Gunpowder grinding wheels from Sycamore Mills in Cheatham County. The wheels were made in England and originally used at the Confederate gunpowder works in Augusta, Ga. They were shown at the 1897 Tennessee Centennial Exposition.

Celebrating 100 Years of Statehood

The 1897 TENNESSEE CENTENNIAL EXPOSITION

In 1897, a year late, Tennessee threw itself a birthday celebration, marking 100 years as the country's 16th state, honoring the traditions of the past while showcasing some of its more "progressive" trends toward the future. Along the way, the Victorians of the Gilded Age couldn't help themselves in having a whole bunch of fun. The summertime event was the Tennessee Centennial Exposition.

The exposition followed in the footsteps of the highly successful 1893 Columbian Exposition in Chicago and the 1895 Cotton States Exposition in Atlanta. A financial recession had hit the country in 1893; politicians were fighting over gold versus silver and tariffs; war loomed with Spain over Cuba and The Philippines; women's groups were demanding the vote; and various temperance organizations were calling for liquor prohibition. Northern interests were heavily invested in developing (exploiting) the mineral, timber, and other natural resources in the state, in addition to the hiring of cheap labor.

Thus the exposition was devised not only to mark the state's 100th anniversary but to boost and promote the state's economy. It was also a public relations effort by the monopolistic railroad companies to gain more favor with the public. The railroads were a major supporter of the exposition. President John W. Thomas and Director General Eugene C. Lewis were railroad men serving as officers of the executive committee. Major Wilbur Fisk Foster was the Director of Works and R.T. Creighton was the Engineer in Chief.

Due to some political bickering but mostly financial concerns, the event was held one year late, in the summer of 1897 instead of 1896. The exposition attracted 1,786,714 attendees and met all expenses (admission was 50 cents for adults, 25 cents for children; half fare after 7 p.m.), impressive considering the fact that a yellow-fever epidemic was raging in certain parts of the country.

Chosen as the site for the exposition was the 200-acre West Side Park, about two miles from downtown and accessible by electric streetcar. The park was a former fairgrounds and harness racing course, and before that a mustering grounds for troops in the War of 1812, the Mexican War, and the Civil War. The park's clubhouse was converted into a restaurant for the event. The site was incorporated as Centennial City, with its own mayor (Norman Farrel) and aldermen, police force, hospital (plus a separate facility for the colored), power plant, telephone service, and post office. Beer and wine sales were allowed but no hard liquor (although one agricultural exhibit was a working moonshine still).

Formal ceremonies were held on June 1-3, 1896. A parade eight miles long with 10,000 participants drew a crowd of 125,000 spectators. The exposition grounds and buildings were nowhere near completion. The construction of Centennial City took 16 months and included 35 major structures, four lakes, several restaurants, a 55-acre military camp, train and street car terminals, and a power plant that consumed 30 tons of coal per day and generated electricity for 18,000 lamps, 458 arc lights, limited air-conditioning, hundreds of fans, and all the other machinery. The buildings were all constructed of wood and plaster and were designed to be demolished following the conclusion of the event. Amusements and rides known as the Vanity Fair were erected in the northwest corner of the park.

"The President will now press the button that will start the machinery." With that announcement on May 1st, 1897, President William McKinley pushed a button in the White House that sent a telegraphic signal to the grounds in Nashville, where a cannon boomed, the main gates were opened to anxious crowds, and the giant iron wheels in the Machinery Building began turning (powered by six Morrin Climax Vertical Boilers).

Six weeks later, the President himself, a native of Ohio, and the First Lady, along with an entourage of politicians and press, would visit the exposition on Ohio-Cincinnati Day (there were many theme days at the fair). The First Couple were greeted by 50,000 well-wishers and attended several receptions, both together and separately. During one of the receptions, spectators gasped when Mrs. McKinley was over-

The 1897 TENNESSEE CENTENNIAL EXPOSITION

Statue of John Thomas

The prominent statue near The Parthenon on an elaborate stone platform is that of John W. Thomas (1830-1906), president of the Nashville, Chattanooga & St. Louis Railroad and Chairman of the Committee overseeing the 1897 Tennessee Centennial Exposition. The statue was erected in his memory in 1907 by railway employees. He is described as "an efficient man of affairs, upright and eminent citizen, Christian and a gentleman."

John W. Thomas Day drew nearly 100,000 people to the grounds.

come by the stifling summer heat and fainted. The President calmly placed a handkerchief over her face and continued his speech, much to the bewilderment of the crowd.

Unknown to most, Mrs. McKinley was an epileptic, whose seizures produced facial contortions. The President was a faithful caregiver to his wife. According to his biographer, "He was tireless in ministering to her mental and physical comfort. His attitude toward her repellent symptoms of facial convulsions was so casual as to appear indifferent. He always sat beside her in the dining room or parlor. At the first sign of rigidity, he was alert. He threw his handkerchief or napkin over her convulsed face, removing it when she relaxed."

Before leaving Nashville on June 12th, President McKinley held a reception in the U.S. Government Building, shaking the hands of hundreds of well-wishers (McKinley was a practiced expert in handshaking). Four years later, in September 1901, McKinley was shot and killed under similar circumstances—at a reception at the Pan-American Exposition in Buffalo, N.Y.

Not all of the exposition proceedings were sober and serious. One of the main attractions was a highwire artist known as Professor Arion, who at night rode a bicycle over a live 500-volt trolley wire strung 75 feet above the ground (without a safety net). Minus rubber tires, the bicycle produced showers of sparks, in addition to the 50 lights bulbs strung on the bike. He also wore an illuminated costume. The highwire act competed with the thousands of electric lights (a new novelty) strung over the grounds, outlining the contours of the buildings, and reflecting in the lakes and pools. Tragically, Professor Arion would lose his life later that year during a similar performance on Long Island, N.Y. in front of thousands of people.

A feat of scientific "magic" was performed regularly at the Hygiene and Education Building, where scientists from the University of Tennessee demonstrated the mysterious properties of X-rays. Tennessee Governor Robert Love Taylor marvelled at an X-ray of his hand; photographs of hand, foot, and arm X-rays were routinely printed on the front page of *The Nashville Sun.*

The 1897 TENNESSEE CENTENNIAL EXPOSITION

Crowds at the exposition were generally well-behaved, but there were exceptions. On May 24th (Kentucky Day) about 100 drunken members of the Kentucky Legion tried to take over the Vanity Fair. The minor riot was quelled by Colonel Eastman G. Curry and his Centennial Guards. In another incident, five young ladies in the Vanity Fair Beauty Show were arrested for violating an ordinance "prohibiting the appearance in public places of women in indecent dress."

Major demonstrations of mock violence were performed. Five sham battles were conducted during the exposition, including the recreation of battle by Confederate veterans and the re-enactment on August 12 of Custer's Last Stand, in which cavalrymen were routed by members of the Improved Order of Red Men (white guys dressed as Indians).

Huge fireworks displays were produced on Tuesday, Thursday, and Saturday evenings during the fair, best seen from the Giant See-Saw, a gigantic girder contraption that featured passenger cars holding 20 spectators (25 cents per ride) balanced at each end of a long beam 200 feet up in the air. It was Tennessee's version of Chicago's Ferris Wheel. One night the see-saw malfunctioned and left riders stranded in the air for several hours. Thrill-seekers could also catch a lofty ride in Barnard's Airship, a sausage-shaped airbag tethered to the ground.

The most talked-about stomach-turner was The Chute, a tall, wooden incline over which small boats would careen down and then slam their occupants into a shallow pool, causing screams and great eruptions of water. After the fair closed and the pool was drained, workers found dozens of sets of dentures.

Fairgoers also got whoozie inside W. Spain's Palace of Illusions and Mirror Maze. They marveled at the Gettysburg Cyclorama, a circular stone building that featured a huge interior painting "in the round" of Pickett's Charge during the third day of the battle at Gettysburg, Pa. The colossal spectacle had taken 13 artists 16 months to create, using seven tons of paint.

Also spell-binding was Edison's Mirage and the Electric Scenic Theater, consisting of a vitascope, kinetoscope, verascope, and other "moving image" projectors. The audience sat on a revolving disk and saw a different picture every two minutes "reproducing with all the life and action of reality the Grand Opera, the Boulevard des Italians of Paris, the Coronation of the Czar, a watermelon feast, the Corbett-Fitzsimmons fight, and hundreds of others..."

The Vanity Fair was also the place to go international. The Streets of Cairo and the Egyptian Theater featured belly dancers, coochee-coochee girls, swordsmen, acrobats, tumblers, and camel rides. The Cuban Village also featured dancing girls, along with food and shopping, hand-rolled cigars, and rides on ponies, donkies, and two elephants. The Chinese Village had 200 native Chinese workers, an opium den, and the Parade of the Chinese Dragon. The Moorish Palace featured

> *The Cafe of Night and Morning was shaped like a burial vault where scenes from Dante's inferno came to life, including skeletons with blazing red eyeballs.*

domes, arches, and minarets.

The macabre and bizarre could also be experienced at the Vanity Fair. The wax and art museum displayed beautiful, weird, and gruesome objects. The Chamber of Horrors included the Devil's Cave and a View of Hell with Cannibals Roasting a Prisoner and Dinah Brown, the notorious baby farmer of New Orleans. The Cafe of Night and Morning was shaped like a burial vault where scenes from Dante's inferno came to life, including skeletons with blazing red eyeballs. The Satin Theater featured death scenes and a descent into hell. Then the doomed were led down a corridor into white light, satin drapes, and angelic singing—Heaven.

Rounding out the Vanity Fair attractions were the Phantom Swing, the Sideshow, the Gladdish Wheel, the Ocean Wave, the Nebraska Sod House, the Old Plantation, the Colorado Gold Mine, Gorman and Boone's Trained Animal Arena and Ostrich Farm, and the birthplace cabins of Abraham Lincoln and Jefferson Davis.

The Parthenon served as the Nashville-Davidson County Building and was crammed with sculptures and paintings, twelve hundred in total, selected by Theodore Cooley of the Fine Arts Department. The Parthenon had a stone foundation, brick interior walls, and wooden exterior. The pediments were plaster, and the roof was metal with a skylight. The architect was Col. William C. Smith, organizer of the Tennessee National Guard, who died in The Philippines in 1898 leading the 1st Tennessee Regiment against the Spanish. At the east end of the building stood the 40-foot-high plaster statue of the Greek goddess Pallas Athena sculpted by Enis Yandell in Paris and shipped by rail and steamship to Nashville. At the west end was the bronze statue of Commodore Cornelius Vanderbilt by Giuseppe Moretti. Vanderbilt's $1 million donation had founded Vanderbilt University in 1873.

Between The Parthenon and the lake was the Memphis-Shelby County Building shaped like a pyramid, covered with hieroglyphics, and lit by chains of lights at night.

The U.S. Government Building covered 52,500 square feet and housed ten exhibits. It opened almost three weeks late to a 45-gun salute, one for each of the states in the union at the time. The Treasury section featured a second-order operating bivalve lighthouse lens lit by electricity. The Bureau of American Ethnology featured a model of an Indian camping circle built by Kiowa Indians. The Commission of Fish and Fisheries had an aquarium consisting of 22 tanks of fresh and saltwater specimens in a grotto-like passageway. The Navy fea-

The 1897 TENNESSEE CENTENNIAL EXPOSITION

tured a gun made in 1490 and brought to the New World by Cortez, a Gatling gun, a mortar captured at Yorktown in 1781, and a seven-ton anchor.

The Agricultural Building featured seven domes and was fronted by growing cotton and tobacco patches, complete with a small tobacco barn. A tropical exhibit near the Terminal Building featured flower beds, palm, banana, orange, and Indian rubber trees, pineapples, sugar cane, cotton, and Cuban tobacco.

The Minerals and Forestry Building showcased the World's Largest Poplar Tree, weighing 70,000 pounds and more than 600 years old.

Some of the newest practical devices in the Machinery Building were the round-bale cotton press and the automatic gear-cutting machine.

Lake Watauga offered gondola rides passing under the Rialto, an arched bridge with buildings fashioned after the famous structure in Venice. The steamboat *Huck Finn* also plied the waters, built and operated by an enterprising 13-year-old, James Hyde, from Ashland City.

Musical entertainment, concessions, and adult beverages could be enjoyed throughout the grounds. The William Gerst Brewing Co. of Nashville served beer and meals at the Old Viena Pilsener Beer House, the Cafe Militaire and the Gerst Alhambra. Gerst won the exposition's gold medal for the best tasting beer. Their main exhibit featured a 2,500-gallon vat of beer. Diehl and Lord of Cincinnati operated the Lion's Roof Garden restaurant and beer hall.

Concerts were performed in the 6,000-seat Auditorium by Gustan Fischer's Band, the Innes Band, and Victor Herbert's 24th New York Regimental Band. Bells in the massive bellfry rang on special occasions (they are now housed at the Tulip Street Methodist Church in Edgefield).

The 22-foot-tall statue of the Greek god Mercury stood atop the entrance to the Commerce Building. After the expo, the statue stood atop the new Union Station train depot until it was toppled in a thunderstorm. Melted down, the bronze in the statue was used to cast the plaques for the Tennessee Agricultural Hall of Fame at the Ellington Agricultural Center.

The Woman's Building, based on President Andrew Jackson's home The Hermitage, was designed by Sarah Ward-Conley. It featured an open-air restaurant on top of the building. A stained-glass window represented the "Apotheosis of Woman." Although the building and exhibits celebrated the woman's traditional roles as wife, mother, and homekeeper, the Progressive New Woman was also promoted. Among the most heated issues of the time was temperance and women's suffrage. Within ten years, the Tennessee legislature would vote to prohibit alcohol manufacture and consumption in the state (well before National Prohibition) and ten years after that a vote of the Tennessee legislature would successfully complete the requirements for the ratification of the 19th Amendment giving women the right to vote.

The Children's Building, which featured playgrounds and a petting zoo, also showcased a new form of education—a model kindergarten, which held daily classes throughout the exposition. Children from across the state were selected to participate.

The Negro Building was designed in the Spanish Renaissance style and housed 300 exhibitors from 85 cities. Fisk University and Tuskegee University were major participants; the Fisk Jubilee Singers performed several times. Booker T. Washington spoke on Emancipation Day, Sept. 22nd. Negro Day was June 5th.

The Texas Building was a modest recreation of the Alamo, with June 24th designated Texas Day. Descendants of David Crockett, the Tennessean who died defending the Alamo in old San Antonio, gathered there on October 1st.

The Tennessee Centennial Exposition designated many theme days for specific audiences; many diverse organizations took the occasion of the fair to gather and enjoy the fellowship.

October 28th drew the largest single-day crowd to the exposition—98,579 people, a total nearly the size of the entire population of Nashville. This day honored John W. Thomas, president of the expo, and was also Presbyterian Day and Atlanta Day. General William Hicks Jackson was Grand Marshal of the parade, which took three hours to pass. Twenty-eight divisions marched in the parade, including Forrest's Cavalry, Terry's Texas Rangers, and Archer's Brigade, all reviewed by General John B. Gordon of Georgia and other dignitaries. Sham battles, always a popular draw, were also conducted that day.

On three days, June 22-24, the United Confederate Veterans' Days were held, with more than 74,000 attending. Fifty to sixty trainloads of attendees arrived each day in Nashville. Many, of course, were Confederate Army veterans. Their convention was actually held at another new attraction in town—the giant brick Union Gospel Tabernacle downtown. The Confederate veterans participated in sham Civil War battles along with their former enemies, fellow veterans from the Grand Army of the Republic. Rows of tents housed many of the veterans in military camps on the east side of the grounds.

Other organizations, both well-known and obscure, held reunions and conventions during the exposition, including the Supreme Senate Knights of the Ancient Essenic Order, Cotton-Seed Crushers of the South, the Concatenated Order of Hoo-Hoo, Brothers of Friendship and the Sisters of the Mysterious Ten, Improved Order of Red Men, Woodmen of the World, Knights of Pythias, Order of Odd Fellows, Knights Templar Grand Commandery, Grand Lodge African Free (A.F.), and the National Association of Colored Women.

Belle Meade Plantation

Belle Meade Plantation is a 30-acre historic site located six miles southwest of downtown Nashville at 5025 Harding Road. The centerpiece of the property is the Belle Meade mansion built in 1853. The Greek Revival house was home to five generations of the Harding-Jackson family, original owners of the Belle Meade Farm.

In the late 19th Century, the farm encompassed 5,400 acres and was one of the largest private estates in Nashville. The farm was a thoroughbred nursery famous for breeding and training championship race horses. Kentucky Derby winners Funny Cide and Barbaro, and even racing legends Secretariat and Seabiscuit, can trace their bloodlines back to the breeding stock at Belle Meade.

John Harding first purchased the tract in 1807. By 1820, a new Federal-style brick house was built for John's growing family. He named his farm Belle Meade, meaning "beautiful meadow." In the late 1830s John's son, General William Giles Harding, assumed control. At the start of the Civil War the estate encompassed 3,500 acres and was worked by 136 slaves. A secessionist, General Harding was sent north to Mackinac Island prison after Union troops occupied Nashville in February 1862.

The 20th Century brought financial difficulty to the family, and the farm was sold. Most of the farm's acreage was developed into Belle Meade Park. The house was occupied until 1953 when it was sold to the State of Tennessee. The state deeded the 30-acre property to the Association for the Preservation of Tennessee Antiquities. The group opened the site as a museum in 1953. The modern visitors center features a gift shop and bookstore. Special events are scheduled throughout the year.

See Map on Page 74

Cheekwood Gardens and Art Museum

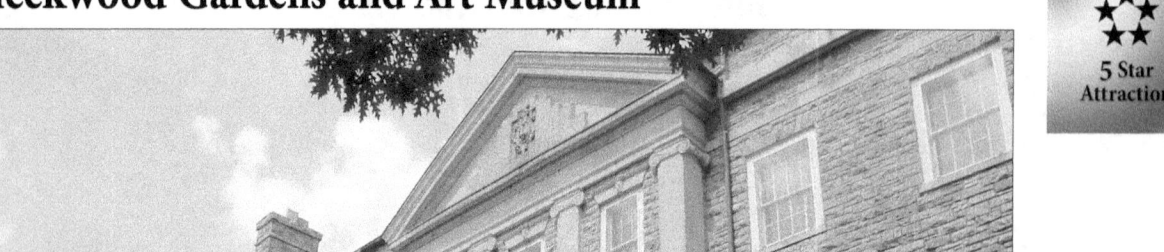

Cheekwood Botanical Gardens and Art Museum is located 8.5 miles southwest of downtown at 1200 Forrest Park Drive near Percy Warner Park. The magnificent 30,000-sq.-ft. Georgian mansion, built in 1933 by famed New York architect Bryant Fleming for coffee tychoons Leslie and Mabel (Wood) Cheek, houses the Ewers-Tyne Collection of Worcester Porcelain, more than 600 pieces of English and American silver, the Cheek dining room with original furnishings, the Permanent Collection of American Art, and special temporary exhibitions, such as the works of Nashville primitive sculptor William Edmondson and the Matilda Geddings Gray collection of Fabergé.

The 100-acre estate features formal gardens, including a water garden and Japanese garden, and a mile-long sculpture trail of 15 artworks. The site also includes the Frist Learning Center, the Botanic Hall, and the Pineapple Room Restaurant and Gift Shop. Cheekwood sponsors a variety of special events throughout the year and offers catering and special-event rentals.

Cheekwood was built for Leslie Cheek, whose father Christopher had moved to Nashville in the 1880s and started a wholesale grocery business. Leslie's relative Joel Cheek developed a coffee blend that was served at Nashville's Maxwell House Hotel. Reportedly President Teddy Roosevelt tasted the Maxwell House coffee during his 1907 visit and proclaimed it "good to the last drop." In 1928 the Cheeks sold their business for more than $40 million. Leslie Cheek used his investment windfall to build the magnificent estate that he called Cheekwood, which opened to the public as an art museum in 1960.

The website is cheekwood.org.

Newsom's Mill

Newsom's Mill (1862) in the Harpeth River State Park in the southwestern corner of Davidson County is built of hand-dressed limestone blocks and serves as a fine example of the art of the mid-19th Century stonecutter. The stone in the mill was taken from a quarry one mile to the south. Stone from Newsom quarries was used in the building of the State Capitol, U.S. Customs House, Hume-Fogg High School, Union Station, and the stone wall around the City Cemetery.

The Newsoms came to Nashville from Virginia in 1800. The first wooden mill built on this spot by William B. Newsom was destroyed by

flooding in 1808. The existing mill was built by son Joseph M. Newsom. For a century the grist mill was the focal point of the community, which was a rail stop on the Nashville and Northwestern Railroad.

In 1905 James B. Ezell bought the mill and replaced the shot water wheel with a more efficient side shot wheel. He also added a generator, which provided electricity for the quarry, rock crusher, and his residence, Harpeth Heights. The home, also built of limestone and located 300 yards to the southwest, was destroyed to make way for Interstate 40. In 1974 the mill was purchased by the state and developed into a park. The day-use park is open 7 to 7 (closes at 5 p.m. Nov. to March). There are no on-site facilities.

Germantown Historic District

The Germantown Historic District contains a wide variety of residential and commercial architecture built between 1820 and 1920. The district is bounded by Jefferson Street, Taylor Street, and Eighth and Third avenues. It now offers many new and renovated housing opportunities, great views of the State Capitol and downtown Nashville, restaurants and shops, and designation as an Inner City Arboretum. Germantown began in 1848 as a platted subdivision and was incorporated into the city in 1865. Centered on the Church of the Assumption the neighborhood became the focus of German immigration in the 1870s and included many skilled craftsmen and butchers. The growing area included several slaughterhouses and packing houses, but as attitudes towards Germans changed with World War One the area slowly fell into disrepair and neglect. In the 1970s, the neighborhood, sparked by church restoration projects, began revitalization. Today the district hosts the annual OctoberFest celebration and many other community events.

The building at 1239 Sixth Avenue North was built in the 1890s and used as a store and residence by the Neuhoff family. It also served as the Fehr Grocery. Decorative brickwork delineates the first and second floors and is used again above the sheet-metal cornice.

Church of the Assumption

The Church of the Assumption at 1227 Seventh Avenue North is Nashville's second oldest Catholic church. It was dedicated in 1859. Father Vogel, together with Jacob Geiger, a master builder and stonecutter in Nashville, is said to have designed the original brick church structure. The rectory was added in 1874 and the school was added in 1879. The present altar, windows, and steeple were added later. Since the Germantown neighborhood was growing around it, most sermons were read in German until World War One. The foundation is made of rough-cut stone and concrete. The exterior walls are red brick. The roof is made of pressed copper. The windows include stained glass. The doors are made of various woods. The double doors on the front facade include ornate Gothic architectural details. This church building was added to the National Register of Historic Places in 1977.

Marathon Village

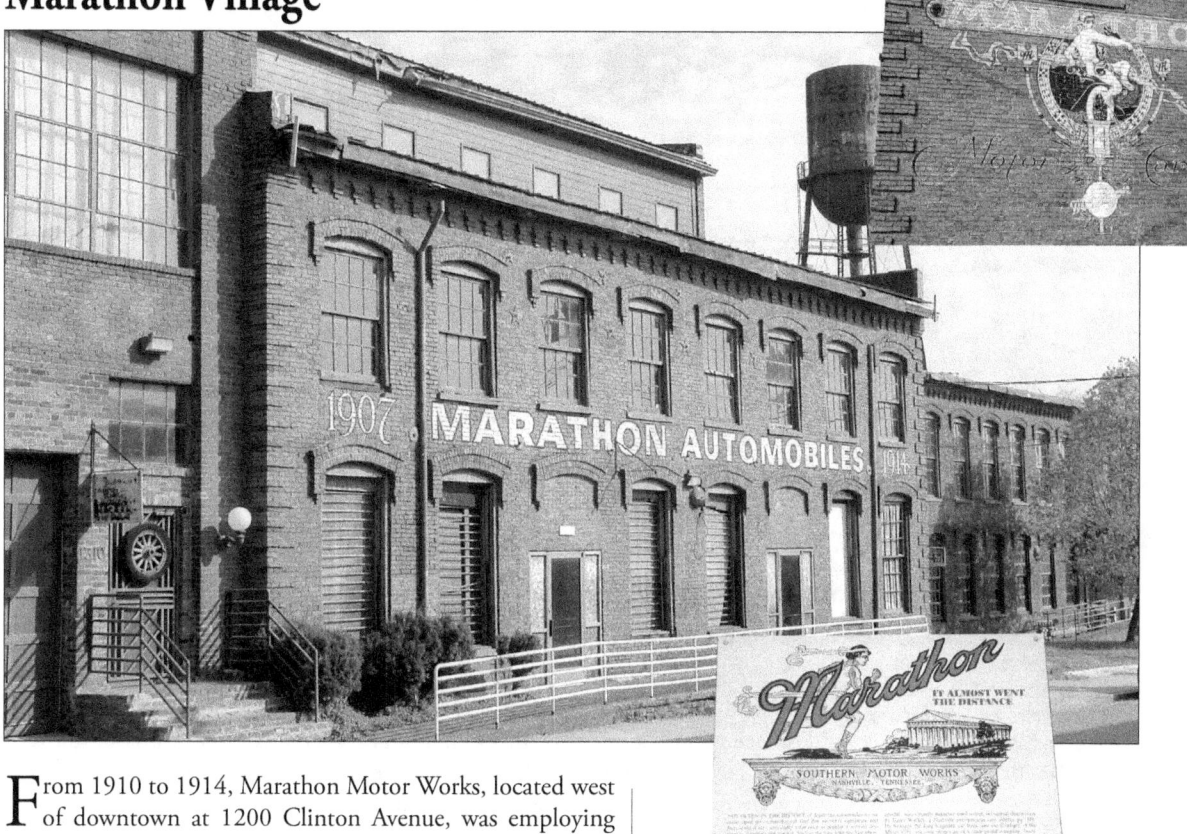

From 1910 to 1914, Marathon Motor Works, located west of downtown at 1200 Clinton Avenue, was employing up to 400 workers and producing up to 200 automobiles per month, establishing themselves as the premier auto builder in the South. There were dealerships in every major American city.

In 1910, Augustus Robinson, owner of the Maxwell House Hotel, brought the automobile division of Jackson, Tennessee's Southern Engine and Boiler Works to Nashville. Operations were set up in the old "Phoenix Cotton Mill" structure built in 1881.

Engineer William Collier designed his first car, initially called The Southern, in 1906. Two models, a rumble-seat roadster and a five-seat touring car, sold for $1,500. Within a few years the line expanded to 12 models on four chassis. The top-of-the-line Champion featured a 45-horsepower engine.

But poor management spelled the doom of Marathon Motors, which stopped building cars in 1914 and shut down completely in 1918. The building was sold in 1922 to Werthan Bag Co. and used to produce cotton bags. Collier continued to operate Southern Engine and Boiler Works until its demise in 1926.

It is believed that there are nine existing examples of Marathon Motors automobiles.

In 1986 entrepreneur Barry Walker bought the property and is developing Marathon Village into commercial space for creative professionals and meeting spaces for rent to various organizations.

In the 1980s Nissan and Saturn established large manufacturing plants in Middle Tennessee; today carmaking is the 10th largest industry in Tennessee.

One of the few remaining examples of a Marathon Motors vehicle, on display at a public event.

Fisk University and Jubilee Hall

The Fisk University Chapel (1892).

Jubilee Hall, 17th Avenue at Meharry Boulevard, built in 1873-76 and designed by architect S.D. Hatch of New York. He achieved a polychromatic effect by interspersing red brick with light stone banding. The facade of the Gothic L-shaped building is symetrical except for the off-center, spired tower.

The Carl Van Vechten Art Gallery. The neo-Romanesque structure built in 1888 as a church once served as the university gymnasium. It was converted to house the Alfred Stieglitz Collection, which includes works by Picasso, Cezanne, Renoir, Toulouse-Lautrec, O'Keeffe, Demuth, Hartley, Dove, and Walkowitz.

Six months after the end of the Civil War, three men—John Ogden, the Reverend Erastus Milo Cravath, and the Reverend Edward P. Smith—established Fisk School in Nashville, named in honor of General Clinton B. Fisk of the Tennessee Freedmen's Bureau, who provided the new institution with facilities in former Union Army barracks near the present site of Union Station. In these facilities Fisk convened its first classes for African-American students on January 9, 1866.

A nine-member choral ensemble of students was formed to tour and raise money for the new school. They left Nashville on Oct. 6, 1871. The singers toured small towns, performing Negro spirituals, not the traditional minstrel show. At one point, in a gesture of hope and encouragement, their leader called them "The Jubilee Singers," a Biblical reference to the year of Jubilee in the Book of Leviticus, Chapter 25.

After gradual acceptance, the singing group was embraced by a wide variety of audiences. In 1872 they sang at the World Peace Festival in Boston and at the end of the year President U.S. Grant invited them to perform at the White House.

In 1873 the Jubilee Singers toured Europe for the first time. Funds raised that year were used to construct the school's first permanent building, Jubilee Hall, now a National Historic Landmark. The beautiful Victorian Gothic building houses a floor-to-ceiling portrait of the original Jubilee Singers, commissioned by Queen Victoria during the 1873 tour as a gift from England to Fisk.

In 1984 Jubilee Hall underwent historic rehabilitation. Of special interest is the Appleton Room, totally refurbished and adorned with a 14th-Century-style ceiling from the Castle Polheim in Austria.

Among the distinguished alumnae of Fisk are W.E.B. Du Bois, the social critic and co-founder of the NAACP; Booker T. Washington, who served on the Board of Trustees; the Work family of composer-musicologists; historian John Hope Franklin; and poet Nikki Giovanni.

Fisk University is located at 1000 17th Avenue North. The phone is (615) 329-8500.

See Map on Page 76

Old State Penitentiary

The old Tennessee State Penitentiary is located about seven miles northwest of downtown on Centennial Boulevard in the Cockrill Bend area.

The grounds are guarded and are not open to the general public. This is not a tourism site. None of the buildings are visible from the street.

Built in 1897, the main administration building bears the appearance of a Gothic castle. At the time of its construction, this facility containing 800 inmate cells was considered one of the most modern and humane prisons in the United States. It was built almost entirely of materials indigenous to the state. The complex consists of the four-story, turreted Administration Building, the main prison building, and the walled compound. The white-brick Administration Building is connected by a passageway to the main prison building. Architectural elements include a central tower with turrets and dormers, conical roofs, arched windows, and decorative corbelling. In 1992, the prison ceased operations, and all remaining inmates were moved to one of the state's other correctional facilities. Since then, the empty building has been used at various times as a movie and television stage. Films such as *Walk the Line* starring Joaquin Phoenix, *The Green Mile* starring Tom Hanks, and *The Last Castle* starring Robert Redford were filmed here, as were music videos for acts such as Big & Rich and Lee Ann Rimes.

Five tiers of cells run the length of the cellblock where the inmates spent most of their time. At the near end of this cellblock there were 24 gunports for the correctional officers to use if necessary.

African-American Historic Sites

FIFTH AVENUE SIT-IN MOVEMENT. Nashville was not the first city to experience non-violent protests at segregated public facilities but the movement here was the most effective. On Feb. 13, 1960, 124 well-dressed Nashville students, who had staged mock sit-ins and prepared well, marched to the Woolworth's, Kress, and McClellan stores downtown, sat at the lunch counters, and asked for service. They were refused, heckled, and spat upon. Later, they added Grants and Walgreens to their list. On Feb. 27, Nashville police arrested 81 students. Black customers boycotted the stores. On April 19th the home of the students' attorney, Z. Alexander Looby, was fire-bombed. Thousands of marchers descended on City Hall, led by Diane Nash, a student leader at Fisk University. Confronted, Mayor Ben West recommended that the lunch counters be desegregated. On May 10, six stores on Fifth Avenue served black customers at their lunch counters for the first time. Days later, in Nashville, the Rev. Martin Luther King called the Nashville sit-ins "the best organized and most disciplined" in the South.

The **FIRST BAPTIST CHURCH CAPITOL HILL** (1895-1972), located at the southwest corner of Charlotte Avenue and Rosa Parks Boulevard, was the headquarters for the Nashville civil rights sit-in movement of the 1960s. The pastor, the Rev. Kelly Miller Smith Sr., was a nationally respected civil rights leader. The sit-ins served as a model for other demonstrations in the South. The present church is located just below Capitol Hill at 933 James Robertson Parkway.

CAMERON-TRIMBLE (1860s) is the oldest surviving African-American neighborhood in Nashville. The name Trimble comes from the owner of the plantation once situated here. Central Tennessee College (1866), later Walden University, located here in 1869 on the corner of First Avenue South and Chestnut Street. Other schools and churches followed. The Cameron-Trimble neighborhood is located in South Nashville bounded roughly by Fourth Avenue South, Lafayette Street, and the railroad tracks near Brown's Creek.

FORT NEGLEY* was built for Union troops in 1862 by impressed free blacks and slave laborers, many of whom died from disease or exposure under horrible working conditions. U.S. Colored Troops who served in the Union Army fought bravely during the Battle of Nashville on Dec. 15, 1864 near **Granbury's Lunette** (190 Polk Avenue near the fairgrounds) and on December 16 at **Peach Orchard Hill** (near I-65/Franklin Pike and Harding Road). Many who made the ultimate sacrifice are buried at **Nashville National Cemetery** near the bronze statue dedicated to the USCT in 2005.

Sites with * have additional information in this publication.

In 1904, the One Cent Savings Bank, now **CITIZENS BANK,** became the first minority-owned bank in Tennessee. Now the oldest continuously operating minority-owned bank in the U.S., Citizens Bank was founded by such distinguished leaders as James C. Napier, Reverend Richard Henry Boyd, and Preston Taylor. The bank first opened in Napier's law office at 411 North Cherry Street (now Fourth Avenue North) near other businesses which served Nashville's black population. Citizens Bank relocated several times over the years; the present main office location of Citizens Bank is 2013 Jefferson Street.

Born about 1883 of former slave parents, **WILL EDMONDSON** worked as a laborer until 1931, when he began to produce primitive limestone carvings. A deeply religious man, Edmondson believed that he was called by God to carve stones and, without formal training, began carving first simple tombstones and later primitive animals, angels, Biblical characters, and even celebrities such as Eleanor Roosevelt. Edmondson was the first black artist to be honored with a one-man exhibit at the Museum of Modern Art in New York City. He died in 1951 and is buried at Mt. Ararat Cemetery. A marker at 1450 Fourteenth Avenue South denotes the former site of his home.

FISK UNIVERSITY* was founded in 1866 as a free school for blacks in Nashville. Jubilee Hall on campus is a National Historic Landmark. The campus also features the Carl Van Vechten Art Gallery and the Fisk Chapel.

GREENWOOD CEMETERY at Elm Hill Pike and Spence Lane was established in 1888 by minister Preston Taylor, founder of Greenwood Park and one of the founders of Citizens Bank. Taylor opened the first black undertaking business in Nashville and operated a casket factory. Outstanding Nashvillians buried in Greenwood Cemetery include Taylor and his wife; three original Fisk Jubilee Singers; Deford Bailey, the first black Grand Ole Opry performer; TSU Coach John Merritt; and civil rights leader Kelly Miller Smith Sr. Located nearby, **MOUNT ARARAT CEMETERY** (1869) in the 800 block of Elm Hill Pike was Nashville's first black cemetery. In 1982, it was acquired by Greenwood Cemetery, restored, and renamed Greenwood Cemetery West. One of the leaders buried there is Dr. Robert Fulton Boyd, a physician and graduate of Meharry Medical College.

African-American Historic Sites

GREENWOOD PARK was established in 1906 by Preston Taylor at Elm Hill Pike and Spence Lane as the first private park for African-Americans. The 40-acre park (which no longer exists) included a clubhouse, theater, skating rink, roller coaster, shooting gallery, merry-go-round, and baseball park (home of the Greenwood Giants). Taylor also maintained a track and stables at the park for the annual Colored State Fair, which attracted 14,000 attendees to the park on a single day.

HADLEY PARK (1912) is thought to be the first public park for African-Americans in the U.S. The 34-acre park at 28th Avenue North and Centennial Boulevard was the site of a speech by Frederick Douglass in 1873. The site was once the antebellum plantation of John Hadley, a slaveowner committed to helping freemen with their new post-Civil War status.

MEHARRY MEDICAL COLLEGE (1876) at 1005 D.B. Todd Boulevard was the first medical education program established for African-Americans in the U.S. and is now the country's largest private institution for the training of black healthcare professionals. More than 3,600 practicing physicians and more than 1,700 practicing dentists are graduates of Meharry. Organized in 1876 as the medical department of Central Tennessee College (later Walden University), Meharry was named for the family that gave liberally to its financial support. In 1900, the name was changed to Meharry Medical College of Walden University, and in 1915 a separate charter was granted to Meharry by the State of Tennessee. In 1931, having outgrown its old plant at First Avenue, South, and Chestnut Street, Meharry moved to northwest Nashville near Fisk University.

HUBBARD HOSPITAL, the primary clinical teaching facility for Meharry, was designed by McKissack & McKissack and completed in 1976. It is named for George W. Hubbard of New Hampshire, who created Meharry Medical School in 1876 along with Dr. John Braden and Dr. W.J. Sneed, and served as its president for 45 years. Hubbard came to Nashville almost by accident during the Civil War during his service as a chaplain with Gen. Sherman's Union army. Hubbard is now known as Metro General Hospital.

MILLIE HALE HOSPITAL (1916) once stood at 523 Seventh Avenue South. A Fisk University graduate and registered nurse, Millie Hale opened a 12-bed hospital for African-Americans who could not afford to go elsewhere. The hospital grew to 75 beds by 1923 and offered nursing training. The hospital auxiliary tended to homebound and needy people in Nashville. Her husband, John Henry Hale, was a professor at Meharry Medical College. The hospital closed in 1938. There is a marker at the site.

The **MORRIS MEMORIAL BUILDING*** (1924) at Fourth Avenue North and Charlotte Avenue was designed by McKissack and McKissack, the first African-American architectural firm in the U.S. This intersection is the heart of the historic African-American business district.

The **NATIONAL BAPTIST PUBLISHING BOARD** was established in 1896 by the Rev. Richard Henry Boyd (1843-1922), a founder of Citizens Bank and Secretary of the Home Mission Board of the Negro National Baptist Convention. Born a slave in 1843, Boyd fought in the Civil War, became an ordained minister, and moved to Nashville from Texas in 1896 to found the publishing board. The purpose of the board was to publish denominational literature relevant to the African-American experience for the Negro National Baptist Convention's member churches. The board was originally located at 523 Second Avenue N., but is now located at 6717 Centennial Blvd.

ROGER WILLIAMS UNIVERSITY, one of four colleges founded in Nashville for freed slaves, began in 1864 as Bible classes in the home of Daniel W. Phillips, a white Baptist minister from Massachusetts. In 1866, the "Baptist College" was renamed the Nashville Normal and Theological Institute. The school was located on Hillsboro Road in 1874, where Peabody College of Vanderbilt University stands today. In 1883, it was renamed Roger Williams University. Forced to close in 1905, the university reopened in 1909 on Whites Creek Pike. In 1929, the school merged with Howe Institute of Memphis (LeMoyne-Owen College). The Whites Creek campus is now occupied by the American Baptist College.

TENNESSEE STATE UNIVERSITY at 3500 John Merritt Boulevard began in 1912 as the Tennessee Agricultural and Industrial State Normal School for the training of African-American teachers. The oldest buildings on campus are Harned Hall (1927), named for Tennessee's first commissioner of education, the old library (1927), and the Women's Building (James E. Elliot Building) (1931). The school became Tennessee State University in 1969. The institution's graduates include noted scientists, college presidents, a U.S. Congressman, elected public officials, and other professionals. TSU's women's track coach Edward Temple produced more Olympic medal winners than any other university coach.

Belmont Mansion

Belmont Mansion, an ornate Italianate villa built in 1850 outside the city limits of Nashville, was the summer home of Joseph and Adelicia Acklen. Belmont or Bellemonte—Italian for "beautiful mountain"—was built on one of the highest hills in Nashville.

The mansion today, located on the campus of Belmont University (1700 Acklen Avenue), is furnished in Victorian opulence with original and period pieces, gilded mirrors, marble statues from Europe, and oil paintings. Guided tours tell about Mrs. Acklen, a strong-willed and beautiful woman who prevailed throughout the Civil War, three marriages, ten children, and the management of one of the largest fortunes in America. An extraordinary character, Adelicia was one of the wealthiest women in the United States, with land holdings in Tennessee, Louisiana, and Texas. The daughter of one of Nashville's pioneers, Oliver Bliss Hayes, at a young age she married an accomplished, much older man, Isaac Franklin, owner of the Fairvue estate near Gallatin, and became wealthy upon his death in 1846.

At the time of the Civil War, the 180-acre estate included formal gardens with statuary and gazebos, a bear house, zoo, deer park, bowling alley, and art gallery. Many lavish formal balls were held in the mansion, usually on moonlit nights.

Joseph Acklen, who was Adelicia's second husband, was forced to flee to Louisiana when Union troops occupied Nashville in February 1862 and he died at their Louisiana plantation. Adelicia was forced to travel there to preserve her property holdings. By plying the Union and Confederate authorities against each other, she was able to sell 2,000 bales of cotton to buyers in London. She traveled abroad after the war to collect her money and spend it on a shopping spree across Europe.

5 Star Attraction

Although the mansion was located at the Union fortification line, it was not damaged during the Battle of Nashville in 1864. The mansion served as the headquarters for Union General Thomas John Wood during the battle. Union scouts used the 105-foot-tall brick water tower to relay signals. Today the tower serves as a carillon, or bell tower, for the university.

The mansion, the second largest antebellum house still standing, features the Grand Salon, the most elaborate domestic room in prewar Tennessee. It is furnished with Corinthian columns, chandeliers, and fine paintings and statuary. A lavish reception for 2,000 guests was conducted there following Adelicia's marriage to her third husband, Dr. William A. Cheatham, in 1867.

The mansion also features a grand staircase, the lavishly furnished tete-a-tete room, upstairs bedrooms, parlors, pantries with original china, the library, and the front hall with the marble statues of "Ruth Gleaning" and "Sleeping Children."

Western Military Institute

The Gothic Collegiate-style building at 724 Second Avenue South on College Hill was designed by Nashville architect Adolphus Heiman and was built in 1853-54 as the Literary Department of the University of Nashville. The limestone building measured 175 by 50 feet and had a composition roof with a parapet wall along the roofline. In the 1850s the building was used by the Western Military Institute. At the outbreak of the Civil War, all of the institute's cadets joined the Confederate army. During the Union Army occupation of the city, the rugged limestone building became Hospital No. 2, housing 300 beds. One room was set aside for "dead-men's knapsacks." The Federal authorities established a total of 25 military hospitals in Nashville, occupying churches, schools, and other structures. Civilians watched from the roof of this building the Battle of Nashville unfold in December 1864. The building has also housed the university's Medical College, Peabody College, and the Children's Museum. Today, it houses Metro Nashville's Planning Department. It is the only remaining building of the original University of Nashville.

Rutledge House

The Rutledge-Baxter House at 101 Lea Avenue at the corner of Rutledge Avenue is a three-story Italianate brick structure sitting on the site of Rose Hill, the home of Henry and Septima Sexta Rutledge. Originally built in 1814, Rose Hill was known for its beautiful terraced gardens. Rose Hill partially burned during the Civil War. Nathaniel Baxter built at this site in the 1860s and incorporated a section of the Rutledge house, which today is a private residence. The home of steamboat captain Thomas Ryman, who built the famous Ryman Auditorium, was across the street.

Geddes Fire Hall

The James Geddes Engine Company No. 6 building at 629 Second Avenue South was the pride of the fire department when it was built in the late 1800s. Named for James Geddes, a civil engineer with the Louisville and Nashville Railroad, it was the last fire hall to use horsedrawn firefighting equipment. The Italianate brick building features a square tower and a round tower, which once housed a steeple with bell. Today the building on College Hill is a private residence.

Litterer Laboratories

The Litterer Laboratories building on Second Avenue South once served as Vanderbilt University's Medical School, complete with operating amphitheater. The south campus, which was to feature a teaching hospital nearby, was abandoned in the 1920s. Originally serving the University of Tennessee Medical School (which moved to Memphis in 1911), the building was bought by Dr. William Litterer in 1915 and donated to Vanderbilt University, which used it into the 1920s. A large building across the street (which survives) was built as Galloway Hospital but never operated in that capacity.

Elm Street Methodist Church

The Elm Street Methodist Church building at the corner of Elm and Fifth Avenue South was built in 1860 and used by occupying Union forces as a military hospital during the Civil War. The ornate clock tower cupola of the church was destroyed by fire in 1925 and not rebuilt. The church closed in 1971. The stained glass windows were removed and used at a now-defunct restaurant on Elliston Place. After renovations, the old church became home to Tuck-Hinton Architects in 1995.

Lindsley Avenue Church of Christ

The Lindsley Avenue Church of Christ (1894) at Second Avenue South is a large Romanesque Revival-style brick building with terra cotta trim designed in the Akron pattern: a semi-circular auditorium surrounded by secondary rooms. Gales, pinnacles, and turrets make this an ornate and picturesque building.

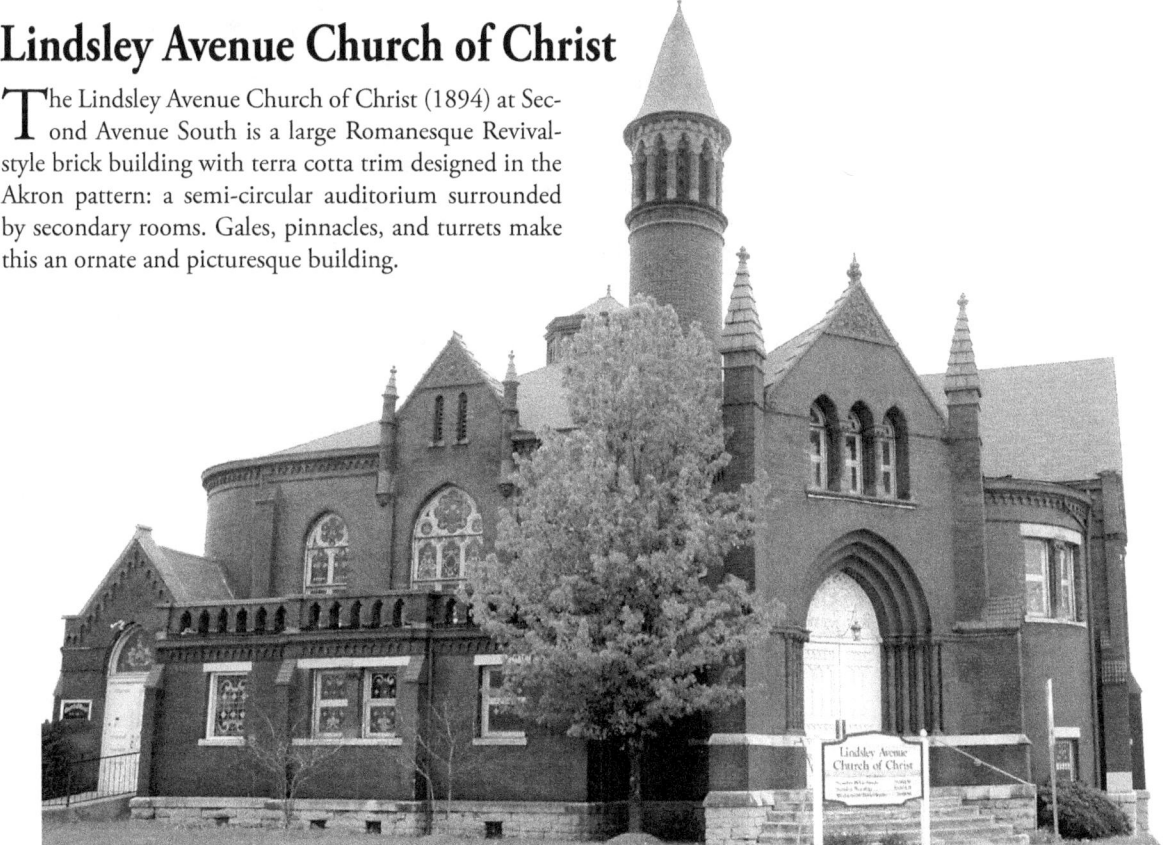

St. Patrick's Church

St. Patrick's Catholic Church at 1219 Second Avenue South was founded in 1891 by the Reverend Timothy C. Abbott, an Irishman who received the title of monsignor from the Pope in 1929. He remained the pastor until his death in 1932. The structure was designed by B.J. and M. Hodge. It served as the church school and center for the celebration of Saint Patrick's Day in the diocese. Irish gypsy clans made annual pilgrimages to St. Patrick's Church to bring their dead kinsmen for final rites and burial at Calvary Cemetery.

Holy Trinity Episcopal Church

The Holy Trinity Episcopal Church at Sixth Avenue South and Ewing Avenue was completed in 1853 as one of the finest examples of 19th-Century Gothic Revival architecture. Willis and Dudley architects of New York used an English village church as their inspiration. It was one of 17 churches built in South Nashville, which was annexed by Nashville in 1854. The octagonal turret, however, was not built until 1887. During the Civil War, Union troops used the rugged limestone building as a gunpowder magazine and as a horse stable, inflicting significant damage. Today, the beautiful "country" church sits on a small, triangular lot surrounded by a commercial and light-industrial section of the city just south of downtown. For information about touring the church, call (615) 256-6359.

Fort Negley

Fort Negley on St. Cloud Hill was the most prominent of the fortifications built around Nashville by the occupying Federal army during the Civil War. It was the largest inland stone fortification built during the war. Nashville became the most fortified city in North America, second only to Washington, D.C. The design by U.S. engineer Captain James St. Clair Morton is elaborate, star-shaped, and European in origin. The fort was named for U.S. General James S. Negley, provost marshal and commander of Federal forces in Nashville at the time.

The fort was built largely by black laborers from October to December 1862. Contrabands (runaway slaves) and free blacks were impressed by the army to build the 23 fortifications around the city. Living conditions were brutal and hundreds of laborers died of disease and exposure. Next to none were ever compensated for their labors.

Fort Negley is 600 feet long, 300 feet wide, and covers four acres. It used 62,500 cubic feet of stone and 18,000 cubic feet of earth. At the southern end of the fort, where attack was most likely, were two massive, bombproof bastions equipped with guns which could be aimed in several directions. Each bastion had tunnels which protected men moving through the works. Casement No. 1 protected a 30-pound Parrot rifle, a cannon which could hurl a 29-pound shell 2.5 miles. There were 11 guns in the fort, operated by 75 artillerymen.

This view looks southwest from Fort Negley across the Franklin Pike along the historic Union fortification line to the present-day City Reservoir and pumphouse, site of the Civil War-era Blockhouse Casino. The 1864 Battle of Nashville was fought in the distant hills to the left (south).

The opening shots of the Battle of Nashville on Dec. 15, 1864, were fired from Fort Negley, although the fort itself was never directly attacked at any time during the war.

After the war, the fort was abandoned and allowed to deteriorate. During the 1930s, WPA work crews reconstructed the fort to an amazing degree, even rebuilding the interior wooden palisades, but those works also eventually fell into disrepair.

Following improvements by City of Nashville Parks, the fort opened to the public in 2004 for the first time in 60 years. Extensive interpretive signage and elevated walkways allow self-guided tours during daylight hours.

A modern Visitors Center opened on the anniversary of the battle in 2007. Admission is free. The phone is (615) 862-8470. The center features interactive touch-screen displays and large maps and photos that tell the story of Nashville during the Civil War. The film *The Fall of Nashville* can be viewed in the auditorium which explains how Nashville became the first major Southern city to fall to Union forces. A computerized kiosk also allows visitors to search for ancestors listed in the National Soldier and Sailor Database.

See Map on Page 77

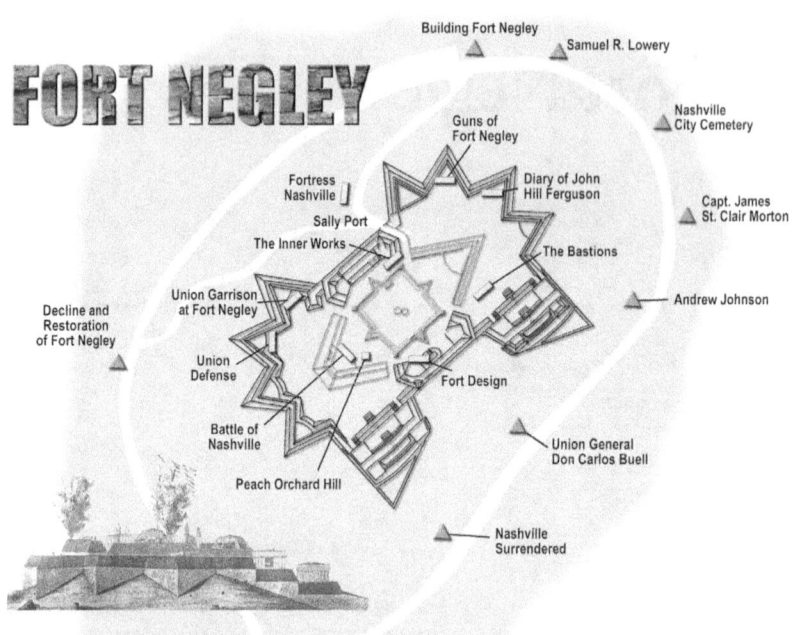

Top: The main gate of Fort Negley Park, built by the U.S. Army Corps of Engineers in the 1930s.
Above: Re-enactors, followed by the general public, march up to Fort Negley during its rededication in December 2004.

Above: The Fort Negley Visitors Center.

Left: A stairway and passage through one of the stone bastions at Fort Negley. Tours are taken on elevated walkways; the ruins themselves are off-limits due to the danger of falling stone.

Battle of Nashville Monument

The Battle of Nashville Monument (also called the Peace Monument) is one of the few monuments dedicated to the soldiers of both sides of the Civil War. Dedicated on Armistice Day in 1927, the sculpture also memorializes the American soldiers who fought in France during World War One.

The monument park is located on Granny White Pike (12th Avenue South) between Battlefield Drive and Clifton Lane just south of the I-440 overpass (no access from I-440).

The memorial was designed by Italian sculptor Guiseppe Moretti on commission from the Ladies Battlefield Association. The white granite obelisk topped with a marble angel stands 40 feet high.

Originally located on Franklin Pike at Thompson Lane, the monument was moved to its present site in 1999 and rededicated by the Tennessee Historical Commission. The park marks the center of the Confederate line on the first day of battle, Dec. 15, 1864. The monument is dwarfed by a witness tree, a basket oak which has been documented as a large tree at the time of the Civil War.

Shy's Hill

Confederate Redoubt No. 1

Confederate Redoubt No. 1 is located on high ground at 3423 Benham Road and represents the northwest salient of the main Confederate line on the opening day of battle. Five small forts were built along the far left (west) flank of the main Confederate line. The forts were typically armed with a battery of two to four Napoleon artillery pieces, 85 artillerymen, and supported by 100 infantrymen. On Dec. 15, 1864, U.S. Army infantry and cavalry attacked and overwhelmed all five forts following an artillery barrage. Redoubt No. 1 was the last to fall. Today the remnants of the earthworks remain. There is interpretive signage and an artillery piece. The site is owned and maintained by the Battle of Nashville Preservation Society.

─────── See Map on Page 78 ───────

On the second day of battle, Shy's Hill was a formidable position occupied by Gen. William Bate's division of Cheatham's Corps on the extreme left flank. Although positioned 600 yards from the hill, the Federals of the XXIII Corps and XVI Corps remained mostly dormant until 4:15 p.m. when Gen. John McArthur ordered McMillen's Brigade to "take that hill." The subsequent charge up the hill resulted in the rout of the entire Confederate army in one of the most decisive battles of the war. The hill was named for Confederate Colonel William Shy, who died defending it. The trailhead to Shy's Hill is located at the historical marker on Benton Smith Road just south of Harding Place. At the side and top of the hill visitors can see remnants of the Confederate earthworks, which were erroneously positioned higher than the military crest. The Battle of Nashville Preservation Society maintains the site.

See *Guide to Civil War Nashville-2nd Edition*, also by Mark Zimmerman, for more extensive information.

Travellers Rest Plantation and Museum

Built in 1799, Travellers Rest at 636 Farrell Parkway was the home of Judge John Overton, a member of the state Supreme Court. The farmhouse began as a two-story, four-room Federal-style clapboard structure with additions built in 1808, 1828, and 1887. Today, the home is furnished in the period of the lifetime of Judge Overton, who died in 1833.

The site includes the mansion and estate, garden, visitors center and video presentation, modern museum, gift shop, outbuildings, and modern meeting hall and auditorium. The phone is (615) 832-8197.

Two guided historic house tours, one self-guided garden tour, and one self-guided Civil War grounds tour are offered. Travellers Rest Plantation and Museum is owned by the Colonial Dames of America in Tennessee and is listed on the National Register of Historic Places.

At the beginning of the Civil War, the home was occupied by Overton's widow (she died in 1862), her son John and his wife Harriet and their children. The farm, worked by 80 slaves, covered 1,050 acres and was valued at $68 million (in today's dollars). When the Union occupied Nashville in February 1862, John Overton fled his home to avoid arrest and imprisonment. Appointed to the rank of colonel by the governor before the war,

Overton offered considerable financial support to the Confederate army.

Confederate General John Bell Hood arrived from Franklin on Dec. 2, 1864 and made Travellers Rest his headquarters. From here, he directed the building of a five-mile defensive line south of the Union-occupied city. Also here, he met on Dec. 8 with Gen. Benjamin Franklin Cheatham, who offered his apologies for miscommunications which allowed the Federal army to escape at Spring Hill on Nov. 29.

At Travellers Rest, Mrs. John Overton proudly hosted a dinner attended by General Hood and five other generals following the marriage of one of Hood's staff officers.

During the Battle of Nashville, the women and children huddled in the cellar awaiting the outcome, General Hood having already relocated his headquarters. The Confederate lines collapsed and the retreating army moved past the house, pursued by Union soldiers. On the night of Dec. 16, Union General W.L. Elliott slept in the same bedroom occupied earlier by Hood.

Tennessee Agricultural Museum

The Oscar Farris Agricultural Museum is located at 440 Hogan Road, between Nolensville Road and Franklin Pike, on the grounds of the state's Ellington Agricultural Center. Housed in a renovated 24,000-sq.-ft. horse barn, the museum contains a blacksmith shop, an extensive collection of farm artifacts, the Tennessee Agricultural Hall of Fame, rural Tennessee prints and folk art sculptures, textiles, a woodworking collection, buggies, wagons, and large items such as the McCormick reaper and Jumbo steam engine. Also exhibited outdoors are log cabins, a small farmhouse, kitchen/herb garden, perennial garden, and nature trail. The center was once part of the Brentwood estate of financier Rogers Caldwell. Admission is free. The phone is (615) 837-5197.

5 Star Attraction

Oscar Farris (1889-1961) served 40 years with the state Agricultural Extension Service, 21 years as Davidson County's extension agent. He was responsible for the first "test and slaughter" control of cattle burcellosis in Tennessee, four years before the practice was accepted nationwide.

Farris worked diligently to create the Agricultural Hall of Fame. Several of the first plaques honoring recipients were cast of metal from the damaged statue of Mercury which had stood atop Union Station. The legislature created the museum in 1957, consisting of artifacts collected over the years by Farris.

Marion Dorset M.D. (1872-1935) discovered a serum for hog cholera. He is the only Tennessean in the National Agricultural Hall of Fame.

Bache & Saxton U.S. Standard Balance (1855), accurate to one ten-thousandth of an ounce, proclaimed to be "the most beautiful specimen of mechanical skill and perfection."

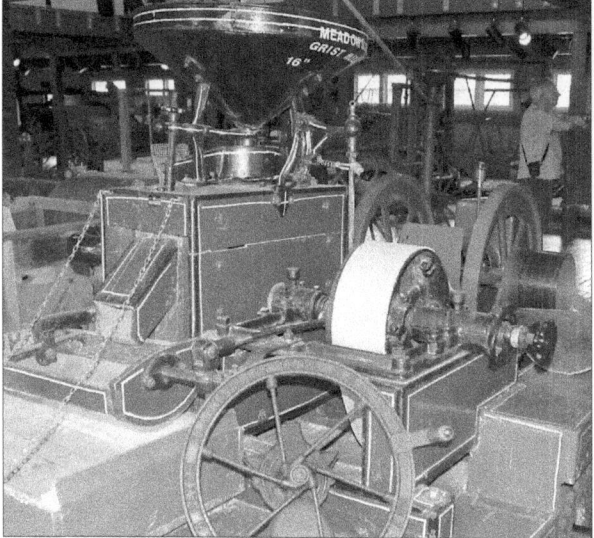

A Meadows steam-powered grist mill from 1906.

The covered wagon exhibit displays the transportation used by the pioneer settlers.

See Map on Page 78

Edgefield Historic District

Edgefield grew during the 1800s as a separate city across the river, a fashionable "suburb" of Nashville for the wealthy. In 1916 a devastating fire destroyed 700 homes and 32 city blocks. Historic Edgefield, Inc. is one of the city's earliest neighborhood associations. Formed in 1976, it worked with the Metro Historical Commission to place the Edgefield Historic District in the National Register of Historic Places and persuaded the city to make it the first locally zoned historic area. The once fashionable neighborhood of Victorian structures and four-square and bungalow-style houses is making a comeback.

The outlaw Jesse James lived for a while in this house at 711 Fatherland Street.

Tulip St. Methodist Church

Tulip Street Methodist Church at 522 Russell Street and the corner of Sixth Street was established about 1860 to serve the Edgefield community. Construction of the current building, designed by Thomas Dismukes and J.E. Woodward, was completed in 1892. The carillon chimes from the 1897 Tennessee Centennial Exposition were installed in the bell tower. The church's twin towers, one square and one round, the extensive use of terra cotta ornamentation, and the wide entrance arch exemplify the Richardson Romanesque architecture popular at the turn of the century. The church survived the great East Nashville fire of 1916 but was heavily damaged by the 1998 tornado. The night of the tornado the bells in the church tower chimed "Amazing Grace" to reassure the community. Most of the tornado damage has been repaired in the community.

See Map on Page 80

Carnegie Library

The East Branch Public Library at 206 Gallatin Pike was designed by New York architect Albert R. Ross and built in 1919. The library was designed in the Beaux Arts style and constructed with a cut limestone exterior. The East Branch Library was one of four libraries built in Nashville using funds donated by philanthropist Andrew Carnegie. The Main Public Library (non-extant) was built with Carnegie funds in 1904 at Union Street and Polk Avenue downtown. The only other surviving Carnegie library is the North Nashville Branch (1915) at 1001 Monroe Street.

Holly Street Fire Hall

The Holly Street Fire Hall or Engine Company No. 14 at 1600 Holly Street and South Sixteenth was designed by the city government's first architect, James Yeaman, and went into service in 1914. The red brick neo-classical structure was the first firehall built to accommodate motorized fire trucks (although it is too small to house today's larger engines). The fire hall was designed to blend in with the neighborhood architecture. Community opposition to plans to demolish the structure saved it in 1980.

Woodland Presbyterian Church

The Woodland Presbyterian Church at 211 North Eleventh Street was built in 1918 after the congregation's second church (1890) was destroyed in the great East Nashville fire of 1916. The church was organized as the First Presbyterian Church of Edgefield in 1858. Repairs were also made to the domed church following the tornado of 1998.

Two Rivers Mansion

TWO RIVERS MANSION at 3130 McGavock Pike (seven miles northeast of downtown Nashville) was constructed in 1859 by David H. McGavock. The mansion is one of the earliest, most significant, and best preserved of the early Italianate-style houses in Middle Tennessee. It is the second house to be erected on the Two Rivers Farm, so named because of its location at the confluence of the Stones and Cumberland rivers. The earlier brick house, built in 1802 by William Harding, also remains. In the 1880s the Two Rivers Stock Farm comprised 1,100 acres with livestock, dairy, and grain growing operations, 15 tenant houses, 13 stables and barns, and 22 other outbuildings. The last heir died in 1965 and the City of Nashville bought the property, preserving the large mansion and original house on a 14-acre tract and using the other acreage for a golf course, park, and two schools. The main mansion can be reserved for private events.

The Hermitage
Home of General Andrew Jackson, 7th President of the United States

The Hermitage is the 1,120-acre estate and home of Andrew Jackson (1767-1845), the seventh President of the United States (1829-37) and the hero of the Battle of New Orleans (1815). The site is a National Historic Landmark, visited by more than 170,000 people each year. The estate has hosted such historical figures as Sam Houston, James K. Polk, the Marquis de Lafayette, Teddy Roosevelt, Lyndon B. Johnson, and Ronald Reagan. During the Civil War, Union soldiers on garrison duty in Nashville made the pilgrimage to the estate to pay homage to The Hero.

The Hermitage: Home of President Andrew Jackson

The first Hermitage was a log cabin in which the Jacksons lived for 17 years before the construction of the mansion. The estate was first called Rural Retreat before being renamed The Hermitage.

The Hermitage is located 12 miles east of downtown Nashville (Exit 221 off I-40, north to 4580 Rachels Lane). Admission is charged. The phone is (615) 889-2941.

The site consists of a modern Visitors Center and Museum, featuring an introductory 21-minute video, exhibits and artifacts, a gift shop, and bookstore. On the grounds are the mansion, smokehouse, gardens, tomb, cemetery, springhouse, slave quarters, the original log cabin, an archeology tour, Tulip Grove Mansion, the Hermitage Presbyterian Church, and the Confederate and Donelson Family cemeteries.

The Hermitage has been lovingly preserved by The Ladies Hermitage Association since 1889.

A replica of a slave cabin is located directly behind the mansion. Cabins for field workers were located throughout the estate.

The Hermitage: Home of President Andrew Jackson

Tulip Grove Mansion was the Greek Revival home of Andrew Jackson Donelson, Rachel Jackson's nephew, and his family. The house sits among tulip poplars.

The tomb in the corner of the garden is the final resting place of General Andrew Jackson and Rachel Donelson Jackson. A small family cemetery lies nearby.

Many special events are held throughout the year, including American naturalization ceremonies.

The original Hermitage was a simple log cabin occupied by Andrew and Rachel Jackson from 1804 to 1821. It was reopened to the public in July 2005 after a six-year, $1.1 million restoration project.

The mansion was built in 1819-21 as a brick home in the Federal style, the center of a plantation which ranged in size from 425 to 1,000 acres and produced corn, cotton, and livestock. A major remodeling in 1831 added a colonnade of ten Greek columns with a facade in the Palladian style. Fire struck in 1834 and the house was rebuilt by 1836, strongly following the Greek Revival style. The interior was completely restored to its 1837-45 appearance, with almost all of the original furnishings. The influence of classical Greek architecture is evident throughout.

At the corner of the garden is the tomb where General and Rachel Jackson lie in rest. Jackson built the Greek-inspired tomb, designed by architect David Morrison, for his beloved wife Rachel, who died in 1828 just before he assumed the Presidency. The love affair between Andrew and Rachel burned bright throughout their marriage. Rachel was the daughter of John Donelson, one of the founders of Nashville. Jackson was buried at the tomb upon his death in 1845. A small family cemetery lies nearby.

The garden was designed by Englishman William Frost in

The Hermitage: Home of President Andrew Jackson

The Hermitage Church in winter.

1819 and features plants and shrubs of the early 19th Century.

The Hermitage was hit hard by a 1998 tornado which felled 1,234 trees but left the historic structures mostly unharmed.

The Tulip Grove Mansion is a Greek Revival house owned by Andrew Jackson Donelson, Rachel Jackson's nephew and President Jackson's secretary during his service in Washington, D.C. The house sits on a rise among tulip poplars, Tennessee's state tree.

The simple brick Hermitage Church nearby was built in 1823 by Andrew Jackson as a favor to his devout wife. He attended services there regularly. Fire gutted the church in 1965, but it was restored and reopened in 1969.

Nearby is the cemetery of the Confederate Soldiers Home (non-extant) and the Donelson family. Also here is the slave cemetery and monument titled *Our Peace: Following the Drinking Gourd*.

Recent archaeology has uncovered foundations of five field slave quarters on the Hermitage estate. Interpretation continues to reveal how these slaves worked and lived. By the 1840s, there were 140 African-American slaves living and working on the Hermitage plantation, by far the largest number of slaves on any farm in Davidson County.

Amqui Station and Visitors Center

In June 2010, the relocated and restored Amqui Station and Visitors Center was dedicated at 301B Madison Street in Madison, Tenn. The Amqui train station was built in 1910 as a switching station for Louisville & Nashville Railroad lines going to the north and the northeast. Amqui is an Indian word meaning "parting of the ways." The station was two stories, the bottom being a waiting area and the top being the control or switching room. The station was abandoned in 1978 and was bought by country music star Johnny Cash, who relocated the old depot next to his House of Cash up the road in Hendersonville. His wife, June Carter Cash, used the depot as an antiques shop. In 2003, when Cash died, the City of Madison bought the station and had it moved back to the vicinity of its original location. The phone is 615-891-1154.

The Old Stone Bridge crosses Manskers Creek off North Dickerson Road in Goodlettsville. The one-lane bridge is still functional. The bridge was used by the stagecoach line which operated from Nashville to Louisville. The stagecoaches ceased operations upon the advent of the railroads in the 1850s.

See Map on Page 79

Bowen-Campbell House

The Bowen-Campbell House is located in Goodlettsville adjacent to the Mansker Station Frontier Life Center in Moss-Wright Park. It is the oldest brick structure in Middle Tennessee, built in 1787 by Captain William Bowen, who had been awarded a land grant for his service in the Revolutionary War. He and his wife Mary had ten children. Eventually they owned 4,000 acres.

Bowen died in 1804 and is buried in a family cemetery behind the house. Bowen's grandson, Brig. Gen. William Bowen Campbell (1807-1867), born in the house, served in the Seminole, Mexican, and Civil wars, one term as governor, and three terms as U.S. Congressman. He is buried in Lebanon, Tenn.

One of Bowen's sons, William Russell Bowen, lived in the house until 1835, when it was sold out of the family. In 1960 it was abandoned and deteriorated. The Bowen-Campbell House Association rescued the landmark and opened it for tours in 1980. About 70 percent of the woodwork is original, as are almost all of the floorboards.

The gravesite of Captain William Bowen, a Revolutionary War soldier, in the family cemetery. The burial plot is bounded by an elaborate stone wall.

See Map on Page 79

Historic Mansker's Station Frontier Life Center

The Historic Mansker's Station Frontier Life Center is located at 705 Caldwell Lane in Goodlettsville's Moss-Wright Park. The site includes the Visitors Center, the replica Mansker's Station (fort), and the Bowen-Campbell House.

The station was built by Kasper Mansker in 1779. The replica fort is approximately one-third the size of the original, lacking only the full number of individual cabins which would have been in the original station. Living history demonstrations are scheduled on a regular basis.

The 18th-Century Colonial Fair is held the first weekend in May and features dozens of sutlers, re-enactors, musicians, and artisans.

Mansker built his first station on the west side of the creek. Due to increasing Indian attacks Mansker left the station in the winter of 1780-81. Indians burned it to the ground. In 1783 he returned and built a second station on the east side of the creek. He lived here with wife Elizabeth and others, including pioneer Isaac Bledsoe. Mansker was one of the signers of the Cumberland Compact. In his sixties, he volunteered to fight at the Battle of New Orleans with Andrew Jackson. He lived at his home in Sumner County until his death in 1821 at age 75.

Re-enactor of Native-American warrior at a Mansker's Station living history demonstration.

See Map on Page 79

Clockwise from Upper Left:
Wyatt Center at George Peabody College.
Disciples of Christ Historical Society.
Old Nashville Union Stock Yards, Inc.
Main Entrance of Percy Warner Park.
Upper Room Chapel and Museum.

Selected Historic Nashville Sites

WEST END

GEORGE PEABODY COLLEGE of Vanderbilt University is located between Eighteenth and Twenty-First avenues, south of Edgehill Avenue. The college was established in 1875 in the College Hill area of town to train teachers following the devastation of the Civil War. International philanthropist George Peabody endowed the $2 million Peabody Education Fund to aid public education in the former Confederate states. The college has been known as Tennessee State Normal College, Peabody Normal College, and George Peabody College for Teachers. The school, now a National Historic Landmark, moved to its present location in 1914. The oldest buildings on campus are the Greek Revival-style Industrial Arts and Home Economics buildings (1914) and the Psychology building (1915). Peabody College merged with Vanderbilt University in 1979. The domed Wyatt Center for Education, originally the Social-Religious Building, was built in 1915 by Ludlow and Peabody. All the campus buildings face inward onto a large wooded commons. **Map on Page 73.**

The **DISCIPLES OF CHRIST HISTORICAL SOCIETY** at 1101 Nineteenth Avenue South serves as the library and archives of the 19th-Century American religious unity movement which became the Christian Church (Disciples of Christ), Christian Churches, and Churches of Christ. The Tudor Gothic stone facility was completed in 1958 as the Thomas W. Phillips Memorial. The architects were Hoffman & Crumpton and Hart, Freeland & Roberts. The sculptor was Puryear Mims. Gus Baker was the stained glass artist. The library of the historic Stone-Campbell Movement contains 37,000 volumes and 25,000 congregational records. The facility was placed on the National Register in late 2006. **Map on Page 73.**

The **UPPER ROOM CHAPEL AND MUSEUM** is located at 1908 Grand Avenue near the Vanderbilt University campus. Begun as a daily devotional guide during the Depression, The Upper Room has evolved into a global ministry, with headquarters established in Nashville in 1953. The chapel features a wood carving of Leonardo DaVinci's *The Last Supper*, created by 50 craftsmen working for 14 months under the direction of sculptor Ernest Pellegrini. It was carved from linden (basswood) and walnut and is 17 feet wide and 8 feet high. The museum also features a 20-foot-tall stained-glass window, oil paintings, icons, porcelains, tapestries, and manuscripts. The winter exhibit is 100 nativity scenes and the spring exhibit is 75 Ukrainian decorated eggs. **Map on Page 73.**

The site of **McCONNELL FIELD** is interpreted at the McCabe trailhead of the Richland Creek Greenway, located off Sloan Road at the entrance to McCabe Golf Course. McConnell Field became Nashville's first municipal airport in 1927 after the city purchased 131 acres of land along Richland Creek from Warren Sloan. The airport was named for Lt. Brower McConnell, a pilot in the Tennessee National Guard's 105th Squadron, who died in an air crash in 1927. Limitations were tight. Overshooting the railroad embankment on the south side could result in rolling off the runway and into the Cumberland River. Nashville's first airmail and passenger flight took off on Dec. 1, 1928 when a Fairchild FC-2W biplane continued on its journey from Chattanooga to Chicago, carrying two passengers and 17 sacks of mail. The airfield quickly became obsolete and was converted into a city park in 1938, named in honor of Parks Commissioner Charles McCabe. Today it is a municipal 18-hole golf course and city greenway. **Map on Page 74.**

DUTCHMAN'S CURVE, marked with signage at a pull-off on the Richland Creek Greenway, is the site of the nation's deadliest railway accident. On July 9, 1918 at 7:30 a.m., two steam locomotives pulling multiple cars and each traveling at 50 mph collided head-on about five miles west of Union Station. Casualties totaled 101 persons, many black construction workers headed to the Old Hickory munitions plant, with about the same number injured, many severely. Fifty thousand spectators were drawn to the ghastly scene as horse-drawn carts stacked with corpses made repeat trips to local morgues. William Floyd, the engineer of one of the trains, was killed the day before his scheduled retirement. **Map on Page 74.**

PERCY WARNER PARK and **EDWIN WARNER PARK** total 2,684 acres of woodlands nine miles southwest of downtown Nashville. Together they form the largest municipal park in Tennessee. The acreage includes picnic areas, scenic roadways and overlooks, hiking trails, equestrian center and horse trails, cross-country running courses, golf courses, athletic fields, and nature center. The parks, listed on the National Register of Historic Places, are used by half a million people each year. Developed in 1927 to 1930 by three men—Luke Lea, Percy Warner and Edwin Warner—the parks were enhanced in the 1930s by the federal Works Progress Administration to include seven limestone entrances, two stone bridges, miles of dry-stacked stone walls, shelters, and a steeplechase course. The main entrance gates at the end of Belle Meade Boulevard were a gift from Mrs. Percy Warner and were designed by Nashville architect Edward Dougherty. A multi-tiered allee designed by landscape architect Bryant Fleming climbs 875 feet up the front hill. Other park entrances are located at Highway 100, Chickering Road, and Old Hickory Boulevard. The Nature Center is located at 7311 Highway 100, just south of Old Hickory Boulevard. Each spring, the racetrack hosts the popular Iroquois Steeplechase. **Map on Page 74.**

KELLEY'S POINT BATTLEFIELD was the site of the largest sustained battle between Confederate cavalry and the Union "brown water" navy. The battle occurred at Bell's Bend in the Cumberland River, nine miles west of Nashville, during the two weeks before the Battle of Nashville. On the river bank, four artillery pieces under the command of Lt. Col. David C. Kelley effectively blocked the Cumberland River against seven heavily armed Union gunboats from Dec. 2-15, 1864. Confederate cavalry and Federal gunboats clashed in six separate engagements. During the fourth engagement, on Dec. 6, 1864, the *U.S.S. Neosho* was hit more than 100 times by cannon fire without sinking. The ironclad narrowly avoided disaster when an unexploded Confederate shell breached the ship's iron plating and lodged in its gunpowder magazine. Pilot John Ferrell and quartermaster John Ditzenback were later awarded the Congressional Medal of Honor for saving the Union colors aboard the *Neosho* when the flag was shot away by Confederate gunfire. Nashville was one of the largest Civil War battlefields in geographical size. From Bell's Bend in the west to the Confederate positions on the Tennessee & Chattanooga Railroad in the east was a distance of 14 miles. Today, six acres

Clockwise from Upper Left:
Werthan Mills
Old Schaub House
Old Isaac Litton High School
Idlewild Mansion
Fall School
Edgehill Polar Bears
Grassmere Historic Farmhouse

Selected Historic Nashville Sites

of Kelley's Point Battlefield are preserved and interpreted as part of the city's Brookmeade Park Greenway. The Battle of Nashville Preservation Society was instrumental in saving the riverside site, which is surrounded by commercial development. **Map on Page 74.**

NORTH NASHVILLE

The **STOCK-YARD BUILDING** at 901 Second Avenue North in Germantown (1924) was the headquarters for the Nashville Union Stockyards. For 50 years the livestock corrals in the vicinity sold cattle, hogs, sheep, and mules. The building featured hallways lined with pink Italian marble trimmed in cherry wood. The main floor housed trading companies as well as a bank, Western Union office, barbershop, saloon, and private gambling room with a 10-foot-long craps table. The commissioner's office was on the upper level and the livestock auctions were on the lower level. The building opened in 1974 as one of Nashville's finest restaurants. **Map on Page 76.**

The old **WERTHAN BAG CORPORATION** building at 1400 Rosa Parks Avenue (8th Avenue North) is one of the few remaining examples of Nashville's 19th-Century industrial infrastructure. The complex of buildings was constructed between 1871 and the late 1880s for the Tennessee Manufacturing Co. owned by Samuel Morgan. Today the buildings are being renovated and marketed as residential lofts. The textile mill employed 268 employees, each earning about $5 per week, and produced "sheeting, drills, and shirtings." The buildings housed 400 looms and 13,820 spindles. The main brick building on Eighth Avenue resembles the Tower of London with four square Norman towers at the corners. The rest of the structures were fenestrated to allow maximum use of natural light. **Map on Page 76.**

The **OLD SCHAUB HOUSE** at 924 Jefferson Street in North Nashville was the home of Mrs. Mary Ann Schaub, who boarded William Strickland while he was working as architect of the Tennessee State Capitol. Strickland and his dog Babe stayed at the house, which was beyond the limits of town, during a cholera epidemic in 1849. Strickland died in 1854; Mrs. Schaub lived in the brick cottage until her death in 1889. The building is now situated in a commercial district northwest of the Bicentennial Capitol Mall State Park. **Map on Page 76.**

MADISON

ISAAC LITTON HIGH SCHOOL opened its doors on Oct. 25, 1930 with a faculty of five teachers. The school closed its doors in 1971. The property was once owned by Isaac Litton, the grandfather of Judge Litton Hickman, who served from 1918-1950 and is known as the founder of the modern Tennessee State Fair. The elder Litton was born in Ireland in 1812 and his family came to Nashville about five years later. As an adult, he owned the West Nashville Planing Mills and Lumber Co. and the Litton and Pulliam Undertakers and Casket Dealers. During the Civil War he refused to take the allegiance oath and was shipped south. Eventually he returned to Nashville. Five hundred Litton High students served as soldiers in World War Two and 31 made the supreme sacrifice for their country and classmates. In 1964 the Litton High "Marching 100" Band performed in the Macy's Thanksgiving Day parade in New York City. In 1959 they performed at the movie premier of *Journey to the Center of the Earth*, starring Nashville native Pat Boone.

Litton High School's main building and the north wing were demolished in 1993. All that remains today is the gymnasium. Plans call for a multi-million-dollar renovation into a youth and community center. The Isaac Litton Alumni Association can be reached at www.isaaclittonhigh.com. **Map on Page 79.**

The **IDLEWILD MANSION** at 712 Neeleys Bend Road in Madison (also known as the Robert Chadwell House) was built around 1874 and is an outstanding example of Italianate architecture. Its construction illustrates the Italian Villa style in a farmhouse. Italianate detailing was not often favored for rural farmhouse construction but is more often encountered in urban settings. In that respect Idlewild is unique in Davidson County. The house is a private residence. **Map on Page 79.**

SOUTH NASHVILLE

EDGEHILL POLAR BEAR PLAZA at 12th and Edgehill avenues near the I.W. Gernert Homes features concrete polar bears, each five feet tall and weighing 600 pounds. They were crafted by Gio Vacchino of the Mattei Plaster Relief Ornamental Co. in 1930 for use as advertisements for the Polar Bear Frozen Custard shops on Gallatin Road and West End Avenue. The shops closed after World War Two. Edgehill resident Zema Hill bought the bears and placed two in front of a funeral home and two in front of his home at 1408 Edgehill Ave., where they stood for 60 years. **Map on Page 77.**

FALL SCHOOL at 8th Avenue South and Chesnut Street was built in 1898 and was in continuous use until a merger in 1970 when it became Fall-Hamilton Elementary, which is currently located on Wedgewood Avenue. It is the oldest standing school building in Nashville. Fall School was named for Philip Slater Fall, a prominent businessman and member of the Board of Education from 1865-1867. The school had no bell; a flag was put out in each front fence corner to signal that school was open. The outstanding feature of the building is a 60-foot-tall octagonal atrium with a water fountain and cupola. The renovated school building was purchased by the Church of Scientology in June 2008. **Map on Page 77.**

GRASSMERE HISTORIC FARM is located on the grounds of the Nashville Zoo at 3777 Nolensville Road. The phone is (615) 833-1534. Admission to the zoo is required to visit the house site. The home was built by Colonel Michael C. Dunn around 1810, making it the second oldest residence in Davidson County that is currently open to the public. It was built in the Federal style, without the ornate front and back porches seen today. The house was occupied by six generations of the family. After the Civil War, William and Lavinia Shute renovated the home, changing the style from Federal to Italianate and adding the porches. Also added at that time were the smokehouse, kitchen, and three-tiered garden behind the home. Primary crops were sweet potatoes, corn, wheat, and hay. Swine and cattle were raised, and flowers and apples from the gardens were sold. The farm prospered late in the 1800s. From the 1930s until 1985, the Croft sisters, Elise and Margaret, lived in the home. After Margaret died in 1974 and Elise passed away in 1985 the Children's

Clockwise from Upper Left:
1947 Tatra T-87 at the Lane Motor Museum.
Sunnyside Mansion at Sevier Park.
David Lipscomb Houses.
Stewart's Stone Wall.
Sculpture of Battle of the Barricade.
Old Hillsboro Fire Hall and Tollhouse.
Cane Ridge Cumberland Presbyterian Church.
Brentwood Hall at Ellington Agricultural Center.

Selected Historic Nashville Sites

Museum by prior agreement received the property for use as a nature study center. The museum opened a wildlife park, which closed for financial reasons in 1995, and the property reverted to Metro ownership. The Nashville Zoo began management of the property in 1996 and the old Croft home was restored by the Metro Historical Commission and the Metro Parks Department. Tours of the house and farm are offered. The main garden area includes heirloom flowers and plants, a second tier of vegetables, and a revived orchard. An herb garden is located behind the kitchen. Heirloom roses are located at the back of the main garden. Numerous daffodils, irises and azaleas brighten the farm grounds. The Master Gardeners of Davidson County work in the gardens most Monday, Wednesday, and Saturday mornings, weather permitting, and are available to give tours and answer questions about the plants and their care. **Map on Page 78.**

The **LANE MOTOR MUSEUM** features 150 automobiles and motorcycles, mostly of foreign production, housed in the former 132,000-sq.-ft. Sunbeam Bakery building at 702 Murfreesboro Road. It houses the largest collection of European vehicles in the U.S. The museum was created in 2002 by collector Jeff Lane and opened to the public in 2003. The museum tries to maintain all vehicles in running order. Admission is charged. The phone is (615) 742-7445. Special events can be held at the facility. The former bakery building dates to 1950 and features high ceilings, natural light, and hand-crafted brick and maple wood flooring. The main display floor covers 40,000 square feet. **Map on Page 78.**

Brightly painted **SUNNYSIDE MANSION** is located in Sevier Park on 12th Avenue South (Granny White Pike), just north of the I-440 overpass. Located between the lines, Sunnyside served as a military field hospital following the 1864 Battle of Nashville. During recent renovation, bullet holes and cannonball tracks found in the walls indicated that the house was heavily fired upon during the battle. Also found was the foundation of the oldest part of the home—a one-story log cabin built around 1820. Mary Childress Benton, the sister-in-law of statesman Thomas Hart Benton, lived here before the Civil War. She and her husband Jesse had left town after a duel with William Carroll and a subsequent gunfight at a Nashville tavern in which his brother shot Andrew Jackson. Mary returned to Sunnyside after her husband died in 1852. A 20th-Century owner, Granville Sevier, added brick wings and built the stone office; his heirs sold the property to the city after his death in 1945. The Greek Revival house was recently renovated for use as offices of the Metro Nashville Historical Commission. **Map on Page 78.**

Located on the campus of **DAVID LIPSCOMB UNIVERSITY** (3901 Granny White Pike), the log cabin was home to educator and religious leader David Lipscomb and wife Margaret Zellner Lipscomb until 1882. The Associated Ladies for Lipscomb moved it to the modern campus from Bell's Bend in 1985. In 1903 the Lipscombs built the brick Avalon as their final home, and gave their surrounding farm as the campus for the Nashville Bible School, founded by Lipscomb and J.A. Harding in 1891. After Lipscomb's death in 1917, the school was renamed David Lipscomb University. **Map on Page 78.**

STEWART'S STONE WALL is marked by a Metro Historical Commission sign at 4616 Leland Lane. Major General William Loring's division of Stewart's Corps fought behind the stone farm wall on the second day of the Battle of Nashville, Dec. 16, 1864. All Federal attacks were beaten back until the Confederate line was broken a mile to the west. The division retreated south through the hills toward Brentwood. **Map on Page 78.**

The **BATTLE AT THE BARRICADE** was fought on the night of Dec. 16, 1864, immediately following the Battle of Nashville. U.S. cavalry commanded by Col. George Spaulding attacked Confederate cavalry under Col. Edmund Rucker at a hastily built barricade of fence rails and logs across the Granny White Pike. During the melee in the dark, the commanders fought each other on horseback and somehow managed to exchange sabers in the process. Rucker was shot by an infantryman and captured; his arm had to be amputated. During the night, it is said that Rucker convinced U.S. Gen. James Wilson that Confederate cavalry commander Nathan Bedford Forrest was nearby with his troopers (he wasn't). Wilson called off his pursuit of fleeing Confederates until dawn on Dec. 17th. By Christmas day, nearly 15,000 Confederates managed to cross the Tennessee River in northern Alabama, thus ending a ten-day, 100-mile fighting retreat in the dead of winter. A historical marker is located on Granny White Pike at the entrance to Richland Country Club. A battle scene by Brickstone Studios, Inc. is portrayed at the entrance to a subdivision on Princeton Hills Drive off Murray Lane in Brentwood. **Map on Page 78.**

The **OLD HILLSBORO PIKE FIRE HALL** located at 2219 21st Avenue South was constructed on property acquired by the City of Nashville on July 16, 1929, and was completed in 1930. The building was built in the Tudor Revival style popular in the adjoining neighborhood. The building is no longer in use as a fire hall. The sideyard once featured a concrete goldfish pond which attracted the neighborhood children. Today, traces of earthworks constructed by Union troops occupying the city during the Civil War can be seen. A marker notes the location of the Hillsboro Pike tollgate and tollhouse once operated by the Nashville and Hillsboro Turnpike Co. The toll for a horsedrawn carriage was 25 cents. **Map on Page 78.**

CANE RIDGE CUMBERLAND PRESBYTERIAN CHURCH at 13411 Old Hickory Boulevard was built in 1859, replacing a log structure which occupied land donated by Edwin Austin and Thomas Boaz in 1826. The church features twin entrance doors, one for men and one for women. One of the best known pastors was Hugh Bone Hill, who also preached at the Jerusalem Church in Rutherford County. Isaac Johnson, a Revolutionary War soldier, died in 1839 and is buried in the church cemetery. Directions: Take I-24 south to Old Hickory Boulevard exit (Exit 62) and turn right. Drive about half a mile and turn right onto Old Hickory Blvd. and proceed about one mile to the church on the right at Cane Ridge Road. There is a historical marker.

BRENTWOOD HALL (1927) was the home of financial wizard Rogers Caldwell (1890-1968), the "J.P. Morgan of the South." He began his empire selling bonds and founded the Bank of Tennessee in 1919. He bought insurance companies, textile mills, oil companies, and department stores, and expanded his bond operations into commercial real estate. He developed a lavish and extravagant lifestyle which included construction of Brentwood Hall, which was patterned af-

Clockwise from Upper Left:
Edgefield Baptist Church.
Old Gallatin Road Fire Hall.
Exhibits at Tennessee Central Railway Museum.
Old Warner Public School.
Old East Nashville High School.
Statue of Jere Baxter at Jere Baxter Middle School.

Selected Historic Nashville Sites

ter The Hermitage. His empire collapsed following the stock market crash of 1929. He was indicted on several charges in Tennessee and Kentucky but managed to avoid any convictions (one was never re-tried after appeal). He resided at Brentwood Hall until 1957, when the state was forced to seize the property. Buford Ellington, a former commissioner of agriculture, was elected governor in 1958 and set up offices in the then-abandoned house to organize his administration. The 207-acre estate became headquarters for the Tennessee Department of Agriculture in 1961. **Map on Page 78.**

EAST NASHVILLE

EDGEFIELD BAPTIST CHURCH is located at 700 Russell Street in the historic neighborhood of Edgefield. The congregation was first organized in 1867 with 31 members. Construction of this church began in 1905, and the first service was held inside the sanctuary in 1907. Adjoining educational facilities were added in 1948. The building plans were drawn by Wheeler, Runge, and Dickey, and the architectural style is consistently Gothic throughout the exterior and interior. The church has towers at each corner and a gable bay with a large window at the center of each street facade. All of the door and window openings have pointed arches. The foundation of the church is made of stone, while the exterior walls are brick. The roof is composed of asphalt shingles, and the windows are stained glass. A unique feature of the interior is the solid wooden door separating the two auditoriums. The door can be raised and lowered by means of cables operated by an electric motor. The original structure was placed on the National Historic Register in 1977 as part of the Historic Edgefield community. **Map on Page 80.**

The old **WARNER PUBLIC SCHOOL** at 626 Russell Street was built in 1892 to replace the old Main Street School. It is named for James C. Warner, a member of the Edgefield Board of Education before Edgefield was annexed by Nashville in 1840. The original building was destroyed by the great fire of 1916. The current building was opened in 1918 and was renovated in 2004 after being damaged by a tornado in 1998. Today it houses the Warner Elementary Enhanced Option School. **Map on Page 80.**

The **EAST HIGH SCHOOL** (now the East Literature Magnet School) at 110 Gallatin Road was completed in 1932. Designed by Marr and Holman, a prominent Nashville architectural firm of the time, the building exhibits stylistic Art Deco characteristics. Perhaps its most famous graduate is media celebrity Oprah Winfrey. The former East Junior High School next door was completed in 1937 and designed by George Waller. It was part of the first phase of a large school construction project undertaken by the city with the aid of Public Works Administration funds. The four-story building exhibits Art Deco and Classical Revival details. The earliest building on the campus is the Gillespie-Malone house, which was moved from its original site fronting Gallatin Road to its present location to make way for the construction of East High in 1931. The house was constructed in 1915 in the Classical Revival style and clad in limestone. **Map on Page 80.**

The **GALLATIN ROAD FIRE HALL** for Engine No. 18, now abandoned, is located at 1220 Gallatin Road near Douglas Avenue. The brick structure was built circa 1930 and has remained virtually unmodified. The fire hall was located along a major road serving areas that were experiencing suburban home construction in the 1920s and 1930s. In May of 1807, the city formed its first volunteer fire-fighting unit. The Nashville Fire Department was organized as a paid department on July 24, 1860, with John S. Dashiell as its first chief. The first horsedrawn steam fire engine was called the *Hamilton*, named after J. M. Hamilton, who was a prominent hardware man of the time. Two other horsedrawn engines, the *Eclipse* and the *Deluge*, were also in service. In 1861, a hook and ladder company was added. Nashville's first motorized fire engine arrived in 1912. Since 1860, Nashville has grown from six square miles to 533 square miles. There are now 39 fire stations. **Map on Page 80.**

Educating the public about the role of railroads, in addition to offering scenic rail excursions, is the mission of the all-volunteer, non-profit **TENNESSEE CENTRAL RAILWAY MUSEUM**. The small museum and gift shop, housed in the former railway's master-mechanic's office, is located at 220 Willow Street off Hermitage Avenue, just east of downtown. The phone number is (615) 244-9001. The museum houses offices, a library, and a rapidly expanding collection of railroad material, including the largest collection of Tennessee Central Railway artifacts to be found anywhere. The TCRM currently owns several passenger cars, cabooses, work/camp cars, boxcars, motorcars, baggage cars, locomotives, and a passenger business car. The museum operates passenger excursions to various destinations in central Tennessee with the cooperation of local railroads. The Tennessee Central Railroad was organized by capitalist Jere Baxter in 1893 to link Nashville with Knoxville via the Cumberland Plateau and to compete with the giants of the day—the Louisville & Nashville Railroad and the Southern Railway. Baxter was born in 1852, the son of a prominent Nashville politician, Judge Nathaniel Baxter. While still in his twenties, he became president of the Memphis and Charleston Railroad Company and helped organize companies promoting the development of coal fields in northern Alabama and eastern Tennessee. He was involved in the founding of South Pittsburg, Tenn., and Sheffield, Ala. Baxter, Tenn. is named for him. After completion of the route to Knoxville in 1898, Baxter began work on a line from Nashville to Memphis. Competition was fierce and when Baxter died in 1904 at age 54 of kidney disease, his dream of an independent railway died with him. **Map on Page 81.**

The **JERE BAXTER STATUE** stands in front of the Jere Baxter Middle School at 350 Hart Lane. In 1907, three years after his death, a statue was erected of him at West End and Broadway. His inscription reads: "That I love my country, the marks I have left upon it shall be my best testimony." **Map on Page 79.**

CLOVERBOTTOM MANSION, located at 2941 Lebanon Road in Donelson, is home to the Tennessee Historical Commission. The large, 23-room Italianate mansion was built in 1858 by Dr. James Hoggatt on land inherited from his father, Capt. John Hoggatt, a Revolutionary War soldier. Pioneer John Donelson had settled in this area of the Stones River bottoms, followed by Andrew Jackson, who married Donelson's daughter, Rachel. By the Civil War, the Hoggatt plantation comprised 1,500 acres. The estate was acquired by the state in 1947 and completely renovated in 1994. It is open to the public only by appointment. **Map on Page 81.**

Top to Bottom:
Cloverbottom Mansion.
Buchanan Log House.
Colemere Mansion.
J. Percy Priest Dam and Powerhouse.

Selected Historic Nashville Sites

The **BUCHANAN LOG HOUSE** at 2910 Elm Hill Pike (seven miles east of downtown) was built by pioneer James Buchanan in 1800-1809 of chesnut logs, poplar floors, and limestone fireplaces. In 1810, Buchanan married Lucinda East, and their family eventually totaled 16 children, necessitating additions to the home. All 16 children lived to adulthood. Buchanan died in 1841 at the age of 78 and is buried in the family cemetery across the street. Behind the main house is the two-story, two-room loghouse built by Buchanan's son Addison and moved here from its original site a quarter-mile away. Judge Thomas N. Frazier bought the house in 1865. The judge was impeached during Reconstruction for opposing the ratification of the 14th Amendment. He was restored to office in 1870. His son, James B. Frazier, served as governor in 1903-1905 and as U.S. Senator from 1905 to 1911. The Buchanan Log House site is owned by the Donelson-Hermitage Chapter of the Association for the Preservation of Tennessee Antiquities. The facility is available for weddings, receptions, and parties. The phone is (615) 871-4524. **Map on Page 81.**

COLEMERE MANSION at 1400 Murfreesboro Pike (southwest corner of the Nashville airport) was built in 1930-31 after the original mansion burned in 1929. The original was built by Col. E.W. Cole in 1893 upon his retirement as president of the N.C. & St.L. Railroad. The current Southern Colonial structure was designed by Russell Hart, inspired by the Arlington mansion in Natchez, Miss. From 1948-73 it functioned as the Colemere private social club. The mansion now serves as a restaurant. **Map on Page 81.**

The **J. PERCY PRIEST DAM** was built by the U.S. Army Corps of Engineers in 1963-68 on Stones River about seven miles from its mouth on the Cumberland River. The dam is easily visible from Interstate 40 east of downtown. Motorists can drive across the dam on Bell Road. The site includes a Visitors Center, parking lot overlook, boat ramp, and trailhead for a Metro Nashville Greenway. The earth and concrete dam is 2,716 feet long and 130 feet high and created a lake 42 miles long with 213 miles of shoreline. Nineteen thousand acres of public land is included in the project, plus four marinas and 21 recreational areas. The lake is heavily used for recreational activities, and the dam, along with Old Hickory Dam on the Cumberland River upstream from downtown, has alleviated much of the traditional flooding in the area. The dam also includes one electrical generator capable of producing 70 million kilowatt-hours per year. The dam and lake were named for eight-term Congressman J. Percy Priest (1900-1956). In a nefarious criminal plot a dynamite bomb was exploded at the dam in November 1978. The blast tore doors from a tunnel but caused no structural damage. The perpetrators planned to breach the dam, flood Nashville, and then plunder the city. **Map on Page 81.**

The **OLD HICKORY LOCK AND DAM** was built by the U.S. Army Corps of Engineers in 1952-54 about 25 miles upstream from downtown Nashville on the Cumberland River. Old Hickory Lake extends 97 miles upstream to Cordell Hull Dam near Carthage, Tenn. and includes 440 miles of shoreline. The dam is 98 feet high and 3,750 feet long. The navigational lock measures 84 by 400 and raises or lowers vessels 60 vertical feet in about 13 minutes. The lock accommodates relatively heavy barge traffic. The dam's power plant includes four electric generators with a capacity of 420 million kilowatt-hours annually. **Map on Page 81.**

DELUGE • J. Percy Priest Dam near Nashville in mid-April 2010, the gates closed and the drainage basin nearly bone dry. Twelve days later, storms from the Gulf Coast dropped more than 14 inches of rain in 36 hours and inundated much of Middle Tennessee with flooding on a scale seen once every one thousand years. The flash flooding took nine lives and inflicted more than $1.5 billion in damages. But before the dam was built, flooding was an annual event.

OLD HICKORY VILLAGE is the historic housing development associated with the 1918 Old Hickory gunpowder plant and subsequent industrial development by E.I. du Pont de Nemours and Co. At the village triangle is the Depression-era U.S. Post Office building, monument to the original families of Hadley Bend and historic cemetery. Renovated buildings, such as the branch public library, and houses of differing architectural styles can be found throughout the resurgent satellite city. **Map on Page 81.**

Historical Markers
Metro Nashville Historical Commission

Adolphus Heiman 1809-1862
Born Potsdam, Prussia. Came to Nashville 1838. Lived in home on this site. Architect, Engineer & Builder. Designed Univ. of Nash. Main Bldg., Central State Hosp. Main Bldg., Suspension Bridge over Cumberland River; Masonic Leader; Adj. U.S. Army Mexican War; Col. 10th Tenn. Inf. Reg. C.S.A. Civil War. Buried in Confederate Circle, Mount Olivet Cemetery.
Location: 900 Jefferson Street

Albertine Maxwell
Regarded as the symbol of dance in her adopted hometown of Nashville, Ellen Albertine Chaiser Maxwell (1902-96) operated the Albertine School of the Dance (1936-80). She had danced with Chicago Opera, Adolf Baum Dance Co., and Ruth St. Denis Dance Co. Founder and director of the Les Ballets Intimes with Nashville Ballet Society (1945-80), Maxwell was also a founding member of the Southeastern Regional Ballet Assn. (1955). Her studio in her home, 3307 West End, no longer stands.
Location: 3307 West End Avenue

Assumption Church
Nashville's second oldest Catholic church, dedicated Aug. 14, 1859, its rectory on right was added in 1874, school on left in 1879. The present altar, windows, and steeple were added later. The Germantown neighborhood grew around it; sermons were often in German until World War I. The parish has produced many nuns and priests, including Archbishop John Floersh and Cardinal Stritch.
Location: 1227 Seventh Avenue, North

Belle Meade Golf Links Historic District
Platted in 1915 by developer Johnson Bransford, Belle Meade Golf Links is one of the early subdivisions that arose from the dissolution of the world-famous Belle Meade Plantation. This small residential district represents early 20th century subdivision design and is listed in the National Register of Historic Places.
Location: Intersection of Windsor Dr. and Blackburn Ave.

Belle Vue
The original log part of this house was built about 1818 by Abram DeMoss and named for the house his father, Lewis DeMoss, built in 1797 overlooking the Harpeth River a mile southwest. In time the name was given to the Nashville and Northwestern Railroad depot and to the U.S. Post Office. Thus the Bellevue community owes its name to this historic site.
Location: Bellevue, 7306 Old Harding Road
Note: The original log part of this house is now thought to have been built by John Garrett. The left front section was built by Thomas Harding around 1802, and the right section which connected the two sections of the house was built about 1820 by Abram and Betsy DeMoss. It was named for the house his father, Lewis DeMoss, built about 1800 overlooking the Harpeth River a mile southeast.

Belmont-Hillsboro Neighborhood
When Adelicia Acklen's estate was sold in 1890, the Belmont Mansion and its grounds became Belmont College. Other portions, and parts of the neighboring Sunnyside Mansion property, were subdivided into residential lots by the Belmont Land Co. In 1900-1910, streetcar lines were built running to Cedar Lane on Belmont Boulevard and to Blair Boulevard on 21st Ave. The neighborhood became a National Register Historic District in 1980.
Location: Belmont Boulevard and Beechwood Avenue

Belmont Mansion
This mansion, designed by an Italian architect, and built in 1850 by Joseph A.S. Acklen and his wife Adelicia, was the center of an extensive estate. Massive gates on Granny White and Hillsboro Pike and tree-lined driveways enhanced the 180 acres that included greenhouses, gardens, zoo, lake, and the largest private art gallery in the South. [Note: Belmont is now known to be the work of Adolphus Heiman. The first section of the house was completed in early 1853, and the total acreage of the plantation was closer to 175 than 180 acres.]
Location: Belmont University, mansion entrance

Black Churches of Capitol Hill
1. First Baptist Church, Capitol Hill (1848) 2. Gay Street Christian Church (1859) 3. Mount Olive Missionary Baptist Church (1887) 4. St. Andrews Presbyterian Church (1898) 5. St. John A.M.E. Church (1863) 6. Spruce Street Baptist Church (1848). These six churches stood within 1/6 mile of this marker. These six Black churches stood in the center of Nashville's prosperous Black business district before the Capitol Hill Redevelopment Program. Several began before the Civil War as "missions" or Sunday School classes of earlier white churches. All boasted memberships of over 1,000 by 1910 and claimed the city's most prominent Black business and professional families. All but one moved in the 1950s, and all continue to serve the Nashville community.
Location: James Robertson Parkway and Charlotte Pike

Blackwood Field
In 1912 the State rented land west of Shute Lane and erected two hangars here for the 105th Observation Squadron, Tennessee National Guard. The airfield of about 100 acres was named for H. O. Blackwood, who gave $1,000 to aid the project. The first airmail flight was from here to Chicago July 29, 1924. Airplanes used the field until 1928.
Location: Hermitage, Shute Lane, 0.3 mile off Lebanon Road

Bradley Studios
In 1955, brothers Owen and Harold Bradley built a recording studio in the basement of a house on this site. They added another studio here in an army Quonset Hut, producing hits by Patsy Cline, Red Foley, Brenda Lee, Marty Robbins, Sonny James, and others. Columbia Records purchased the studios in 1962. The studio established its reputation in the music industry with hits by stars including Johnny Cash, Bob Dylan, Roger Miller, George Jones, and Tammy Wynette. Donated by the Mike Curb Foundation.
Location: 804 16th Avenue South on Music Row

Buchanan Log House
James Buchanan (1763-1841) built this two-story single pen log house with hall and parlor plan c1807. The single pen log addition was added c1820 to accommodate the Buchanan family's sixteen children. The house displays a high level of craftsmanship and is one of the best examples of two-story log construction in Middle Tennessee. The house was restored and placed in the National Register of Historic Places in 1984.
Location: Elm Hill Pike in front of Buchanan Log House

Cane Ridge Cumberland Presbyterian Church
Cane Ridge Cumberland Presbyterian Church, built in 1859, replaced a log building which occupied land donated by Edwin Austin & Thomas Boaz in 1826. One of the best known pastors was Hugh Bone Hill, who also preached at the Jerusalem Church in Rutherford County. Isaac Johnson, a Revolutionary War soldier, died 1839 and is buried in the church cemetery.
Location: Antioch, 13411 Old Hickory Boulevard

Capt. Alexander Ewing "Devil Alex"
Early settler of N.W. Davidson Co. Served in Revolutionary War as Aid-de-Camp to Gen. Green. Wounded at Guilford. Earned nickname and 2666 acres. Built and owned first brick plantation house in area, 1/4 mile East. Later built Ewing Mansion on Buena Vista Pike. He and his wife Sarah are buried directly across in Ewing Plantation cemetery.
Location: Ewing Drive at Knight Road

Captain John Rains
On Christmas 1779 he led his family and livestock across the frozen Cumberland and settled in this vicinity. In 1784 he built a fort that enclosed the spring 75 yards east. At James Robertson's orders he often led a company of scouts against Indians. His home was on this hill until he died in 1834, age 91.
Location: Rains Avenue and Merritt Street

Captain Ryman's Home
On this site stood the residence of Captain Thomas Green Ryman, owner of the Ryman steamboat line and builder of the Union Gospel Tabernacle, renamed Ryman Auditorium after his death in 1904. The Queen Anne frame house with a slate roof, seven gables and two turrets, served as the home of Captain and Mrs. Ryman and their seven children from 1885-1926. The house was razed in 1940.
Location: 500 block, Second Avenue South

Cardinal Stritch
Samuel Stritch, born Aug. 17, 1887, southwest corner Fifth and Madison, entered Assumption School at age 7. Ordained when 22, he sang his first Mass here, was priest in Memphis and Nashville, Bishop of Toledo, Archbishop of Milwaukee, Archbishop of Chicago. Named Cardinal in 1946, he was called to Rome in 1958 to head Catholic missions, thus became first American member of the Roman Curia.
Location: 1227 Seventh Avenue, North

Chickasaw Treaty
In 1783, Chickasaw chiefs met with white settlers at a spring 100 yards north and agreed on land rights—the Cumberland country for the settlers, the Tennessee River lands beyond the Duck River ridge for the Chickasaw. This tribe became firm friends with James Robertson and his people, but the settlements suffered many more raids by Cherokees and Creeks.
Location: Morrow Road and Terry Drive

Christ Church Cathedral
Organized in 1829, Christ Church was Nashville's first Episcopal parish. The present Victorian Gothic church, designed by Francis Hatch Kimball of New York, opened for services on Dec. 16, 1894; the tower, by local architect Russell E. Hart, was added in 1947. Designated the Cathedral for the diocese of Tennessee at the 1995 Diocesan Convention.
Location: 900 Broadway

City of Edgefield
The portion of East Nashville known as Edgefield, the name suggested by Gov. Neill S. Brown, was incorporated as a city Jan. 2, 1869. Its approximate bounds were

Shelby Ave., Sevier St., So. 10th St., Berry St., Cowan Ave., and the river. Its first mayor was W.A. Glenn and its last was S. M. Wene. It was annexed to the City of Nashville Feb. 6, 1880.
Location: East side Woodland Street Bridge

Clover Bottom Mansion
Built in 1858 by Dr. James Hoggatt on land inherited from his father, Capt. John Hoggatt, a Revolutionary War soldier, this fine Italian villa-style home is centered in an area of local historical significance. John Donelson settled early in this rich Stone's River bottom area, followed by Andrew Jackson, who married his daughter, Rachel.
Location: Donelson, 2930 Lebanon Road

Cornelia Fort Airport
Cornelia Fort (1919-43), Nashville's first woman flying instructor volunteer, Army's WAFS, WWII, was the first woman pilot to die on war duty in American history. "I am grateful that my one talent, flying, was useful to my country" she wrote shortly before her death. Miss Fort was lost in a crash over Texas flying a basic-trainer plane, BT 13-A, across the United States.
Location: Airpark Drive

Craighead House
This Federal-style home was built c1810 for John Brown Craighead and his first wife Jane Erwin Dickinson. Craighead was the son of early Nashville settler the Rev. Thomas Craighead. In 1823, Craighead married Lavinia Robertson Beck, youngest daughter of Nashville founders Charlotte and James Robertson. Major additions to the house were made in 1824, 1919, and 1998. Developers purchased the Craighead estate in 1905 and planned the present-day Richland-West End neighborhood.
Location: Westbrook Avenue

Cumberland Park
The Cumberland Fair and Racing Association sponsored harness racing here 1891-1894. The great match race between Hal Pointer of Tennessee and Direct of California occurred Oct. 21, 1891. Direct won all three heats in record time for a pacing race. Arion, Directum, Kremlin, Robt. J. raced here. Running races 1893-1906 preceded the State Fair 1906.
Location: State Fairgrounds, northwest corner of grandstand

Customs House
President Rutherford B. Hayes laid its cornerstone in 1877. Designed by Treasury Department architect W. A. Potter, it was occupied in 1882 by collectors of customs and internal revenue, U.S. courts, and Nashville's main post office. Addition to rear began in 1903, wings in 1916. Declared surplus in 1976, then given to the city. It was renovated by the development firm that leased it.
Location: 701 Broadway

Devon Farm
Home of John Davis, early surveyor, who came from N.C. to Nashville in 1788. Davis was an Indian fighter & scout in the State Militia until 1795. He settled on Big Harpeth in 1795-96 and that year built a 1½ story home of handmade brick. The farm, named for Devon cattle bred here, has been owned by seven generations of Davis-Hicks descendants. [Note: Recent research shows that this home was built by Giles Harding, who came to Davidson County from Virginia and purchased this tract of land in 1798. Harding's son, Morris Harding, married Fanny Davis, daughter of John Davis. John Davis lived in the area about three miles northwest of the Harding Place. The Hardings had no children, and Fanny's nephew Edward Hicks, a well-known breeder of Devon cattle, inherited the farm after his aunt's death and changed its name from "Oak Hill" to "Devon Farm."]
Location: East side of Hwy. 100 past Edwin Warner Park near Devon Farm entrance

Disciples of Christ Historical Society
Library and archives of the 19th c. American religious unity movement which became: the Christian Church (Disciples of Christ); Christian Churches; and Churches of Christ. Located here, 1958, in the Thomas W. Phillips Memorial. Architects: Hoffman & Crumpton; Hart, Freeland & Roberts. Sculptor: Puryear Mims. Stained glass artist: Gus Baker.
Location: 1101 Nineteenth Avenue, South

Dry-Stack Stone Walls
Dry-stack stone walls, a Scots-Irish building tradition adapted by slaves in the early 19th century, were common throughout Middle Tennessee. During the 1864 Battle of Nashville, Brigadier General Henry Jackson was captured at this wall on the Middle Franklin turnpike after the Confederate line collapsed at Shy's Hill.
Location: 4708 Granny White Pike

Dutchman's Curve Train Wreck
The deadliest train wreck in U.S. history occurred on July 9, 1918, when two crowded trains collided head-on at Dutchman's Curve. The impact caused passenger cars to derail into surrounding cornfields, and fires broke out throughout the wreckage. Over 100 died, including many African-American workers journeying to work at the munitions plant near Old Hickory.
Sponsored by the Bellevue Harpeth Historic Association
Location: White Bridge Road at Richland Creek Greenway Trailhead

East Nashville Fire
Nashville's worst disaster by fire occurred Wednesday, March 22, 1916. It began at 11:47 a.m. in the rear of Seagraves Planing Mill, 80 yards west, and was swept eastwardly by 44 to 51 mph gales. It was brought under

control at 4:30 p.m. near South Tenth and Dew Streets. 648 buildings were burned, 1 life was lost and 3,000 left homeless.
Location: 211 North First Street

Edmondson Home Site
Will Edmondson, born about 1883 of former slave parents in the Hillsboro area of Davidson County, worked as a railroad and hospital laborer until 1931, when he began his primitive limestone carvings. Working without formal training, he produced some remarkable sculptures which won high praise in exhibits across the U.S. He died in 1951.
Location: 1450 Fourteenth Avenue, South

Edwin Warner Park 606.7 acres
Edwin Warner (1870-1945) succeeded his brother Percy on the Park Board in 1927 and served for eighteen years. He personally directed the acquisition of most of the Warner Park acreage and supervised WPA development of the property. Warner organized a major Victory Garden program in the park during WWII. Park land west of Old Hickory Blvd. was renamed in his honor in 1937.
Location: Highway 100 at Edwin Warner Park entrance

Eighth Avenue South Reservoir
This 51-million-gallon reservoir was built 1887-89 on Kirkpatrick Hill, the site of Federal Fort Casino during the Civil War. It is elliptical in shape with axes of 603 and 464.4 feet. Perimeter of wall is 1,746 feet and water depth is 31 feet. Rupture in east wall occurred at 12:10 a.m., Nov. 5, 1912. The interior was waterproofed in 1921. Designated as a National Water Landmark by AWWA, 1971.
Location: Eighth Avenue South, on entrance steps to reservoir

Ezell House
In 1805 Jeremiah Ezell (1775-1838) moved here from Virginia and purchased 17 acres of land on Mill Creek. In 1816 he served on the Court of Pleas for Davidson County. In 1888, his grandson, Henry Clay Ezell, built this brick vernacular Queen Anne style house. His large farm was known for breeding fine mules from stock imported from Spain.
Location: Corner of Old Ezell Road and Donelson Pike / Harding Place

Frederick Stump 1723-1822
Frederick Stump, an early settler in the Fort Nashborough area, came from Pennsylvania by way of Georgia. He was a Revolutionary War soldier and noted Indian fighter. He owned a larger plantation along Whites Creek where he operated a mill and inn and rented land to other settlers. This log house is reputed to have been his home where he operated the inn.
Location: 4949 Buena Vista Pike

First Airfield
E. L. Hampton's pasture became "Hampton Field" when transient airplanes began landing here during the first World War. About 2,000 feet long from here west, bounded north and south by Golf Club Lane and Woodmont Boulevard, it continued in use as Nashville's first airfield about five years until the opening of Blackwood Field in 1921.
Location: 2305 Hampton Avenue

First Baptist Church
Organized in 1820, this is the church's third downtown location. The elaborate Gothic tower is all that remains of the Matthews & Thompson building that stood at this location from 1886 to 1967. The Baptist Sunday School Board, now one of the world's largest publishers of religious materials, was organized here in 1891. Edwin Keeble Associates designed the new building, which opened in 1970.
Donated by First Baptist Church
Location: 108 Seventh Ave. South

First Baptist Church East Nashville
Founded in 1866 under the direction of Rev. Randall B. Vandavall, First Baptist Church East Nashville built this Classical Revival building between 1928 and 1931, during the height of Rev. W.S. Ellington's career. Nashville artist Francis Euphemia Thompson painted the distinctive baptistry murals in the 1950s and 1960s. At that time the church served as a frequent meeting place for the African-American community during the Civil Rights Movement.
Donated by FBC East Nashville
Location: 601 Main Street

First Steam Locomotive
On Dec. 13, 1850, the first steam engine, Tennessee No. 1, ordered by the Nashville and Chattanooga Railroad, arrived at the wharf on the steamboat *Beauty* from Cincinnati. The one-mile trip on improvised tracks from the wharf to the S. Cherry St. crossing required 4 days of mule power. A one-mile trial run was made from this point on Dec. 27, 1850.
Location: Fourth Avenue South and Hart Street

Fort Negley Site
The guns of Fort Negley, commanding three turnpikes to the South & Southeast, opened the Battle of Nashville, Dec. 15, 1864. This site was selected by Capt. J.S. Morton as the key strongpoint in the Federal line around the city. The European style fort named for General James S. Negley was built of stone, logs, earth & railway iron.
Location: Chestnut Street and Ridley Avenue

General Thomas Overton 1753-1825
Gen. Thomas Overton served in the Revolutionary War and as Inspector of Revenue in N.C., the same position held by his brother Judge John Overton in Tenn. He was one of Gen. Jackson's seconds in duel with Chas. Dickinson. This grave plot was a part of his homeplace, "Soldier's Rest," where he lived from 1804 until his death in 1825. [Thomas Overton died in 1824. His will was recorded on September 3, 1824.]
Location: Old Hickory, Donelson Avenue

Germantown Historic District
European immigrants established Germantown, the first suburb in North Nashville, in the 1850s. Large brick townhouses stood next to modest workers' cottages, illustrating the area's economic and social diversity. World War I and changes in public attitude began decades of decline. Renovation projects at two historic churches began the neighborhood's revitalization in the 1970s. Germantown became a National Register Historic District in 1979.
Location: NW corner of Jefferson St and 6th Ave. North

Glendale Park
Here, near the center of a 64-acre woodland park owned by the Nashville Railway and Light Co., the Glendale streetcar line turned back toward town. The park opened in 1888 to attract passengers for the railway—originally steam, electric after 1893. A zoo was added in 1912. The park closed in 1932, a casualty of automobiles and the Depression.
Location: 4300 block of Lealand Lane

Granny White Grave
Grave of Lucinda "Granny" White, who settled here in 1803 on 50 acres of land. She died in 1815 at about age 73. Granny White Tavern stood 200 ft. to the north. Famous for its food, brandy, and comfortable beds, it attracted travelers from the Natchez Trace, four miles to the west. Grave restored by General James Robertson Chapter D.A.R.
Location: 5100 block of Granny White Pike in median of Granny White Gap subdivision
Note: Granny White's tavern was perhaps four miles from the Natchez Trace Road, but not the Natchez Trace.

Grassmere
Col. Michael C. Dunn, a landowner and sheriff, built a home in the Federal style ca. 1810. A grandson-in-law, William D. Shute, received the farm in 1859 and named it Grassmere. Intact following the Civil War, the house was renovated and an Italianate porch added ca. 1880. Margaret and Elise Croft, 5th generation descendants, lived here until their deaths. Wishing to preserve the farm, the sisters gave it to future generations as a "nature study center."
Location: 3777 Nolensville Road

The Harpeth Hall School
On Sept. 17, 1951, Harpeth Hall opened as an independent girls' college preparatory school on the former P.M. Estes estate. Susan Souby headed the first school of 161 girls. Originating with Ward Seminary (1865-1913); Belmont College for Young Women (1890-1913); and the Ward Belmont School (1913-1951), Harpeth Hall continued Nashville's tradition of superior single-gender education. Motto: Let us lift up the mind and spirit.
Location: 3801 Hobbs Road

Heaton's Station
On this bluff in 1780, pioneers who came with James Robertson built Heaton's (also called Eaton's) station. It and two other forts (Freeland's and Nashborough) withstood all Indian attacks and saved the Cumberland settlements. On the river below were successively a buffalo ford, ferry, and Lock No. 1. The home of Amos Heaton stood 100 feet north.
Location: Lock and Baptist World Center Roads

Hillsboro Toll Gate No. 1
Ten yards north stood toll gate and toll gate house erected by Nashville and Hillsboro Turnpike Co., incorporated in 1848. Charges to travel macadamized road could not exceed: horse or mule, 3¢; 10 sheep, 20¢; 20 meat cattle, 25¢; carriage drawn by pair of horses or mules, 25¢. Toll removed in 1903. Toll gate house, enlarged, stands 20 yards northwest.
Location: 2219 Twenty-First Avenue, South

Holy Trinity Episcopal Church
This building, renowned for its pure Gothic architecture and harmony of proportions, was designed by Wills and Dudley of New York, in a style suggesting an English village church. The cornerstone was laid May 7, 1852, by Bishop James Otey. The church was used as a powder magazine by the Union Army for several months during the Civil War. [Note: The exact date in May 1852 of the laying of the cornerstone is still disputed. Three dates are possible: May 6, May 7, and May 29.]
Location: Ewing Avenue, Lafayette, and Sixth Avenue South

Houston's Law Office
Sam Houston, a native of Virginia, moved to Nashville in 1818 to study law with Judge James Trimble. Houston practiced in Lebanon, Tenn., before returning to Nashville to serve as District Attorney (1819-21). In 1821, he opened a law office near this site. He was elected a U.S. Congressman (1823-27), Governor of Tenn. (1827-29), and President of the Republic of Texas (1836-38). Donated by the Nashville Bar Association in 1999.
Location: 400 block of 2nd Avenue N. at the Criminal Justice Center

Hyde's Ferry Turnpike
Here was toll-gate #2 of the Hyde's Ferry Turnpike Co., chartered in 1848 to build a road from Nashville to Ashland City and Sycamore Mills. Richard Hyde's ferry crossed the Cumberland River 2.6 miles southeast, where the railroad bridge is now. Davidson County paid $10,000 for its part of the road in 1901. Cheatham County bought its portion and freed it from tolls in 1916.
Location: Hyde's Ferry Road and Cato Road
[Note: Davidson County paid $10,000 for its part of the road on January 3, 1902.]

Jackson's Law Office
Andrew Jackson settled in Nashville in 1788 and served as Atty. Gen. until 1796. Lawyer John Overton owned a building here (1791-96) and shared office space with his friend Jackson. Jackson was Tennessee's first Rep. to Congress (1796) and state Superior Court judge (1798-1804). He led U.S. troops to victory at the 1815 Battle of New Orleans and was elected President in 1828. Donated by the Nashville Bar Association.
Location: Fourth Avenue North and Union Street

James Carroll Napier
James C. Napier (1845-1940), Nashville Negro lawyer, educator, member of the city council, delegate to four Republican national conventions. Registrar of the U.S. Treasury, 1911-1915, was a trustee of Fisk, Howard, and Meharry; advocate of public schools; and founder of the One-cent Savings Bank, later the Citizens Savings Bank and Trust Co. [Note: Napier resigned as Registrar of the U.S. Treasury in 1913.]
Location: 648 Claiborne Street

John Trotwood Moore 1858-1929
Tennessee novelist, poet, co-author, four-volume history, "Tennessee, the Volunteer State"; publisher, "Trotwood Monthly"; author of short stories; breeder and judge of livestock; teacher, lecturer; beloved companion and raconteur; President, Tennessee Historical Society; State Librarian and Archivist, 1919-1929; lived in his home Arden Place on this site.
Location: 4425 Granny White Pike

Johnson's Station
A double log house and a few log cabins, partially picketed, stood here about 1790. On May 9, 1793, 4 children on their way to the spring were attacked by Indians. Three were scalped and killed. One escaped. The home of Charles Bosley, wealthy pioneer and a member of the Nickajack Expedition, later stood on this site.
Location: West side of Harding Rd. near Richland Creek near Overbrook School
Note: Two of the four children were actually killed.

Julia McClung Green 1873-1961
Dedicated educator who served Davidson County public schools 57 years as a teacher, the first Supervisor of Elementary Education 1911-1944 and Director of Character Education, Miss Julia oversaw schools countywide. A progressive, she pioneered school hot lunch and health programs for children, local affiliation with national education organizations, and the local PTA movement.
Location: 3500 Hobbs Road

J. W. Price Fire Hall
Constructed in 1892 for Hose Company #1, this building is one of the earliest extant fire halls in Nashville. The upstairs housed firefighters while the lower floor stabled the company's two horses. R. C. Burk served as the first Captain. The fire hall was renamed for J.W. Price, a local businessman, c1910. In 1993, the building reopened as a branch of the Nashville Public Library, and is named for State Legislators Charles and Mary Pruitt.
Location: 117 Charles E. Davis Boulevard

Lake Providence Community
Soon after the Civil War, freed slave families established farms and dairies in this community named for Lake Providence Missionary Baptist Church. The church was founded in 1868 by Rev. Larry A. Thompson, a traveling missionary. The first church building and school stood nearby. Many roads in this area are named for African-American settlers.
Location: 4500 block Nolensville Road

Luke Lea Heights
Luke Lea (1879-1945) envisioned this park, gave to the city in 1927 the original 868 acres, and asked that the land be named for his father-in-law, Percy Warner. Founder of the Nashville Tennessean newspaper, Lea was a key developer of Belle Meade, a U.S. senator, organizer and colonel of the 114th Field Artillery, WWI. To honor him the Park Board named a high hill and overlook Lea Heights.
Location: Belle Meade Blvd. at Warner Park entrance

Lockeland Spring
Located 250 yards S.E., this famous pioneer spring served Lockeland mansion on site of present school building. Home built by Col. Robert Weakley in early 1800s and named for his wife, daughter of Gen. Matthew Locke of Salisbury, N.C. Spring water won prize at St. Louis Exposition in 1904, for its "unique mineral composition and salubrious quality."
Location: 100 South Seventeenth Street

Major Wilbur Fisk Foster 1834-1922
Chief Engr. Army of Tenn. C.S.A; Construction Engineer on first R.R. Bridge in Nashville; City Engineer of Nashville and member of American Society of Civil Engineers; Di-

rector of Works at the Tennessee Centennial Exposition, 1897, and Co-Founder of Foster & Creighton Co.; Elder, First Presbyterian Church; 33rd Degree Scottish Rite Mason.
Location: Centennial Park, by Lake Watauga

Mansker's First Fort
Here on west bank of the creek that he discovered in 1772, Kasper Mansker and other first settlers built a log fort in 1779. John Donelson's family fled here in 1780 for safety from Indians. Mansker abandoned the fort in 1781 and moved to Fort Nashborough. He returned in 1783, built a stronger stockade on east bank of the creek a half mile upstream, and lived there until he died in 1820.
Location: Goodlettsville, Long Hollow Pike before turning off to Moss-Wright Park

Marathon Motor Car
The Marathon motor car was manufactured here 1910-1914 by the Southern Motors Works (later called Marathon). Four models, all touring cars, were powered by engines of 4 cylinders, 30-35 hp and 6's of 50 hp, with wheelbases from 9'8" to 12'5". The plant closed operations in 1914 due to financial difficulties but continued a parts and service business until 1918.
Location: Twelfth Avenue North and Clinton Street

McConnell Field
In 1927 the City bought 131 acres from Warner Sloan and made this the Nashville airport, named for Lt. Brower McConnell, Tennessee National Guard pilot who died that year in an air crash. The hangars were 50 yards east. Aircraft outgrew the field in the 1930s and moved to Sky Harbor and Berry Field. The Park Board began the golf course in 1939.
Location: Trailhead of Richland Creek Greenway at entrance to McCabe Golf Course, Sloan St.

Mill Creek Baptist Church and Graveyard
Mill Creek Baptist Church, mother church of Southern Baptists in Davidson County, occupied two meeting houses at this site from 1797 until the early 20th century. Here, in 1833, Baptists formed the first Tennessee Baptist Convention. The church's graveyard includes the graves of many early settlers of both African and European descent.
Location: Glenrose Avenue at Dodge Drive

Mount Pisgah Community
In 1867, Jane Watson deeded land to several African-American families, many of them her former slaves. First called Watson Town, the community became known as Mt. Pisgah by 1871. The Methodist Episcopal Church North organized a church here in 1866 and bought an acre of land from William Holt in 1869 for a church and school building. The second church building, used 1916-1979, stood along the Owen & Winstead Pike, now Edmondson Pike. Donated by the Mt. Pisgah United Methodist Church.
Location: Edmundson Pike at Mt. Pisgah Road

Mrs. John Donelson
After Col. John Donelson was killed in 1785, his widow and family continued to live here in a log house. In 1789 lawyers Andrew Jackson and John Overton boarded with the Donelsons. Here Jackson met Rachel, the Donelson's youngest daughter. They married in 1791 and lived here until they acquired their own home across the Cumberland in 1792.
Location: Madison, Gallatin Road and Two Mile Pike

Mud Tavern
The Mud Tavern Community developed around the crossroads of the Elm Hill and McGavock Turnpikes. The name derives from the mud and log inn at the crossroads where early 19th century travelers found rest and refreshment. Mud Tavern later became a lively rural community, with a railway stop, schools, post office, and general store, which thrived until overtaken by 20th century commercial development.
Location: Elm Hill Pike at Briley Parkway

Nashville Centennial 1780-1880
The Centennial Exposition on this site in 1880 from April 23 through May 30 marked a century of progress since the founding of Nashville. There were parades, oratory, music; historical, art and commercial exhibits; theatrical performances, and "the grandest display of fireworks ever seen in Nashville."
Location: Broadway and Eighth Avenue South
[Note: According to the May 30 edition of the *Daily American*, the actual closing day of the Centennial Exposition was May 29, 1880.]

Nashville Fire Department
The city's first fire-fighting force of volunteers was formed in May 1807. The first paid Dept. was organized on July 29, 1860, with J. S. Dashiell as chief. Three horse-drawn steam engines were bought. A telegraph alarm system was installed in 1875. Chief A. A. Rozetta used the first auto Nov. 21, 1910. First gasoline-driven engines were used Sept. 1912.
Location: 506 Second Avenue North

Nashville General Hospital
Opened on this site February 1890, with a capacity of 60 beds. Doctor Charles Brower of the University of Nashville Medical Department was appointed Superintendent. In 1891, a school of nursing was opened with Miss Charlotte E. Perkins as Superintendent. This was the first

training school for nurses between the Ohio River and New Orleans.
Location: Hermitage Avenue
[Note: The city hospital opened its doors on April 23, 1890 and has since been demolished.]

Nashville Plow Works
Site of a farm implement factory operated by Messrs. Sharp and Hamilton, previous to the War Between the States. With the outbreak of hostilities they reversed the Biblical injunction and produced swords of excellent quality for the Confederacy. With the coming of the Federal Army, the making of swords was discontinued.
Location: Eighth Avenue South and Palmer Place

The Nashville Race Course
The Nashville Race Course, the "Burns Island Track," 1828-1843, was 0.6 of a mile north. Here Oct. 10, 1843, was run the then-richest race in the world, the $35,000 Peyton Stakes, 4-mile heats, promoted by Bailie Peyton. The winner, owned by Thomas Kirkman, was renamed "Peytona." Ten Broeck and Thora also raced here.
Location: Metro Center, Cumberland Bend and Great Circle Road

Nashville Sit-Ins
Formerly located at this site was First Baptist Church, Capitol Hill, headquarters of the 1960s Sit-In Movement, led by Rev. Kelly Miller Smith. Strategy sessions, non-violence workshops, mass meetings, victory celebrations, and administrative office were here. The well-disciplined Nashville sit-ins served as a model for civil rights demonstrations throughout the South.
Location: Eighth Avenue North and Charlotte Pike

Nashville's First Radio Station
June 1922, Boy Scout John H. DeWitt, Jr., started Nashville's first radio station (WDAA) on the Ward-Belmont Campus. Assisted by music teacher G.S. deLuca, he broadcast Enrico Caruso records to the opening of the River and Rail Terminal on the river at Broad Street. DeWitt was WSM radio station's chief engineer, 1932-1942, and president, 1947-1968.
Location: Belmont University, Freeman Hall

Neill S. Brown 1810-1886
Located 125 yards north is the site of Idlewild, home of Neill S. Brown, native of Giles County and fourteenth governor of Tennessee, 1848-1850. The only governor to live in East Nashville, he is credited with naming the city of Edgefield. Appointed United States Minister to Russia in 1850, and in 1870 was a member of the State Constitutional Convention.
Location: 809 Main Street

Newsom's Mill
The original Newsom's Mill was located upstream and was destroyed by flood in 1808. Joseph M. Newsom constructed this turbine-powered grist-mill in 1862 of hand-dressed limestone cut from Newsom's Quarry, a mile south. Newsom's stones are found in many important buildings in the city of Nashville.
Location: Highway 70 and Newsom's Station Rd. near the Cheatham Co. line

Oglesby Community House
Built 1898, the Mary Lee Academy, the second school in the Oglesby Community, was named for its first teacher, Miss Mary Lee Clark. The county bought the school in 1906. The name changed to Ogilvie in honor of the land donor, Benton H. Ogilvie, and later became Oglesby. In 1943, the schoolhouse was given back to the Oglesby Community.
Location: Old Hickory Boulevard and Edmondson Pike

Old Hickory Powder Plant
Site of the $87,000,000 Old Hickory Powder Plant built and operated in 1918 by the E. I. duPont deNemours Co., for the United States Government, to make smokeless gunpowder for the Allied Armies in World War I. By the time of the Armistice Nov. 11, 1918, the plant, 75% complete, was producing 750,000 lbs. of powder every 24 hours.
Location: Old Hickory, Swinging Bridge Road and Cinder Road

Old Hickory Triangle
This intersection, known as "The Triangle," served as the commercial core of Old Hickory from the 1920s through the 1940s. A variety of shops were located here, including a grocery, bank, general store, barber shop, restaurants, and doctors' offices, as well as the bus station and YMCA. The Public Works Administration built the Colonial Revival Post Office in 1934-35.
Location: Old Hickory Village Triangle

Parmer School
In 1927 8.25 acres of the Belle Meade Plantation were acquired from its owner Walter O. Parmer to use for a new school. Parmer School opened that fall as a one-room school with grades 1-3. In 1928 the school was transformed into a modern brick building with 4 classrooms adding grades 4-8. By 1951 there were 18 classrooms. The school closed in 1982 and burned in 1985. The stone and brick archway was left as a reminder of the school's history. The property became a public park in 1986.
Location: Parmer Park on Leake Avenue

Percy Warner Park - 2058.1 acres
Percy Warner (1861-1927) was a pioneer in electric utilities and hydroelectric development in the South. As

chairman of the Park Board, he expanded Nashville's park system. Preservation of this natural area was one of his greatest civic projects. Named in his honor by the Park Board in 1927, this land constitutes the largest municipal park in Tennessee.
Location: Belle Meade Boulevard at Warner Park entrance

Powder-Grinding Wheels

These wheels used by the Confederacy to grind gunpowder at Augusta, Ga., in 1863-1864 were made in Woolwich, England, and were shipped on the blockade runner "Spray" via Mobile. After the war, Gen. Miles purchased them for use at Sycamore Powder Mills, Cheatham County. They were exhibited at the Tennessee Centennial Exposition in 1897.
Location: Centennial Park, northeast corner in rear of park

Randall Jarrell, 1914-1965

Distinguished poet, critic, novelist, and teacher. Born in Nashville; Hume-Fogg graduate 1931; Vanderbilt bachelor's and master's degrees. Served in U.S. Army Air Corps in World War II. Wrote about losses of war and childhood innocence. Poet Laureate at Library of Congress, 1956-58. Winner of National Book Award for poetry, 1960.
Location: Hume-Fogg High School, 700 Broadway

RCA Studio B

RCA Records established a recording studio in this building in November 1957, with local offices run by guitarist-producer Chet Atkins. Its success led to a larger studio, known as Studio A, built next door in 1964. Studio B recorded numerous hits by Elvis Presley, the Everly Brothers, Roy Orbison, Don Gibson, Charley Pride, Jim Reeves, Dolly Parton, and many others. Along with Bradley Studios, Studio B is known for developing "The Nashville Sound." Donated by the Mike Curb Foundation.
Location: 1611 Roy Acuff Place on Music Row

St. Patrick Catholic Church

Erected in 1890 and named for Ireland's patron saint, this Second Empire style church was built to serve South Nashville's growing Irish Catholic population. Until 1954, the Sisters of Mercy taught a grade school here. Since the 1890s, the Irish Travelers, a unique clan of American nomads, have come here periodically for weddings and funerals.
Location: 1219 Second Avenue South

Saint Thomas Hospital

On April 11, 1898, at the request of Nashville Bishop Thomas Byrne, the Daughters of Charity opened Saint Thomas Hospital on this site in the former home of Judge J. M. Dickinson. Named for Byrne's patron saint, the hospital began as a 26-bed "refuge for the sick," opened a new building in 1902, operated a School of Nursing, and grew to 333 beds before moving in 1974 to 4220 Harding Road. Opposite side: Engraving of Saint Thomas Hospital.
Location: Hayes Street and 20th Avenue North

Samuel Watkins, 1794-1880

Brick manufacturer and builder, who at the age of 15 fought under Gen. Jackson in the Creek campaigns and at the Battle of New Orleans, left at his death in 1880 this site and $100,000 as an endowment for a school later called Watkins Institute. A pioneer school for adult education, it has been in continuous operation since 1885. [Note: Samuel Watkins' tombstone indicates that he was 88 years old when he died in October 16, 1880. He would have been 20 during the Creek campaigns of fall 1813. Although Watkins Institute was organized as early as 1885, classes did not begin until 1889.] (This is not the same Sam Watkins, Confederate Soldier of Company H.)
Location: 601 Church Street, wall marker

Scottsboro

In 1869, Tom Scott opened a general store 500 yards to the southwest on Old Hyde's Ferry Pike that also served as a post office and public gathering place. Scott's Store became the center of this farming community, which stretches north to Joelton and south to the tip of Bells Bend. The unincorporated crossroads community was called Scott's Store until 1902, when it was renamed Scottsboro.

Bells Bend (opposite side)

Bells Bend, first known as White's Bend, is an 18-square-mile area encompassed by a U-shaped bend in the Cumberland River. Numerous archaeological sites indicate that the area has been inhabited for at least 10,000 years. Bells Bend has thrived as an agricultural community since the early 19th century with land owners that included Montgomery Bell and David Lipscomb. The Clees family operated a mill and ferry service beginning in the 1870s. Clees Ferry ceased operation in 1990.
Location: Old Hickory Boulevard at Ashland City Highway

Site of First Store

Lardner Clark came from Philadelphia in the early 1780s with ten horses packed with piece goods, needles, and pins. He established Nashville's first drygoods store in 1786, on a site 30 yards east. The building, which served as store, tavern, and dwelling, faced south and was known as "the house with the piazza."
Location: 214 Second Avenue North, wall marker
Note: Davidson County records show Lardner Clark suing customers for unpaid bills as early as 1783.

Site of Original Gas Works

The Nashville Gas Light Co., founded March 1850, with General Washington Barrow, President, built first gas works in Tennessee for manufacturing gas from coal.

First street lamp was lighted Feb. 13, 1851, at Second Avenue, North, and Public Square. First gas stove was used in 1894. Natural gas piped from Texas was first used in Nashville on August 5, 1946.
Location: 800 Second Avenue North

Site of Waterworks Plant
The City's present waterworks was inaugurated at this site Oct. 1, 1833. The pumping station was erected on the lower river bluff and the reservoir on the upper grounds. German engineer, Albert Stein, designed and supervised construction. The system cost $55,000, the first bonded debt of the City. A new plant was in operation and this site was abandoned by April 1891.
Location: Hermitage Avenue

Sunnyside
Home of Mrs. Jesse Benton, widow of Jesse Benton who left Nashville after a feud with Andrew Jackson. Built in the 1840s, restored in the 1920s by Col. Granville Sevier. Two log cabins east of the house, reputed to have been built by the French for trade with the Chickasaw and Choctaw Indians, may be the oldest structures in Metropolitan Nashville.
Location: Granny White Pike and Kirkwood Avenue in Sevier Park
[Note: Deedbook research indicates that the house was built in the 1850s. Documentary and archaeological evidence supports a 19th-century date for the construction of the log cabins.]

Tanglewood Historic District
The Tanglewood Historic District is a rustic style suburban development from the 1920-1940s built by Robert M. Condra, a prominent Nashville builder. Natural materials are featured in this popular Arts and Crafts substyle that harmonizes with the landscape. Tanglewood is located at the site of a late 1700s settlement known as Haysborough.
Location: Madison, 4908 Tanglewood Drive North

Temple Cemetery
The Temple Cemetery was established in 1851 with the purchase of three acres by the Hebrew Benevolent Burial Association and still serves Nashville's first Jewish congregation, The Temple, Congregation Ohabai Sholom. It blends early urban burial ground practices with picturesque elements of later Victorian garden cemeteries. The Temple Cemetery was listed in the National Register of Historic Places in 2004.
Location: 2001 15th Avenue North

Tennessee Ornithological Society
On October 7, 1915, Dr. George Curtis, Albert F. Ganier, Judge H.Y. Hughes, Dr. George R. Mayfield, Dixon Merritt, and A.C. Webb met at Faucon's Restaurant, 419 Union Street, approximately 25 feet east of here, to found the Tennessee Ornithological Society. T.O.S. was chartered by the state for the purpose of studying Tennessee birds. A journal, The Migrant, publishes accurate records of birds across the state. The Birds of the Nashville Area has local records. T.O.S. is the state's oldest conservation group in continuing existence. Donated in memory of B.B. Coffey (1870-1966).
Location: Union Street and Fifth Avenue North, wall marker

The Seeing Eye, Independence and Dignity Since 1929
The Seeing Eye, the world-famous dog guide training school, was incorporated in Nashville January 29, 1929, with headquarters in the Fourth and First National Bank Building at 315 Union St. Morris Frank, a 20-year-old blind man from Nashville, and his guide dog, Buddy, played a key role in the school's founding and subsequent success. It was Frank who persuaded Dorothy Harrison Eustis to establish a school in the United States.
Location: Commerce Street at 3rd Avenue North

Timothy Demonbreun
Jacques-Timothe De Montbrun, born on Mar. 23, 1747, in Boucherville, Quebec, was the first white man to live in the Nashville area. Beginning in 1769, he spent several winters here trading for furs. He served as Lieut. Gov. of Illinois Country, 1783-86. He became permanent resident of Nashville in 1790, operating store and tavern. Died at home on this site, Oct. 30, 1826.
Location: Broadway and Third Avenue, North, wall marker

Tolbert Fanning, 1810-1874
In 1844, noted educator, evangelist, and agriculturalist Tolbert Fanning started Franklin College, a liberal arts school near this site where boys farmed to cover tuition. In 1855 he co-founded the Gospel Advocate, a religious journal. Fanning's wife, Charlotte Fall, began Fanning Orphan School for girls here in 1884. Their aim was to put education within the "reach of every youth."
Location: Briley Parkway and Vultee Boulevard

Tolbert Hollow
George Tolbert, a farmer, bought 97½ acres here in 1897 that became known as Tolbert Hollow. He was a former slave who, according to family tradition, purchased his own freedom. Tolbert worked 45 acres by 1880 and cut and sold wood with his sons. Land ownership signified true freedom for blacks after the Civil War. Generations of Tolbert's descendants continued to live on his land.
Location: 576 Old Hickory Boulevard

Transfer Station Site
Site of electric street railway transfer station 1902-1940. Electric streetcar service began formally on April 30,

1889, replacing mule-drawn streetcars which had served the city since 1866. Final run for electric streetcars was Feb. 2, 1941, on Radnor line. Operation of bus system began Aug. 4, 1940, on Hillsboro-Sunset line.
Location: Third Avenue North and Deaderick

Two Rivers Mansion
Built in 1859 by David H. McGavock, this mansion stands on land inherited by McGavock's wife, Willie, from her father William Harding. The smaller house to the left was built in 1802. Dr. James Priestley's Academy, established about 1816, was located on the 1,100-acre farm one mile from the mansion on the Cumberland River Bluff.
Location: Donelson, 3130 McGavock Pike

Una Community
The Una community developed around the crossroads of Smith Springs Road and Old Murfreesboro Pike in the early 19th century. The local postmaster changed the community name from Rowesdale, or Rosedale, to Una in 1882, honoring a Peabody college student much loved by local residents. Home to schools, churches, a general store, and a service station, this bustling tightly-knit rural community was supplanted by suburban development by the end of the 20th century.
Sponsored by Metro Council member Vivian Wilhoite
Location: Smith Springs Road and Old Murfreesboro Road

Union Station
Erected by Louisville and Nashville Terminal Company and dedicated Oct. 9, 1900, the Romanesque style building of Bowling Green limestone and Tennessee marble was designed by L&N Chief Engineer Richard Montfort. A monument to the grand days of rail travel, the beloved station was renovated in 1986 into an elegant hotel by Union Station, Ltd.
Location: 1001 Broadway

United Nations Visit to Nashville
On June 7, 1976, 101 permanent representatives of the United Nations made a historic and unprecedented group visit to Nashville at the invitation of Tennessee Governor Ray Blanton and Nashville Mayor Richard Fulton. During the visit, the United Nations representatives attended a forum at nearby Vanderbilt University, a special Tennessee luncheon in Centennial Park, and a special performance of the Grand Ole Opry. United Nations Secretary-General Kurt Waldheim was presented the Cordell Hull Peace Award by the State of Tennessee and Vanderbilt University during the visit.
Location: Centennial Park near Parthenon

Vauxhall Garden Site
Located immediately south, this fashionable place of entertainment was established by Messrs. Decker & Dryer in 1827 and operated for more than a decade. It covered several acres and included a ballroom, dining hall and miniature railroad. Pres. Jackson was honored here on several occasions. John Bell made his famous "Vauxhall Garden Speech" here May 23, 1835.
Location: Demonbreun Street and Ninth Avenue South

Vine Street Temple
Nashville's Jewish community began in the 1840s. Many early families were immigrants fleeing oppression in Germany, Russia, and Poland. Completed in 1876, the Vine Street Temple, with nine Byzantine domes was Nashville's first synagogue, for 80 years a symbol of the city's strong Jewish presence. In 1955, the Reform congregation moved to West Nashville where it and other Jewish congregations continue today.
Location: Commerce St. and Seventh Ave., North

Votes for Women
On August 18, 1920, Tennessee became the 36th state to ratify the 19th Amendment to the U.S. Constitution, thereby giving all American women the right to vote. After weeks of intense lobbying by national leaders, Tennessee passed the measure by one vote. The headquarters for both suffragists, wearing yellow roses, and anti-suffragists, wearing red roses, were in the Hermitage Hotel.
Location: Union Street and Capitol Boulevard

Watkins Park
Land once known as Watkins Grove was given to the city in 1870 by brick maker and contractor Samuel Watkins. It served as a site for political gatherings, school commencements and concerts. This became Nashville's first public park in 1901. Park Board chairman E.C. Lewis planned landscape features including a stone entrance and fence, walkways, flowerbeds, and benches, which were built with materials donated by citizens. In 1906, the Centennial Club opened the city's first playground here, setting a precedent for public recreation facilities elsewhere in the city. Improved by the Works Progress Administration in the 1930s, Watkins Park was a park for black Nashvillians from 1936 until the 1960s, when the park system was desegregated.
Location: 616 17th Avenue North

Waverly Place
On the high ground about 100 yards east stood Waverly, home of A.W. Putman, writer and authority on pioneer James Robertson. Hence the name "Waverly Place" which resulted from a syndicate promotion in the 1880s by J. F. Yarbrough, H. W. Grantland, W. M. Morrison, John White, Baxter Smith, C. L. Ridley, Percy Warner, J. C. Warner and J. F. Wheless.
Location: Eighth Avenue South and Benton Avenue

"Western Harmony"

Music publishing in Nashville began in 1824 when "The Western Harmony" was published by Allen D. Carden and Samuel J. Rogers. A book of hymns and instruction for singing, it was printed by Carey A. Harris on the press of his newspaper, the Nashville Republican, on College Street (now Third Avenue) in this vicinity.
Location: Third Avenue North and James Robertson Parkway

West End High School

One of Nashville's best examples of Colonial Revival style, this building was designed by Donald Southgate and opened in 1937. Public Works Administration funds supported its construction during a major city school building project of the 1930s. Principals William H. Yarbrough (1937-54) and John A. Oliver (1955-68) built a reputation for academic and athletic excellence. It became a middle school in 1968.
Donated by the West End High School Alumni Association, Inc.
Location: West End Middle School, Elmington Park, 3529 West End Ave.

William Gerst Brewing Company

The Nashville Brewery opened here in 1859 operating under several names and owners until William Gerst acquired it in 1893. Gerst brewed some of the South's finest ales and lagers until Prohibition, when sodas and malt beverages were bottled. William Gerst died in 1933, the year prohibition ended, and his four sons resumed operations using the popular "Brewed in Dixie" slogan. Gerst Brewery closed in 1954 due to national competition.
Location: Sixth Avenue South and Mulberry

William Walker

Born May 8, 1824, Walker moved to this site from 6th Ave. N. in 1840. In early life he was doctor, lawyer, and journalist. He invaded Mexico in 1853 with 46 men and proclaimed himself Pres., Republic of Lower California. Led force into Nicaragua in 1855; was elected its Pres. in 1856. In attempt to wage war on Honduras was captured and executed Sept. 13, 1860.
Location: Fourth Avenue, North and Commerce Street

Woodbine

An early settler of this area was James Menees, at whose home Mill Creek Baptist Church was formed in 1797. James Whitsitt, first pastor, served over 50 years. Earlier known as Flat Rock, in 1939 this place was renamed Woodbine, after the David Hughes Estates once located on Nolensville Road. In 1919 the L&N Railroad began operation of Radnor Yards.
Location: Nolensville Road and Whitsitt Avenue

Woodmont Estates

Created in 1937 from the G. A. Puryear farm. It was once part of Samuel Watkin's country estate. Olmsted Bros. Landscape Architects designed the roads and lots to flow naturally with the hills, valleys, and brook. Residential development was made possible by the 1915 construction of a concrete road. Known by 1918 as the first documented concrete road in Tennessee.
Location: West Valley Brook and Bear Road

Historical Markers
Tennessee Historical Commission

3 A 10
Buchanan's Station
One of Cumberland settlements, established here in 1780. The fort was attacked Sept. 30, 1792, by about 300 Creeks and Lower Cherokees under Chiachattalla. Aided by the heroism and efficiency of Mrs. Buchanan and other women in the stockade the attack was repulsed and Chiachattalla was killed.
Location: U.S. 70S, turn north at Spence Lane, at dead end go east 1 mile

3 A 81
Hunter's Hill
On Cumberland River, two miles north, was Andrew Jackson's plantation, Hunter's Hill, which he bought in 1796 and where he lived until 1804 when he sold it to Colonel Edward Ward and removed to the adjoining tract to which he gave the name of the Hermitage. The Hunter's Hill house was destroyed by fire in 1903.
Location: U.S. 70N, at Lebanon and Shute roads

3 A 168
New Hope Baptist Church
Organized in 1846 by Elders Peter and Thomas Fuqua, New Hope Baptist Church is one of the oldest churches in the Nashville Baptist Association. In 1847, one mile south of here, a log church edifice was erected. It was destroyed by fire in 1871. This present building was built in 1872 on a site donated by W.E. Hagar and J.T. Gleaves. Bricks were handmade on the premises for the solid walls. The Rev. G.W. Hagar, the longest-serving pastor (1861-79), is recognized for his efforts in rebuilding the church. He is buried in the church cemetery.
Location: Hermitage, 6010 New Hope Road

3 A 13
The Hermitage
Home of Andrew Jackson (1767-1845), Major General in the Army, hero of the Battle of New Orleans, and seventh President of the United States. It was originally built in 1819; partially burned in 1834, during Jackson's second term, replaced by the present building in 1835. He died here and is buried in the garden.
Location: TN45, Old Hickory Boulevard, at Hermitage exit

3 A 11
Tulip Grove
Designed by Jos. Reiff, who was also the builder of the Hermitage. This house was built in 1836 for Andrew J. Donelson, Jackson's namesake and secretary. A West Point graduate, Donelson was at one time minister to Prussia, and held other offices. In 1856 he was a candidate for vice-president on ticket with Millard Fillmore.
Location: U. S. 70N, Lebanon Road

3 A 54
Confederate Cemetery
Most of the 483 Confederate soldiers buried here were veterans who died while in the Confederate Soldiers' Home which stood about 1 mile north of here. Also buried here is Ralph Ledbetter, former slave and bodyguard to a Confederate officer during the war.
Location: U.S. 70N, Lebanon Road, west of cemetery gate

3 A 16
Clover Bottom
In 1780, the Gower party, tending Middle Tennessee's first cotton crop, were killed or captured by Indians. On nearby Stone's River some flatboats were built for Aaron Burr's abortive expedition. The famous match races between Andrew Jackson's "Truxton" and Capt. Jos. Erwin's "Plowboy" were run on racetrack in river bottom, 1805-06.
Location: U.S. 70N, west of Stone's River

3 A 115
Sherrod Bryant
With a certificate of freedom praising his industry and morality, Sherrod Bryant (1781-1854) moved here from Granville County, N.C., before 1840. A farmer, he was probably the wealthiest free Black in Tennessee by 1850, owning land and slaves worth $25,000. An area nearby became known as Bryant Grove. He is buried in Bryant Town Cemetery, Donelson, Tenn.
Location: Couchville Pike, west of Rutherford County line

3 A 32
Demonbreun's Cave
Jacques-Timothe De Montbrun, French Canadian fur trader and later lieutenant governor of the Illinois Country, visited in this area as early as 1769. On at least one occasion he took refuge in the cave [upstream from here] when attacked by Indians. He settled in Nashville in 1790, living there until his death in 1826.
Location: Riverfront Park, 1st Avenue

3 A 95
Belmont Domestic Academy

On the present site of Two Rivers High School, Belmont Domestic Academy, a girl's boarding school, was founded in 1815. It was conducted by Mr. and Mrs. John J. Abercrombie in a large frame house formerly the residence of David Buchanan. Among the young ladies who attended the school after it moved to Nashville in 1817 was Sarah Childress, who became the wife of James K. Polk.
Location: Two Rivers High School

3 A 105
Hill McAlister
1875-1959

A native of Nashville, Hill McAlister was elected City Attorney in 1905. In 1911 he was elected to the State Senate where he supported legislation in areas of health, education, and labor. He later served five terms as State Treasurer and two terms as Governor, 1933-37. Governor McAlister died in Nashville.
Location: Ben Allen Road, at entrance to State Office Building

3 A 145
The Harris Music Building

This Italianate structure was built ca. 1876 as the home of Richard Harris, an entrepreneur and owner of Harris Furniture Co. In the late 1880s, he became the first Black trustee of Fisk University. W.G. Waterman, a Fisk professor, became owner of the house, and in 1909 he conveyed ownership to Fisk. In 1927, the building became the Music Annex. In 1991, the Music Annex was rededicated as the Harris Music Building.
Location: 17th Avenue North and Phillips Street

3 A 164
Engine Company No. 11

Organized January 15, 1885, Nashville's first African-American fire unit, Engine Company No. 4, was located at 424 Woodland St. On January 2, 1892, Capt. C.C. Gowdy, hoseman Harvey Ewing, and reel driver Stokely Allen were killed while battling a fire which destroyed a full city block in the business district, along 3rd Avenue North. Funeral services for the fallen firefighters were held in the State Capitol building on January 6, 1892. In 1923, Engine Co. 4 moved to North Nashville and became Engine Co. 11. In 1966, Engine Co. 11 moved to its present location.
Location: 1745 18th Avenue North

3 A 125
William Edmondson
(c. 1883-1951)

Born c. 1883, William Edmondson, a native Nashvillian and renowned primitive sculptor, worked exclusively in limestone. In 1937, he became the first African American to be given a one-man show by the Museum of Modern Art in New York City. His visions in stone are now held in major museums throughout America. In June of 1981, for the opening of its new facilities, the Tennessee State Museum honored him with a 125-piece exhibition.
Location: 17th Avenue North and Charlotte, William Edmondson Park

3 A 143
Richardson House

This house, listed in the National Register of Historic Places, was built in 1905 as the home of Reuben B. and Mary Knowles Richardson. Richardson, who served as Capt. of Eng. Co. No. 4 from 1893 to 1923, was one of the first Blacks to obtain this rank in Nashville. In 1923, Eng. Co. No. 4 moved from Woodland St. to 12th Ave. No. and Jefferson St., and became Eng. Co. No. 11. In 1930, the name of the building housing that company was changed to Reuben B. Richardson Hall.
Location: 1017 16th Avenue South

3 A 129
Greenwood Park

At this location in 1905, Preston Taylor, a Nashville businessman, religious leader, and former slave, established the first park to serve Nashville's Negro community. Greenwood Recreational Park included a ball park, swimming pool, amusements, and picnic facilities. The park served as the site of the Negro state fair and Boy Scout summer camp. Greenwood preceded the city's public park for Blacks by 7 years and remained open until 1949.
Location: Spence Lane between Elm Hill Pike and Lebanon Road

3 A 144
Confederate Circle at Mount Olivet

After the War Between the States, the women of Nashville bought land at Mount Olivet, and formed Confederate Circle. The remains of about 1,500 Confederate soldiers were moved here from area battlefields. Seven Confederate generals were buried in or around the circle. They are William B. Bate, William N.R. Bealle, Benjamin Franklin Cheatham, William H. Jackson, George E. Maney, James E. Rains, and Thomas Benton Smith. Other prominent Nashville Confederates, Colonels Adolphus Heiman and Randall McGavock, lie nearby. A 45-foot granite monument marks the center of the circle.
Location: 1101 Lebanon Road

3 A 80
The Children's Museum

One of the largest Children's Museums in the country, with exhibits of North American animals, birds, flowers, minerals, fossils and local history. A Planetarium, Art Gallery, live animals and other exhibits feature the ever-changing world around us.
Location: Lafayette Street and 2nd Avenue South

3 A 132
Nashville Blacks in the Civil War
From October-December 1862, on this hill, Black laborers helped the Union Army build Fort Negley. In November, Blacks helped defend the unfinished fort against Confederate attack. During the Battle of Nashville (December 1864), nearly 13,000 Black soldiers aided in the defeat of the Confederates. By 1865, Blacks had assisted the Union Army in building 23 fortifications around Nashville.
Location: Fort Negley Boulevard

3 A 57
Albert Gleaves
Born here Jan. 1, 1858, a graduate of the Naval Academy in 1879, he commanded the USS Cushing in the War with Spain. In 1917 took command of the Cruiser and Transport Force, U.S. Navy, which convoyed Allied troops to France without the loss of a man. In 1919 was commander-in-chief, Asiatic Fleet. He held the Distinguished Service Medal, Japanese Order of Sacred Treasure, 1st Class, Chinese Order of Weng Hu, 1st Class, and French Legion of Honor. He died Jan. 6, 1937.
Location: 9th Avenue South and McGavock

3 A 106
William Carroll
1788-1844
A native of Pennsylvania, William Carroll moved to Nashville in 1810. He became a successful merchant and hero of the War of 1812. William Carroll served longer as Governor, 12 years, than anyone else in the history of the state. Under his leadership the Legislature passed laws in areas of criminal justice, fiscal policy, and education. Tennessee's "Business Governor" died in Nashville.
Location: Old City Cemetery, 4th Avenue South

3 A 35
City Cemetery
First established in 1822, the remains of many early settlers were brought here for permanent burial. Among the more than 20,000 persons buried here are Gen. James Robertson, Gov. William Carroll, Sec. of Treasury George W. Campbell, Lt. Gen. Richard S. Ewell, Brig. Gen. Felix K. Zollicoffer and Capt. William Driver.
Location: 4th Avenue South at Oak Street

3 A 109
Governors' Mansion
A residence built on this site in 1910 served as the residence of the governors of Tennessee from 1921 until 1949, when a residence on Curtiswood Lane was acquired by the state. Governors who lived here were Alfred Taylor, Austin Peay, Henry Horton, Hill McAlister, Gordon Browning, Prentice Cooper, and Jim McCord. The building was used as offices before being razed in June 1979.
Location: U.S. 70, West End Avenue, west of Vanderbilt Plaza Hotel

3 A 108
Anne Dallas Dudley
1876-1955
Anne Dudley played a significant role in the ratification of the Nineteenth Amendment by the State of Tennessee. A native of Nashville, she served as president of the Nashville Equal Suffrage League, 1911-15; president of the Tennessee Equal Suffrage Association, Incorporated, 1915-17; and as vice president of the National American Woman Suffrage Association, 1917. May 1, 1916, Anne Dudley walked from downtown Nashville to Centennial Park to demonstrate her support for the right of women to vote.
Location: U.S. 70, West End Avenue in front of the Parthenon in Centennial Park

3 A 36
Cockrill Spring
The house of John Cockrill, an early settler, stood about 60 yards north, near a large spring, whose waters ran northeast into Lick Branch, which emptied Great Salt Lick, around which Nashville was founded. A blacksmith shop stood under the great oak tree nearby. The spring was a stopping place for travelers along Natchez Trace.
Location: West End Avenue, Centennial Park

3 A 93
The Parthenon
Erected as the central structure of the Tennessee Centennial Exposition, 1897, this is the only full-scale reproduction of the fifth century B.C. Athenian temple and is exact in almost every detail to the original. The idea of reproducing this magnificent building was conceived by Major E. C. Lewis, Director General of the Exposition. The building served as a gallery of fine arts during the commemoration.
Location: West End Avenue, Centennial Park

3 A 37
Cunningham House
The house which formerly stood here was headquarters for a succession of commanders following occupation of Nashville by Federal forces in 1862. These included Major Generals Don Carlos Buell, William S. Rosecrans, Ulysses S. Grant and George H. Thomas. Chief of Staff to Rosecrans was Brig. Gen. James A. Garfield.
Location: 221 6th Avenue North

3 A 33
Fort Nashborough
The original stockade fronted on the river slightly north of here, covering an area of about two acres. In that enclosure, May 13, 1780, representatives of this and other settlements met and adopted the Cumberland Compact for government of the new settlement. About 500 yards

west, Apr. 2, 1781, settlers, assisted by dogs, drove off the Indians in the Battle of the Bluffs.
Location: First Avenue North

3 A 42
Freeland's Station

On this site stood one of the principal stations of the Cumberland Settlements. Felix Robertson, son of Col. James Robertson and the first white child born in the Settlement, was born here, Jan. 11, 1781. On Jan. 15 the fort was heavily attacked by Indians, who were repulsed and driven westward.
Location: 1400 8th Avenue North

3 A 31
Great French Lick

In 1710, a French trader from New Orleans had a trading post near the salt and sulphur spring which attracted game of all kinds. His successor was Charles Charleville, who died here in 1780, aged 84. The spring was about 300 yards southwest; the trading post was on this spot.
Location: Jefferson Street, 5th Avenue North

3 A 94
Sulphur Dell

Nashville's first (1885) and last (1963) professional baseball was played in the Athletic Park which formerly occupied this block. Traditionally baseball was introduced in Nashville in 1862 by soldiers of the Union army of occupation who played the game here. This low-lying area, originally called Sulphur Spring Bottom, was first called "Sulphur Dell" by local sports writer, Grantland Rice. In 1963 this was the oldest playing grounds still in use in professional baseball.
Location: 4th Ave. North east of state park

3 A 96
Fisk University

Fisk University, founded in 1866 by the American Missionary Association, was chartered in 1867 to provide higher education for men and women regardless of race. Named for General Clinton B. Fisk, assistant commissioner of the Freedman's Bureau for Kentucky and Tennessee, it was originally housed in army barracks. The first permanent building, Jubilee Hall, was completed in 1876, and built with funds raised in American and European concert tours by the Fisk Jubilee Singers.
Location: 1000 17th Avenue North

3 A 119
Fisk Memorial Chapel

Fisk Memorial Chapel, designed by New York architect William Bigelow, was erected in 1892 in memory of General Clinton B. Fisk, a founder of the University. The religious and cultural center of the campus, the Chapel has welcomed foreign dignitaries, outstanding concert artists, and renowned lecturers, such as Booker T. Washington and Dr. Martin Luther King, Jr.
Location: 1000 17th Avenue North

3 A 136
Carl Van Vechten Art Gallery

This building, completed in 1889, was the first gymnasium built at any predominantly Black college in the United States. In 1949, it was rededicated as an art gallery and named in honor of Carl Van Vechten, a New York music critic, author, photographer, and art collector who encouraged Georgia O'Keefe to donate to Fisk University part of the art collection of her late husband, Alfred Stieglitz.
Location: Fisk University, 1000 17th Avenue North

4 D 41
Samuel Allen McElwee
1858-1914

Born a slave in Madison County, Samuel McElwee began teaching school in Haywood County at the age of 16. In 1882, he was elected to the Tennessee House of Representatives and one year later was graduated from Fisk University. The only African American elected from Haywood County, Samuel McElwee served three successive terms in the legislature, promoting uniform education and justice. In 1884 and 1888, he was a delegate to the Republican National Convention. McElwee moved to Nashville in 1888 after he was defeated for re-election by force of arms.
Location: Jackson Street and 17th Avenue North

3 A 120
Jubilee Hall

Erected in 1876, Jubilee Hall was the first permanent structure built on the Fisk University campus. Named for Fisk's world-famous Jubilee Singers, this Victorian Gothic structure is sometimes called "frozen music." Jubilee Hall is a National Historic Landmark and a memorial to the spirituals and the singers who sang them.
Location: 1000 17th Avenue North

3 A 121
The Little Theatre

The Little Theatre, circa 1860, is the oldest structure on the Fisk University campus. Erected as part of a Union Army hospital barracks during the Civil War, it was known as the "Railroad Hospital." The interior was remodeled for use as the Fisk campus theater in 1935.
Location: 1000 17th Avenue North

3 A 122
Academic Building at Fisk University

The Academic Building at Fisk University was designed

by Nashville architect Moses McKissack and was made possible by a gift from philanthropist Andrew Carnegie. On May 22, 1908, William H. Taft, later 27th President of the United States, laid the cornerstone. This building served as the first library at Fisk.
Location: 1000 17th Avenue North

3 A 137
Thomas W. Talley

Recognized during his lifetime primarily as a chemist, teacher, and administrator at Fisk University, Thomas W. Talley (1870-1952) was also Tennessee's first African-American folklorist. A native of Bedford County, he began collecting folk songs about 1900, and published many of them in Negro Folk Rhymes in 1922. Later, he compiled the state's first collection of Black folk tales, Negro Traditions. Talley was also a skilled singer and composer.
Location: Fisk University, 1000 17th Ave. North

3 A 155
Talley-Brady Hall

Talley-Brady Hall was named for well-known African-American chemists Thomas Talley and Saint Elmo Brady, both graduates of Fisk University. Talley was chairman of the chemistry department from 1902 to 1927. In 1916 Saint Elmo Brady was one of the first African Americans to receive a Ph.D. degree in chemistry. An internationally recognized authority in the field of alkaloids, Brady was chairman of the chemistry dept. from 1927 to 1952.
Location: 1016 D.B. Todd Boulevard

3 A 141
James Weldon Johnson Home

This Dutch Colonial house was built in 1931 for James Weldon Johnson. He served as U.S. Consul to Venezuela and Nicaragua, editor of the New York Age, and field secretary of the NAACP. Johnson's poem, "Lift Every Voice and Sing," set to music by his brother, J. Rosamond Johnson, is renowned as the Negro National Anthem. Johnson occupied the Adam K. Spence Chair of Creative Literature and taught creative writing at Fisk University from 1931 until his death in 1938.
Location: D.B. Todd Boulevard and Hermosa Avenue

3 A 153
Arna Wendell Bontemps
1902-1973

At this site lived Arna W. Bontemps, one of the most prolific contributors to the Harlem or Negro Renaissance. From 1943 to 1965, Bontemps, an award-winning poet, playwright, novelist, biographer, historian, editor, and author of children's books, was head librarian of Fisk University. During his tenure, the Fisk University Library became a rich repository for the study of African-American culture and history.
Location: 919 D.B. Todd Boulevard

3 A 159
The John Wesley Work Home

In 1937 this Victorian-style house became the home of John W. Work III. A teacher and composer for 39 years, he served his alma mater by enriching the Fisk musical traditions. Director of the Jubilee Singers, Work III, a serious composer, completed more than 100 compositions. He was not only an acclaimed composer and choral conductor, but also a recognized author, educator, and ethnomusicologist. His father, John W. Work II, composer of the Fisk alma mater, "The Gold and Blue," was known as the rescuer and preservationist of Negro religious music. Work II's book, Folk Songs of the American Negro, was one of the first extensive studies on the origin and development of religious African-American music by a descendant of an ex-slave who lived during the time many of the songs had their beginnings.
Location: 17th Avenue North and Meharry Boulevard

3 A 154
Cravath Hall

This neo-Gothic structure first served as the Erastus M. Cravath Memorial Library. Named for Cravath, the university's first president (1875-1900), it was designed by Nashville architect Henry Hibbs and built in 1929-30. The interior walls depict several murals by Aaron Douglas, the leading Harlem or Negro Renaissance painter and founder of the Fisk Art Department.
Location: 1015 17th Avenue North

3 A 142
Ella Sheppard (Moore), 1851-1914

Ella Sheppard, an original Fisk Jubilee Singer, lecturer and teacher, was born on February 4, 1851. She entered Fisk in 1868, and was selected to join the group of nine singers that set out on October 6, 1871 to raise funds to save the school. She also served as pianist and assistant director for this group which introduced spirituals to the world. After seven years, the Singers had raised $150,000 and brought the cause of Black education to the attention of millions. Her home stood on this site.
Location: 17th Avenue and Jackson Street

3 A 133
Zephaniah Alexander Looby, 1899-1972

Z. Alexander Looby, attorney, statewide civil rights leader, and a founder of the Kent College of Law, Nashville's first law school for Blacks since the 1890s, is credited with desegregating the city's airport dining room and public golf courses. In 1951, he and Robert E. Lillard were the first Blacks elected to the city council since 1911. A member of the Metro Charter Commission, Looby retired in 1971 after having served under both forms of government.
Location: Metro Center Boulevard, Z. Alexander Looby Library and Community Center

3 A 157
Desegregating Nashville's Lunch Counters
After the predawn bombing of attorney Z. Alexander Looby's home, approximately 3000 civil rights leaders and students from Tennessee State, Fisk, Meharry, American Baptist College, and Pearl High School marched along this route on April 19, 1960, to meet with Mayor Ben West at the courthouse. In response to Diane Nash, a leader of the student sit-ins, the mayor recommended that store owners end segregated lunch counters. On May 10th, under an agreement between Black leaders and city merchants, Nashville became the first major southern city, outside of Texas, to begin desegregating its public facilities.
Location: D.B. Todd Boulevard and Jefferson Street

3 A 158
TSU's Reserve Officers' Training Corps
Established in April 1919, the Reserve Officers' Corps at Tennessee State University (then Tennessee Agricultural and Industrial State Normal School) was one of the first ROTC units at an African-American college. Under First Lieutenant Grant Stuart, emphasis was placed on military science and preparing African-American officers as leaders.
Location: John Merritt Boulevard and 33rd Avenue North

3 A 156
Frankie J. Pierce
Frankie J. Pierce was born during or shortly after the Civil War. In 1921, she founded the Tennessee Vocational School for Colored Girls and served as its first superintendent until 1939. The founding of this school was aided by the Negro Women's Reconstruction Service League and the City Federation of Colored Women's Clubs which she organized. Prior to the modern civil rights movement, Pierce led her club members in a march on city hall in protest of the city's segregated public facilities. Frankie J. Pierce died in 1954.
Location: 2700 Herman Street

3 A 124
Tennessee State University
Established in 1912 for the education of Negro citizens, Tennessee State University merged with UT-Nashville in 1979 and has become a major comprehensive urban university. Development from normal school to university progressed as follows: TN A&I State Normal School (1912-1922); TN A&I State Normal College (1922-1927); TN A&I State College (1927-1951); TN A&I State University (1951-1969); Tennessee State University, beginning in 1970.
Location: 2904 John Merritt Boulevard

3 A 113
Alpha Kappa Mu Honor Society
Founded at Tennessee A&I State College, November 26, 1937, to give more recognition to talented Negro scholars. The first meeting was called by Dr. George W. Gore, Jr., Dean and sponsor of the local honor society. AKM now has 76 chapters nationally and has held membership in the Association of College Honor Societies since 1952.
Location: Tennessee State University, 3500 John Merritt Blvd.

3 A 147
Pearl High School
Named for Joshua F. Pearl, the city's first superintendent of schools, Pearl was established in 1883 as a grammar school for Negroes and was located on old South Summer Street. It became a high school in 1897 when grades 9 thru 11 were transferred from Meigs School. In 1917, the 12th grade was added and Pearl moved to 16th Ave. No. and Grant Street. In 1936, the school moved to this location. In 1966, the first year that the TSSAA was fully desegregated, Pearl's boys' basketball team won the state championship. Considered one of the leading Black academic high schools in America, Pearl was closed in 1983, as a result of court-imposed busing. In 1986, this facility became the site of the Martin Luther King Magnet High School for Health Sciences and Engineering.
Location: 17th Avenue North and Jo Johnston

3 A 123
Hubbard House
Built about 1921 from donations of Meharry Medical College alumni and trustees, Hubbard House served as the retirement home of Dr. George W. Hubbard, a founder and head of Meharry for 44 years. Listed on the National Register of Historic Places due to its architecture and its link to Dr. Hubbard, this building is the last remnant of the original Meharry campus.
Location: 1109 First Avenue South

3 A 152
Hulda Margaret Lyttle (1889-1983)
In 1913, Hulda M. Lyttle was one of three graduates in the first nursing education class of Meharry's G.W. Hubbard Hospital. In 1916, Lyttle returned to Meharry as Director of Nurse Training. Between 1921 and 1938, she served as superintendent of the hospital and of nurses, and director of the nursing school. In May 1938, Lyttle was appointed dean of Meharry's School of Nursing, the medical school's first African-American female dean of an academic division and one of the first African-American deans of nursing in the United States.
Location: Hulda Lyttle Hall, Meharry Medical College, D.B. Todd Blvd.

3 A 151
Hadley Park
In 1912, Nashville officials purchased 34 acres of land to provide a public park for Negro citizens. Originally a part of the John L. Hadley plantation, Hadley Park was dedicated on July 4th. It is considered the first public park in the United States for African Americans. Named for either the pioneer African-American physician Dr. W.A. Hadley or John L. Hadley, supporter of freedmen after the Civil War, Hadley Park continues as a benchmark in the community's cultural heritage.
Location: 28th Avenue North

3 A 126
Immaculate Mother Academy
In 1904, a Philadelphia nun and heiress, Mother Mary Katherine Drexel, purchased this site for Immaculate Mother Academy, which included a primary school and the first Catholic secondary school for Black students in Tennessee. Holy Family Catholic Church was moved here in 1919, and the primary school was renamed for it. Immaculate Mother became a fully accredited high school in 1940. Until their closing in 1954, the schools were staffed by the Sisters of the Blessed Sacrament of Bensalem, PA.
Location: 7th Avenue South and Drexel Street

3 A 26
James K. Polk
The house which stood about 100 feet west was built in 1815 by Felix Grundy. James K. Polk bought it while President in 1847. He came home to it on expiration of his term of office and died here, June 15, 1849. His widow occupied it until her death in 1891. It was later owned by Jacob McGavock Dickinson, Secretary of War, 1909-1911, and a descendant of Grundy.
Location: 211 7th Avenue North

3 A 77
Maxwell House Hotel
On this site stood the Maxwell House Hotel built by John Overton in 1859. It was destroyed by fire on Christmas Day, 1961. After wartime use as barracks, hospital and prison, it was formally opened as a hotel in 1869. Presidents Andrew Johnson, Rutherford Hayes, Grover Cleveland, Theodore Roosevelt, William McKinley, William Howard Taft, and Woodrow Wilson lodged here, as did a host of celebrities from the world of business, politics, the arts, and the military services.
Location: 4th Avenue North, Old Third National Bank Building

3 A 78
Downtown Presbyterian Church
From 1814 to 1955 this was the site of the First Presbyterian Church. President Andrew Jackson was received into the church in 1838. James K. Polk was inaugurated governor here in 1839. The building designed in the Egyptian style by William Strickland, architect of the State Capitol, was dedicated in 1851. When the First Church moved, the Downtown Church was organized.
Location: 5th Avenue and Church Street

3 A 139
Sarah Estell
Sarah Estell, a free Black woman in the slavery era, ran an ice cream parlor and sweet shop near here. She overcame the many hurdles faced by free persons of color, and her venture thrived. Her catering firm met the banquet needs of the city's firemen, church socials, and political parties from 1840-1860.
Location: 217 5th Avenue North

3 A 46
William Driver
Born 1803 in Salem, Mass., and a sea-captain at 21, he retired in 1837. Coming here for his wife's health, he brought with him the flag given him in 1831, which he had nicknamed "Old Glory," the first known use of the term. This flag was flown from the Capitol when Federal troops took Nashville in 1862. Capt. Driver died in 1883.
Location: 511 5th Avenue South

3 A 43
Nashville Female Academy
Occupying five acres extending north and westward, this school was founded in 1817. First principal was Dr. Daniel Berry, of Salem, Mass. It suspended in 1862, Federal troops occupying the buildings. Reopening a short distance southward as Lanier Female Academy, it later returned to its own site. It closed finally in 1878.
Location: Church and McLemore streets

3 A 97
United Daughters of the Confederacy
On this site was the regular meeting place of the Frank Cheatham Bivouac, United Daughters of the Confederate Veterans. It was here on Sept. 10, 1894, Caroline Meriwether Goodlet called together a group of women and organized the National Daughters of the Confederacy. A year later the name was changed to the United Daughters of the Confederacy.
Location: 311 Church Street

3 A 38
Nashville Inn
First hostelry on this spot was established by Maj. William T. Lewis, 1796. It became Winn's Inn in 1806, the Nashville Inn a few years later. Among its many distinguished guests were the three sons of the Duke of Orleans. Andrew Johnson, then governor, was living here when the

inn was destroyed by fire in 1856.
Location: North side of Public Square

3 A 74
Holy Rosary Cathedral

Near here in 1820 the first Catholic Church in Tennessee was built by Irish Catholic workers then building a bridge over the Cumberland River. In 1830 a brick structure known as the Holy Rosary Cathedral succeeded the frame building. Here Bishop R.P. Miles, first Bishop of Tennessee, was installed Oct. 15, 1838. When St. Mary's Cathedral was built in 1847, Holy Rosary Church became St. John's Hospital and Orphanage. The site was sold to the state in 1857.
Location: Capitol Hill

3 A 34
State Capitol

Designed by William Strickland, a Philadelphian who designed St. Mary's Catholic Church and the First Presbyterian Church here, as well as many buildings elsewhere. Building was commenced 1845, completed 1855. Strickland died in 1854, and is buried in the capitol's north wall. His son, Francis, supervised completion.
Location: Entrance to Capitol

3 A 50
State Museum

This museum contains the collection of the Tennessee Historical Society (chartered 1849), successor to the Antiquarian Society (chartered 1819). Also included are relics of Tennesseans in peace and war, exhibits of the state's flora, fauna and industry, and exhibits from foreign countries.
Location: Capitol Boulevard

3 A 41
Talbot Tavern

Established by Thomas Talbot, in 1804, the inn which stood here was later known as the City Hotel. The trustees of Cumberland College, later the University of Nashville, habitually met here. A dinner was given here for Aaron Burr in 1806. Here, in 1813, was the fight between Jesse and Thomas H. Benton, and Generals Jackson and Coffee. Jesse Benton and Jackson were wounded, the latter seriously.
Location: East side of Public Square

3 A 53
Frank Maxwell Andrews

Born in a house which stood here, Feb. 3, 1884, he graduated from the Military Academy in 1905. Originally a cavalry officer, he transferred to the Air Corps in 1917. In 1941 he commanded the Caribbean Defense Command, later U.S. Air Forces, Middle East; then was commanding general, European Theater of Operations. At the time of his death in Iceland, May 3, 1943, he held the Distinguished Service Medal, Distinguished Flying Cross, Air Medal and Order of the Crown of Italy.
Location: Lea Avenue

3 A 130
Sampson W. Keeble

Sampson W. Keeble, barber, businessman, and civic leader, became the first African American to serve in the Tennessee General Assembly. Serving from 1873 to 1875, Keeble was appointed to the House Military Affairs Committee and the Immigration Committee. After service in the legislature, he was elected magistrate in Davidson County and served from 1877 to 1882.
Location: 111 Broad Street

3 A 40
University of Nashville

Moving to a building in this area in 1802, Davidson Academy became Davidson College in 1803 and Cumberland College in 1806. Lack of funds closed it in 1816; it reopened in 1822 and became the University of Nashville in 1826. One of its developments was Peabody College for Teachers, which went to its present location in 1911.
Location: 724 2nd Avenue South

3 A 138
Deford Bailey 1899-1982

Bailey, a pioneer of the Grand Ole Opry and its first black musician, lived in the Edgehill neighborhood for nearly 60 years. His shoeshine shop was on 12th Ave., South, near this intersection. His harmonica performance of the "Pan American Blues" inspired Judge George D. Hay to dub WSM's Barn Dance the "Grand Ole Opry." Traveling extensively with Opry musicians, he entertained audiences throughout the South and Midwest. In 1928, he recorded eight sides for RCA Victor during Nashville's first recording session.
Location: 12th Avenue South and Edgehill

3 A 117
Homes of David Lipscomb

This cabin was home, periodically, up to 1882 of educator, editor, and religious leader David Lipscomb and wife, Margaret Zeilner Lipscomb. The Associated Ladies for Lipscomb moved it here from Bell's Bend in 1985. In 1903, the Lipscombs built "Avalon" as their final home, and gave the surrounding farm as the campus for the Nashville Bible School, founded by Lipscomb and J.A. Harding in 1891. After Lipscomb's death in 1917, the school was renamed David Lipscomb College.
Location: 4000 block of Granny White Pike

3 A 51
Vanderbilt University
An independent, privately supported university founded 1873 by Commodore Cornelius Vanderbilt, New York shipping and railway magnate, who gave $1,000,000 to start the university and expressed his wish that it should "contribute to strengthening the ties which should exist between all geographical sections of our common country."
Location: West End Avenue, between 21st and 23rd avenues

3 A 128
Roger Williams University
The Nashville Institute, renamed Roger Williams University, was located on a 28-acre campus next to Hillsboro Pike from 1874 to 1905. It was the largest of the Baptist schools for African Americans, influencing many important educators and leaders. The main building, which was destroyed by two fires in 1905, stood at the top of the knoll.
Location: 21st Avenue South, opposite the Social-Religious Building

3 A 149
Hillsboro Theater
In 1925, the Hillsboro Theater opened as a silent film house with its entrance on 21st Avenue South. The stage arch was decorated by Italian craftsman, Raffaelo Mattei. It was the home of the Children's Theatre of Nashville after 1931, the Grand Ole Opry between 1934 and 1936, and the Nashville Community Playhouse after 1937. It became the Belcourt Cinema in 1966.
Location: 1719 21st Avenue South

3 A 148
Hillsboro-West End
This classic streetcar suburb was developed on farm land as Nashville grew south and west in the late nineteenth century. Built in Bungalow, Tudor, and Colonial Revival styles, many homes from the 1910s and 1920s still stand. The Hillsboro-West End neighborhood is listed in the National Register of Historic Places.
Location: Blair Boulevard and Natchez Trace

3 A 28
Richland
0.6 mile North, James Robertson built a station of the Cumberland Settlements in 1790. In 1797 he built there the first brick house in Middle Tennessee, living meanwhile in a log house about 1 mile N.W. of here. It was called Travelers' Rest until about 1816. The brick house burned in 1902; the log house still stands.
Location: U.S. 70N, Charlotte Pike

3 A 131
Tennessee Baptist Orphans' Home
On July 6, 1891, the Tennessee Baptist Orphans' Home was established at this site. The orphanage was housed in the Hotel Delaware. With the encouragement of Mrs. Roger Eastman, the Tennessee Baptist Convention endorsed the home in 1894 as its official child-caring institution, the forerunner of the Tennessee Baptist Children's Homes.
Location: 4200 Delaware Avenue

3 A 150
Bethlehem Centers of Nashville
100th Anniversary (1894-1994)
Formerly United Methodist Neighborhood Centers, Bethlehem Centers of Nashville began as settlement houses: Wesley House (1894), Centenary Center (1908), and Bethlehem Center (1911). Bethlehem Center was one of the first locations for African American Boy and Girl Scout troops in Nashville. Its Camp Dogwood was the first camp for African American children in this region of Tennessee. In February 1994, the Tennessee State Museum honored the agency with a 100-piece pictorial exhibit.
Location: 1417 Charlotte Avenue

3 A 118
Washington Hall
Inspired by Thomas Jefferson's Monticello and Lord Burlington's Chiswick House in London, John B. Daniels built this Italianate house c. 1914. Colonel Luke Lea, a United States Senator, organizer of the 114th Field Artillery in World War I, and founder of the Nashville Tennessean, lived here from 1936 until his death in 1945. He gave to the people of Nashville 868 acres of land for the creation of Percy Warner Park. One of the leading developers of Belle Meade, he also was instrumental in establishing the American Legion, and, for many years, was active in the public life of the state.
Location: 3700 Whitland Avenue

3 A 29
Belle Meade
Established by John Harding, 1806, on site of Dunham's Station, Cumberland Settlements. This house was built after the first mansion burned in 1853. Here, on one of Tennessee's great plantations, William Giles Harding founded one of the earliest Thoroughbred horse nurseries in the U.S.; his son-in-law, Gen. Wm. H. Jackson, brought it to international prominence. Its great days ended in 1904. Since 1954, it has been Headquarters of the Assn. for Preservation of Tennessee Antiquities.
Location: U.S. 70, Harding Road

3 A 116
Belle Meade Deer Park
Jackson Boulevard follows the contour of the 408-acre Belle Meade Plantation Deer Park, established by John Harding in 1833 or 1834. The park became a favorite picnic spot for Nashvillians. By 1854, it held approximately

200 deer and 14 buffalo. A few deer which survived the Civil War returned and rapidly multiplied. When the park closed in 1904, it held between 250 and 300 deer and a few elk.
Location: TN 100, Jackson Boulevard

3 A 167
Smith Farmhouse

In 1815, James Hifle Smith (1788-1845) and wife, Lucy Greer Smith (1793-1872), came to Pasquotank, Tennessee, from Virginia. They built a 1½ story single-pen log house on this site and opened a general store, which operated until 1975. The farmhouse shows the evolution of three distinct architectural styles. Listed in the National Register of Historic Places, it depicts early Tennessee log construction practices and the influence of the Greek Revival, Victorian, and Bungalow periods of design.
Location: 8600 TN Highway 100

3 A 15
Old Stone Bridge

Immediately to the east is one of the stone bridges over which passed the old stage from Nashville to Louisville. The stage line operated until the railroad was completed.
Location: U.S. 41, over Mansker's Creek, in Goodlettsville

3 B 19
William Bowen Campbell

Born in the brick house 2.2 mile NE, Feb. 1, 1807. Member of State and National Houses of Representatives; also commanded a company in the Seminole War and the "Bloody First" TN Inf. in the Mexican War. Governor, 1851-1853, and member of Congress in 1865. He is buried in Lebanon where he died, Aug. 19, 1867.
Location: U.S. 31W and U.S. 41, in Goodlettsville

3 A 146
William Bowen House, circa 1787

Near Mansker's Creek stands a rare example of Federal architecture built by Capt. William Bowen and Mary Henley Russell. Bowen, an early pioneer and Indian fighter, had served in the French & Indian and Revolutionary wars before moving his family to the Cumberland settlements. The house was restored and placed on the National Register of Historic Places in 1976. A grandson, William Bowen Campbell, served as fifteenth governor of Tennessee.
Location: Sumner County, Goodlettsville, Long Hollow Pike at Conference Drive

3 A 140
First Long Hunters, 1765

Henry Skaggs, his brothers, Charles and Richard, and Joseph Drake, and a group of other long hunters were the first Anglo-Saxons to explore this area. They made their campsite at Mansker's Lick, opening the doorway for the future settlement of Goodlettsville and Middle Tennessee.
Location: In Goodlettsville, Moss Wright Park

3 B 23
Kasper Mansker
1746-1820

Two blocks west is the grave of this renowned frontiersman and Goodlettsville's first citizen. Coming first to the Cumberland Settlements in 1770, he returned in 1780 and built his fort one-half mile north on Mansker's Creek. He repeatedly fought marauding Indians to protect the first white settlers of this region and was made a colonel in the frontier militia. He lived the remainder of his life at his fort which was called Mansker's Station.
Location: U.S. 31W, in Goodlettsville

3 A 14
Mansker's Station

Here, near Mansker's Lick, Kasper Mansker established a station of the Cumberland Settlements in 1780. The road connecting with Nashborough was built in 1781. John Donelson and his family moved here after abandoning his Clover Bottom Station, following the 1780 Massacre. A great game trail ran northeast from the Lick.
Location: U.S. 41, in Goodlettsville

3 A 100
New Bethel Baptist Church

New Bethel Baptist Church (formerly White's Creek) was organized in 1794 six miles north of Nashville on White's Creek Pike, through the labors of Daniel Brown, Joshua White, Nathan Arnett, and Patrick Mooney. It was moved to Dickerson Road in 1837 and the name changed to New Bethel in 1854. It was one of five churches in the organization of Mero District Association, the first one in Middle Tennessee, organized in 1796.
Location: in Goodlettsville, on Dickerson Road

Battle of Nashville Markers

N-1-2
Cavalry Action
Dec. 15, 1864

The right of the main Federal defense line crossed Charlotte Pike here. In the opening phase of the battle, mounted and dismounted cavalry of Wilson's Corps moved out of the Federal works, supporting the advance of Smith's XVI Corps in a turning movement against the extreme left flank of the Confederate positions.
Location: Charlotte Avenue, between 33rd and 35th avenues.

N-1-1
Cavalry Action
Dec. 15, 1864

Forming the outer arc of the main Federal attack, R.W. Johnson's 6th Cavalry Division, Wilson's Corps, here hit Rucker's Confederate Cavalry Brigade, west of Richland Creek. Withdrawing southward to Harding Road, Rucker held his ground there until bypassing Federal infantry forced further withdrawal to Hillsboro Pike late in the afternoon.
Location: 54th Avenue, west of Richland Creek Bridge

N-1-3
Federal Defenses

The hill to the west was a strong point in the system of permanent Federal defenses, started in 1862, which extended to the river on both sides of town. Artillery was emplaced here from time to time.
Location: West End Avenue, in Centennial Park, near the Parthenon

N-1-5
XVI Corps Line of Departure
Dec. 15, 1864

Supported by a division of Wilson's cavalry, A.J. Smith's Corps moved westward astride Harding Road, displacing Ector's Confederate Brigade from positions across the pike northward to the west of Richland Creek. This brigade outposted the Confederate left flank; the main line was along Hillsboro Pike.
Location: West End Avenue, at Orleans Drive

N-1-4
Defense by Ector's Brigade
Dec. 15, 1864

In position from here northward along high ground, Ector's Brigade of French's Confederate Division, commanded by Col. Daniel Coleman, outposted the left of Hood's line. Attacked by the Federal XVI Corps, supported by artillery and part of the Cavalry Corps, it was overwhelmed. It withdrew southeast to Hillsboro Pike.
Location: West End Avenue, at Ridgefield Avenue

N-1-13
Federal Defenses
Dec. 2-15, 1864

Near here, the interior defensive lines ran southwest to cross Harding Pike; the total length of these works was about 7 miles. First garrisoned by Wood's IV Corps, it was occupied Dec. 15 by Donaldson's Division of Quartermaster employees. Part of the breastworks can be seen on Vanderbilt campus, 300 yards west.
Location: 21st Avenue South, at entrance to Vanderbilt campus

N-1-12
Outer Federal Defenses
Dec. 2, 1864

Here the outer Federal defensive line, which stretched 7 miles around the city, crossed Hillsboro Pike. It was used at the commencement of battle on Dec. 15 by Wood's IV Corps as a line of departure for the main attack. Faint traces of the old entrenchments are visible a few yards west.
Location: 21st Avenue South, at Bernard Avenue

N-1-11
IV Corps Drop-Off Line
Dec. 15, 1864

Using the defensive salient 500 yards east, Wood's Corps, with the XVI Corps on its right, swung southwest to envelop the left of the Confederate line, 1½ miles south, and pushed it back in spite of determined resistance. The XXIII Corps (Schofield) followed in support.
Location: 21st Avenue South, at Linden Avenue

N-1-10
Assault on Montgomery Hill
Dec. 15, 1864

500 yards east of here, Maj. Gen. T.J. Wood led an assault by his IV Corps against the Confederate skirmish line on the hill, eventually carrying it. Attacking the main line about 600 yards south, Wood was unable to take it by direct assault, the divisions of Loring and Walthall holding fast until the XVI Corps, moving past their left, forced withdrawal.
Location: 21st Avenue South, at Cedar Lane

N-1-9
Redoubt No. 1
Dec. 15, 1864

Stewart's Confederate Corps held this salient of the left of Hood's defenses. A thin infantry line ran south behind a stone wall on the east side of the pike. After the routing of Ector's Brigade on Harding Pike and successive over-

running of Redoubts 3, 4, and 5 to the south, Stewart's position was flanked; he withdrew southeast toward Granny White Pike.
Location: TN 106 (Hillsboro Pike), near Hampton Avenue

N-1-8
Confederate Outpost
Dec. 15, 1864

100 yards west was Redoubt No. 3 in the Confederate system of detached works beyond the main line. It was overrun by the enveloping attack of Wood's IV Corps from the northwest.
Location: TN 106 (Hillsboro Pike), south of Woodmont Boulevard

N-1-7
Lumsden's Defense
Dec. 15, 1864

0.3 mile west was Redoubt No. 4 in Hood's detached supporting works. Garrisoned by Lumsden's Battery of smoothbore Napoleons, supported by 100 men of the 29th Alabama Infantry under Capt. Foster, it was finally overrun by the assault of 12 infantry and 4 dismounted cavalry regiments, supported by four Federal batteries.
Location: TN 106 (Hillsboro Pike), at Hobbs Road

N-1-6
Taking of Redoubt No. 5
Dec. 15, 1864

Hood's Redoubt No. 5 was on this hill. Couch's division of the XXIII Corps, sweeping to the south of the route of Smith's XVI, captured it and the hills to the east late in the afternoon. Wilson's cavalry, crossing the highway about 2 miles south, advanced rapidly eastward, flanking the Confederate defenses.
Location: TN 106 (Hillsboro Pike), 0.8 mile south of marker N-1-7

N-1-16
Schofield's Jump-Off Line
Dec. 15, 1864

The Federal defensive line ran northeast and southwest through here. It was garrisoned by Schofield's Corps on arrival here after the Battle of Franklin, Dec. 2, and later became a line of departure for the advance into support positions. Cruft's Provisional Division then occupied this line in reserve.
Location: 12th Avenue South, south of intersection with Acklen Avenue

N-1-15
Confederate Defenses
Dec. 15, 1864

Stewart's Corps, Army of Tennessee, held this part of Hood's original line, extending east about 1500 yards, and west and south about 1 mile to Hillsboro Pike. After the turning of his left, about 4:00 p.m., Stewart established a new position extending southward, to the west of Granny White Pike.
Location: Granny White Pike, near Woodmont Boulevard

N-1-14
Confederate Defenses
Dec. 15, 1864

After being outflanked by the advance of the Federal XVI Corps (Smith), Loring and Walthall put their divisions in a defensive line west of this road, facing westward. Here, their determined defense brought Federal advances against the Confederate left to a close for the day.
Location: Granny White Pike, near Shackleford Road intersection

N-2-3
Schofield's Assault
Dec. 16, 1864

The Federal XXIII Corps attacked southeastward from positions about 3/4 mile west. Coordinating with the attack of Smith's XVI Corps, and assisted by pressure by Wilson's encircling cavalry from the south, its action brought about the final collapse of Hood's defenses.
Location: Granny White Pike, at Harding Place

N-2-2
Smith's Assault
Dec. 16, 1864

The Federal XVI Corps attacked southward along this road. After violent artillery bombardment, McArthur's Division took the hill to the west about 4:00 p.m., precipitating the rout of Hood's Army. This hill is named for Col. W.M. Shy, 20th TN Inf., killed in the desperate defense which he commanded.
Location: Granny White Pike, between Harding Place and Sewanee Road

N-2-1
Confederate Position
Dec. 16, 1864

Stewart's Corps, badly mauled during the first day, withdrew at night to a line extending eastward. Lee's Corps, forming the right wing, extended the line across the Franklin Pike. Cheatham's Corps, on Stewart's left, extended the line westward, and following the hills, curved south. Chalmers' Cavalry Division covered the left flank.
Location: Granny White Pike, at Sewanee Road

N-1-18
Federal Defensive Line
Dec. 15, 1864

The Federal defensive line ran NE and SW through here. Ft. Casino was on the hill to the west, Fort Negley to the northeast. Garrisoned on Dec. 2 by Schofield's XXIII Corps, it was occupied by Cruft's Provisional Division when the battle began. The XXIII Corps moved out in support of

the main effort, 5 miles southwest.
Location: 8th Avenue South, on south slope of hill below City Reservoir

N-1-17
Lee's Position
Dec. 15, 1864

Here, Stephen D. Lee's Corps, Army of Tennessee, bestrode the highway and railroad. Cheatham's Corps held the right of the line, which ran northeast about 2 miles to Rains' Hill. After the Confederate left was broken in the afternoon's fighting, Lee's Corps fell back to high ground about 1 1/2 miles south.
Location: TN 6 (Franklin Pike), near Thompson Lane

N-2-4
Confederate Defenses
Dec. 16, 1864

Lee's Corps held the right flank of the line in the final stages of the battle, linking with Stewart to the west. Here it extended east, then south around Peach Orchard Hill. Violent attacks by Steedman's brigades were repulsed bloodily; Lee did not withdraw until the left and center of the Confederate line had collapsed.
Location: TN 6 (Franklin Pike), north of intersection with Elysian Fields Rd.

N-1-19
Cheatham's Line
Dec. 15, 1864

Holding a line running NE and SW and with its right on the N.C. & St. L. R.R. at Rains' Cut, Cheatham's Confederate Corps stood off the attacks of Steedman's brigades. Part of Cheatham's Corps was moved to the support of Stewart's line late in the afternoon; collapse of the left wing forced Cheatham's withdrawal southward during the night.
Location: 4th Avenue South, at Peachtree Street

N-1-21
Steedman's Line of Departure
Dec. 15, 1864

The left of the Federal main defensive line rested on the Cumberland River north of here, extending southeast to the Murfreesboro Pike. From this line, Steedman's Provisional Detachment of six brigades made the secondary attack against the Confederate right. Thomas' main attack was delivered against the Confederate left.
Location: Hermitage Avenue, near entrance to the old General Hospital

N-1-20
Steedman's Position
Dec. 15, 1864

From a line of departure running NE-SW through here, Maj. Gen. Steedman's Provisional Detachment of 6 brigades at 6:00 a.m. launched a holding attack southwestward against the Confederate right, on high ground about 2 miles south. The main attack, about 5 miles west, enveloped the Confederate left after an all-day fight.
Location: Lafayette Street, at Claiborne Street

3-A-21
Hood's Retreat
Dec. 16, 1864

In this neighborhood, late in the evening of his decisive defeat at Nashville, Hood reorganized his army for withdrawal southward. Lt. Gen. Stephen D. Lee's Corps, supported by Chalmers' Cavalry Division, covered the withdrawal, fighting continuously until the army bivouacked near Spring Hill, 21 miles S., the night of Dec. 17th.
Location: U.S. 31 (Franklin Pike), Davidson County, near Brentwood

Confederate Line

Trenches about 20 ft. N of this point, held by Loring's Division, were the center of the Confederate main line before the Battle of Nashville. On Dec. 15, 1864, Redoubt #1, a key artillery salient 200 yds. NW, fired on Federal forces until overrun by General Wood's troops late in the day, when Confederates retreated toward Granny White Pike.
Location: 1808 Woodmont Boulevard

Federal Main Line

On Dec. 16, 1864, the Federal 16th Corps under General A.J. Smith joined the 23rd Corps under Gen. John M. Schofield at this point. From this line at about 4:00 p.m. the 1st Div. launched the assault that broke the Confederate line at the salient on Shy's Hill to the south which resulted in the rout of Hood's Army.
Location: 4515 Shy's Hill Road

Peach Orchard Hill

On Dec. 16, 1864, Gen. S.D. Lee's Corps, Army of Tennessee, held this right flank of Hood's defense line which ran south along the crest of this ridge. Violent artillery fire and infantry attacks by the corps of Wood and Steedman failed to dislodge the defenders who withdrew only after the collapse of the Confederate left and center in late afternoon.
Location: Franklin Road and north side of ridge on Harding Place

Shy's Hill

On this hill was fought the decisive encounter of the Battle of Nashville December 16, 1864. At 4:15 p.m. a Federal assault at the angle on top of the hill broke the Confederate line. Col. W. M. Shy, 20th Tenn. Inf., was killed and Gen. T.B. Smith was captured. The Confederates retreated over the Overton Hills to the Franklin Pike.
Location: 4619 Benton Smith Road

Stewart's Line

Loring's division of Stewart's Corps, Hood's Confederate Army of Tennessee, fought behind this stone wall Dec. 16, 1864. All Federal attacks were beaten back until the Confederate line was broken a mile to the west. The division retreated south through the hills toward Brentwood.
Location: 4616 Lealand Lane

Assault on the Barricade
(Dec. 16, 1864)

During the retreat from Nashville, Colonel Edmund Rucker's brigade attempted to block the Union pursuit by erecting a barricade of fence rails and logs across Granny White Pike, ½ mile south of this spot. During the ensuing night attack by Union cavalry, fierce hand-to-hand fighting took place until the position finally was overrun around midnight, with Rucker defeated and then captured.
Location: Granny White Pike near Richland Country Club

Confederate Final Stand, December 16, 1864

After the withdrawal from the main Confederate line at Peach Orchard Hill, Lt. Gen. Stephen D. Lee formed a battle line across Franklin Pike 400 yards east of here with 200 men from the remnants of Brig. Gen. Henry Clayton's division and two cannons from the Eufaula Light Artillery. This last line of defense halted the Federal pursuit for the night as the Confederate army retreated through the hills to the southwest.
Location: 827 Tyne Boulevard

Notes

Notes